Front Cover:

Detail, *"...AND THEN...THERE WERE THREE!!,"* by Paul Szep. This cartoon appears in its entirety on page 31. The *Bush icon,* also by Paul Szep, that appears on various pages in the book, is derived from the cover cartoon.

Leo E. Heagerty, *Editor*

Jack Ohman, *Project Consultant*

Chronos Publishing

EYES ON THE PRESIDENT
GEORGE BUSH: HISTORY IN ESSAYS & CARTOONS

Chronos Publishing

PO Box 487

Occidental, CA 95465-0487

ISBN: 0-9633624-1-0 Hardcover

ISBN: 0-9633624-0-2 Paperback

Library of Congress Catalog
Card Number: 92-75674 Hardcover

Library of Congress Catalog
Card Number: 92-75675 Paperback

Contents

PREFACE

This book, *Eyes on the President,* is anything but a homogenized or sanitized treatment of the George Bush presidency. It is not a consensus history, nor is it intended as a definitive interpretation of our country's 41st president. Yet, *Eyes on the President* does something substantive: It offers readers an abundance of information essential to understanding the issues and events that transpired during the Bush presidency. *Eyes on the President's* long-term relevance lies in the fact that it will facilitate discussion and inquiry about the many challenges, issues, and decisions that now face the country as we move into the future.

We believe this book will prove rewarding to the political sophisticate and the general reader alike, as it joins mind and heart, fact and intuition, enlivening the process of studying history. The essays in *Eyes on the President* have been written specifically for this book by scholars, writers, and investigative reporters acclaimed for expertise in their subjects. The 210 political cartoons chosen for this book originally appeared in the national press. Altogether, more than 2,000 cartoons were graciously submitted by most of America's greatest political satirists for consideration for inclusion in this book.

The book begins with an appraisal of George Bush, the man and his presidency, by the noted presidential scholar, Thomas E. Cronin. Following are 14 chapters, each devoted to a single issue or event. Each chapter opens with an essay that provides the reader a historic background, pertinent facts, and frank analysis of the subject.

Following each essay is a series of political cartoons. Through the cartoons, *Eyes on the President* captures the responses of the cartoonists to events as they occurred. Like a photograph, the cartoons embody the passion of the moment. It is also worth noting that the political cartoons form more than a historical record of the nation's reaction. They helped to mold that reaction. They are part of the political process.

Each cartoon is accompanied by a short commentary that provides further analysis and perspective to the issue. True to the spirit of the cartoons, the publishers have not shied away from controversial comment where appropriate.

Finally, we hear from the political cartoonist who shares with us his recollections of President Bush, his administration, and the cartoonist's lament at the passing of this Golden Age.

Ultimately, our intent in publishing *Eyes on the President* is to stimulate a greater interest and participation in our nation's democratic process. We firmly believe that this participation should be premised on a well-informed public that understands the significant issues and events facing it as individuals and as a nation. Also, we strive to play a part in a reversal of a dangerous and growing trend in this country to manipulate and manage facts surrounding issues vital to our national well-being. We oppose any usurpation of the public's right to know.

From this retrospective in essays and cartoons, we hope that the American public, in all its diversity, will come to know better the facts and some of the forces behind many of the decisions and actions for which the Bush presidency will be remembered. Armed with this understanding and information, each of us will stand better prepared to make the decisions that face us today.

We are pleased that this book marks the first in a series on the American presidents by Chronos Publishing. These books will form a collection, a history of American presidents, past and to come, in essays and cartoons.■

Introducing the Authors

Thomas S. Blanton, *Iran-Contra Affair*

Thomas S. Blanton is a nationally recognized expert on matters of national security and the Freedom of Information Act. He is the executive director of The National Security Archive, a research and library organization located in Washington, D.C., specializing in freedom of information documents regarding U.S. foreign policy. The National Security Archive requested and later sued to gain release of Colonel Oliver North's diaries regarding Iran Contra in May 1990. Mr. Blanton coauthored *The Chronology: The Documented Day-by-Day Account of Secret Military Assistance to Iran and the Contras.*

Barry Bluestone, *The Economy*

Barry Bluestone is the Frank L. Boyden Professor of Political Economy and a Senior Fellow at the John W. McCormack Institute of Public Affairs at the University of Massachusetts, Boston. Mr. Bluestone is the co-author of *The Deindustrialization of America; The Great U-Turn: Corporate Restructuring and the Polarizing of America;* and *Negotiating the Future: A Labor Perspective on American Business.*

Eugene J. Carroll, Jr., Rear Admiral (Ret.), *Military Spending*

Rear Admiral Carroll is the deputy director of the Center for Defense Information in Washington, D.C., a nonprofit organization that specializes in reporting on defense issues and military spending. He served on General Alexander Haig's staff in Europe from 1977 to 1979. He was the first naval officer to serve as director of U.S. military operations for all U.S. forces in Europe and the Middle East. Rear Admiral Carroll is active in research and analysis concerning major defense and long-term national security issues.

Thomas E. Cronin, *The George Bush Presidency*

Thomas E. Cronin is a widely recognized scholar of the American presidency. He is a nationally known political scientist and writer and is the McHugh Professor of American Institutions and Leadership at Colorado College, in Colorado Springs. Cronin is the author, co-author, and editor of a number of books on subjects such as the American presidency, the election process, operations of American government, state and local politics, and national public policy. Cronin also writes frequently for the *New York Times, Washington Post, Washington Monthly, Science, Public Policy, Political Science Quarterly, Christian Science Monitor, Los Angeles Times,* and *Newsday.* Cronin earned his Ph.D. in political science from Stanford University. He will serve as the 1993 president of the Western Political Science Association.

Robert A. Dodds, *Cartoon Commentaries*

Robert A. Dodds wrote the commentaries for the cartoons in this book. He has been a political science teacher at Santa Rosa Junior College, in Santa Rosa, California, for the past 23 years. He is an Air Force veteran of the Korean War and received his master's degree in history from the University of California at Berkeley.

Joost R. Hiltermann, *The Gulf War*

Joost R. Hiltermann is a human rights consultant who has spent extensive time in the Middle East investigating and reporting on human rights issues. He is a member of the editorial board of *Middle East Report,* a publication of the Middle East Watch, a New York agency that monitors and reports on human rights issues. He has also written for the *Nation,* and *Mother Jones.* Mr. Hiltermann recently returned from Iraq where he monitored and reported on the activities of the Kurdish rebels.

John B. Judis, *Foreign Policy*

John B. Judis is a contributing editor of the *New Republic* and a Washington correspondent for *In These Times.* He is the author of *William F. Buckley, Jr.: Patron Saint of the Conservatives* and *Grand Illusion: Critics and Champions of the American Century.* His articles and opinions have appeared in many journals, newspapers, and magazines, including the *American Prospect, Wall Street Journal,* and *Wilson Quarterly.*

David L. Kirp, *Education*

David L. Kirp is a professor specializing in education policy at the Graduate School of Public Policy, University of California at Berkeley. His books on education include *Learning by Heart: AIDS and Schoolchildren in America's Communities; Educational Policy and the Law; Managing Educational Excellence;* and *Just Schools: The Idea of Racial Equality in American Education.* He is also a frequent contributor to the *Atlantic Monthly, Mother Jones, Nation, Public Interest, Lingua Franca, Los Angeles Times,* and *New York Times.*

Constance Matthiessen, *Health Care*

Constance Matthiessen is a staff reporter for the Center for Investigative Reporting, in San Francisco. She has written widely on the U.S. health-care crisis and environmental issues. Her articles have been published in the *Washington Post, Health (Hippocrates), Mother Jones, Newsday, Denver Post, Nation, San Francisco Chronicle, San Francisco Examiner,* and *Worldpaper.*

Eileen McNamara, *Abortion*

Eileen McNamara is a staff writer with the *Boston Globe Magazine.* As a newspaper reporter, she has written extensively on subjects ranging from the inner-city police beat to politics and Capitol Hill, with an increasing focus on such issues as battered women, abortion, juvenile justice, and infant mortality.

Jefferson Morley, *War on Drugs*

Jefferson Morley has written numerous articles on drugs, drug policy, and the nation's war on drugs. He is an associate editor for the *Washington Post.* His investigative reporting and essays have appeared in the *New York Review of Books, Los Angeles Times, Nation, New Republic,* and *New York Observer.*

Jack Ohman, *The Cartoonist*

Jack Ohman is an editorial cartoonist with The Oregonian newspaper in Portland, Oregon. He lectures widely and appears on national television providing a satirical look at the political scene. Jack has been instrumental in gaining acceptance of this book project within the cartoonist community.

Stephen P. Pizzo, *Savings and Loan Scandal*

Stephen P. Pizzo won the Investigative Reporters and Editors Book of the Year award and the Book List's Non-Fiction Book of the Year for his book *Inside Job: The Looting of America's Savings and Loans.* He is also the author of *The Ethics Gap: Crisis of Ethics in the Professions.* Mr. Pizzo is the West Coast correspondent for the *National Thrift News* and has written widely on the savings and loan and banking industries for the *Arizona Republic, Mother Jones, National Law Journal, New York Times, Penthouse, Playboy, Roll Call,* and *Washington Post.*

Stephanie Saul, *The Supreme Court*

Stephanie Saul is a reporter for *Newsday* at the U.S. Department of Justice in Washington, D.C. Ms. Saul is the recipient of numerous journalism awards for her coverage on government and legal affairs, including the George Polk Award, the National Press Club Award, and the American Bar Association's Silver Gavel Award.

Yvonne Scruggs, *The Cities*

Yvonne Scruggs is the director of the Joint Center for Political and Economic Studies in Washington, D.C., a nonpartisan, nonprofit institution dedicated to helping African Americans participate effectively in the political and economic life of our society. During the Carter administration, she was deputy assistant secretary of the U.S. Department of Housing and Urban Development. She is the former deputy mayor of Philadelphia and former commissioner of Housing of New York State.

Glenn R. Simpson, *The President and Congress*

Glenn R. Simpson is a reporter for *Roll Call,* a Capitol Hill newspaper written for members of Congress. Mr. Simpson is also the congressional correspondent for *Insight* magazine and a contributor to the *New Republic.*

David Weir, *The Environment*

David Weir is the managing editor of *Mother Jones* and a cofounder of the Center for Investigative Reporting. Mr. Weir is the co-author of two books on the environment: *The Bhopal Syndrome: Pesticides, Environment, and Health* and *Circle of Poison: Pesticides and People in a Hungry World.*

1

INTRODUCTION: THE GEORGE BUSH PRESIDENCY: AN APPRAISAL

THE GEORGE BUSH PRESIDENCY

An appraisal   Thomas E. Cronin

George Bush came to the American presidency with a better political résumé and more senior government experience at the national level than any other president of this century. The personable, well-bred, and proper Bush had served in Congress, had represented the United States in China and at the United Nations, had run the Central Intelligence Agency and the Republican National Committee, and had been an advisor to three presidents. Further, he had served an eight-year White House apprenticeship under a very popular president.

In 1988 Bush won a come-from-behind victory, winning 40 of the 50 states for 426 electoral votes to his opponent's 112. Bush won the entire South, the Southwest, all the Rocky Mountain states, most of New England and the Midwest, and the all-important states of California, Texas, Florida, Illinois, Ohio, Michigan, Pennsylvania, and New Jersey. Although his 53.5 percent share of the popular vote fell about 6 percentage points short of Reagan's 1984 landslide, his victory was nevertheless substantial.

Four years later, in 1992, George Bush suffered the worst electoral defeat of any 20th-century incumbent since William Howard Taft, who came in a dismal third in 1912. Voters had turned on Bush for failing to lead the nation out of a prolonged recession and for failing to deal with the profound economic problems that resulted from a decade of supply-side economics—spending and borrowing too much and saving and investing too little.

By 1992, even lifelong Republicans and past supporters faulted Bush for forsaking leadership, for abdicating the agenda-setting responsibilities of the presidency, for being "our Jimmy Carter," and committing "a thousand points of slight." Reagan advisor and Bush supporter Arthur B. Laffer summed it up for many conservatives: "George Bush has not earned the right to be re-elected. His performance has been poor across a wide range of presidential tasks... He had the best résumé in town and turned out to be a "dud."[1]

In 1992 Bush won only 38 percent of the popular vote in a three-way race and captured just 168 electoral votes to Arkansas governor Bill Clinton's 370. In the following appraisal, I examine why Bush ran for the presidency, why he won in 1988, what forces shaped his White House, what legacy he left, and why he was repudiated by the voters—including perhaps as many as 10 million men and women who had supported him just four years earlier.

The Campaign of 1988

Nineteen eighty-eight was a year of peace, prosperity, and Ronald Reagan's farewell ride into the sunset. In many ways, the 1988 election was a referendum on Reagan. Americans liked Reagan even if they believed he was too ill-informed about the issues and only vaguely in charge of the White House staff. He had cut taxes, stood up to the Soviets, and, for the most part, promoted a sense of optimism about America's global mission and its sense of itself. Yes, the deficit and homelessness and poverty and crime and drug abuse and environmental problems had all increased, yet somehow Reagan exuded confidence and hope—and he talked decisively and looked like a president. Perhaps he was only an "acting president," but he was superb at it.

Vice President George Bush offered few fresh policy initiatives as he launched his bid to become the nation's 41st president. Instead, he skillfully associated himself with the successes of the Reagan years. He also promised not to raise taxes and stressed his experience—especially his diplomatic experience in China, at the United Nations, and in dealing with the Soviet Union.

His campaign and political handlers told Bush he had to go on the attack and raise doubts in the voters' minds about the experience and liberal bent of his opponent, Massachusetts governor Michael Dukakis. Bush's campaign was an impressive, and to many people a distasteful, negative attack on Dukakis that often succeeded in portraying the governor as elitist and weak on crime and environmental pollution. Dukakis was denigrated as a Harvard-educated card-carrying member of the American Civil Liberties Union and too sophisticated to encourage the Pledge of Allegiance. Dukakis helped the Republican cause by fighting back tepidly and by

1

seeming so mechanical, wooden, and cold that he earned the epithet "ice man."

In contrast, George Bush often looked as if he were the candidate of conviction, emotion, and even passion. Still, it was never entirely clear why George Bush wanted to be president. Plainly he had been a loyal, perhaps "blindly" loyal in his own words, number-two man.

No one doubts that Bush was a keen competitor or that he valued public service. His stint as one of the nation's youngest fighter pilots in World War II earned him the Distinguished Flying Cross. He had grown up in a strongly partisan family and volunteered in Republican political campaigns all his adult life. He chaired the Harris County (Houston, Texas) Republican Party in the early 1960s. He stood unsuccessfully for the U.S. Senate in 1964. He ran for, and won, a seat in the House in 1966. After four years in Congress, he ran and was again defeated for a U.S. Senate seat. In those days it took courage to run as a Republican in Texas. President Richard Nixon rewarded him for his efforts with the U.N. ambassadorship and his Washington career took off.

Bush was ambitious and restless—his career was rather haphazard, with one job leading to another, and was marked more by opportunism than by policy ideas. Ideology or political philosophy did not seem to motivate his choices or to determine what jobs he took on. He was comfortable with tactics and facts, but ill at ease with strategy and theories. Bush was apparently not well read, rarely talked about books or vision, and was not known to be reflective. He told people in 1988 that he was running for the presidency "because I believe in the honor of it all." And this statement, to Bush, probably meant public

service was important as an end in itself. Good people, like himself, should respond to duty, honor, and country.

Even his close friends were puzzled about what fundamental policy values, if any, motivated his presidential candidacy. From the early 1960s on, Bush had regularly switched positions on issues depending on the views of his constituency or the changing times. He had opposed the passage of the landmark Civil Rights Act of 1964, but later changed his mind. He had endorsed the Planned Parenthood movement in his early career, but then opposed it in the 1980s. He had criticized as reckless Reagan's supply-side economic proposals, but later sang a completely different tune. He, like many a pragmatic politician, changed his views on a host of matters. All this maneuvering made it hard for people to discern what kind of policy leader he would be in the White House.

Ultimately, George Bush would win the 1988 election, not because of his policies or his political philosophy, but because times were good, Ronald Reagan had blessed him, and Michael Dukakis ran an inept campaign. Bush won in large part because the economy was good in 1988 and voters yearned for a continuation of the Reagan years. What kind of president did the American voters think Bush would be? The Gallup Organization's exit interviews on election day 1988 found that only 11 percent believed he would make an "excellent" president. Forty-five percent thought he would make a "good" president. However, another 41 percent suggested he would prove to be only "fair" or "poor." Gallup also asked voters to rank several policy priorities for the newly elected president: reducing the federal budget deficit—44 percent; protecting

American jobs from foreign competition—20 percent; increasing programs to meet the needs of families, such as child care and education—15 percent; negotiating further arms reduction with the Soviet Union—12 percent; improving protection of the environment—8 percent.[2]

Bush's First Year

"I come before you and assume the presidency at a moment rich with promise," George Bush said in his Inaugural Address on January 20, 1989. "We live in a peaceful, prosperous time, but we can make it better."

Presidential scholars agree that a president's first 100 days and first 6 to 10 months are crucial periods for setting the agenda and winning at least a few key legislative victories. Strong 20th-century presidents such as Woodrow Wilson, Franklin Roosevelt, Lyndon Johnson, and Ronald Reagan began with clear goals and pushed Congress to approve bold new programs. Indeed, every new president is in effect invited in the first year to share a vision and a national agenda with attentive Washington, national, and world audiences.

But Bush virtually relinquished any advantage offered by the honeymoon period. He got off to a slow start and appeared more concerned with managing a response to events as they happened than with shaping events by his actions. His early weeks were noted for their caution, pragmatism, and political orthodoxy.

In doing so, however, he encouraged an image of blandness. There was to be no "Bush Revolution" or New Deal or Great Society. Pundits searching for a label suggested it might be the "Beige" or "Bland Deal." Conservative columnist George Will noted the absence of any large purpose or specificity and labeled Bush the "pastel president." A *Wall Street Journal* evaluation of Bush's first 100 days found him blending into the landscape, reacting to events, and allowing Congress or others to set the national agenda. Bush rarely gave the American people a sense of where he wanted to lead, although he was credited with appointing several competent people to his cabinet.[3]

No doubt Bush's caution was dictated in part by his own penchant for prudence and pragmatic incrementalism. He was more inclined to respond than to initiate. Perhaps his training as ambassador and vice president had dimmed his capacity for bold, independent agenda setting.

In this context, Bush has to be understood as an insider and as a Tory. He had served in Congress and in the cabinet. He believed in government. Insiders are seldom, if ever, bold reformers. They tend to be cautious and to push incremental changes if they push changes at all.

An insider appoints fellow insiders, as Bush surely did, and a government of insiders is rarely a government of ideological fervor or bold imagination. Its cautious approach and deliberate intent to lower expectations seem boring because they *are* boring. Bush called it prudence. His critics called it timidity or pallidness.

Instead he spent most of his first year traveling to dozens of states and paying several state visits abroad. His was a visible presidency, long on procedure, protocol, and process and short on vision and big-ticket policy proposals. The American people found Bush an amiable, decent president, yet hardly the stuff of a great presidency.

Bush—What Kind of Leader?

For most of his years in government, George Bush had been on the receiving end of other people's orders. As president he had to reverse roles, take charge, and exercise political, policy, and institutional leadership. People expect a president to define, defend, and promote key values and a vision for the nation. For several reasons, George Bush found living up to this expectation difficult.

First, Bush did not have a clear mandate from voters, as had Reagan, to implement major programs. Moreover, unlike Reagan in 1981, Bush did not have a Republican Senate. His party had even suffered losses in both houses of Congress in 1988—something that rarely happens when new presidents are elected.

So Bush hit the ground hesitating and more confused than confident about what positions or what issues, if any, had helped to elect him, and where he wanted to lead the nation. "He entered office with limited 'political capital,' relatively few 'political advantages' and therefore a weak 'strategic position'," observed political scientist Charles O. Jones.[4]

And Bush had a limited conception of what he wanted to achieve. When pressed by reporters, he would often fall back on bromidic platitudes such as "I would like to have it written that we made major strides towards getting a grip with Congress on the budget deficit." He hoped his legacy would be "a kinder and gentler America as part of a more peaceful, democratic world."[5]

The American people may have been expecting a third Reagan administration. But Bush knew he was no Reagan and, in fact, held a different conception of the office of president. He wanted to be more moderate on issues such as civil rights, the environment, and education. He also wanted to be more of a hands-on, informed president. He prided himself on knowing the names of all the Republicans in Congress and the state party chairs. He placed great stock in close, personal relationships with dozens of foreign leaders.

If Reagan was a wholesaler, Bush was a retail man. He would be Mr. Inside to Reagan's Mr. Outside. His would be a rounding not a sharpening leadership. Loyalty, personal loyalty, was his first principle of governing. His leadership style was as devoted to personal diplomacy as it was devoid of ideological purpose.

Some Bush advisors, and perhaps Bush himself, believed the time was ripe for inaction. They felt it was prudent to downsize both the government and the presidency—except, of course, for the commander in chief's responsibilities. It was as if Bush preached and practiced the motto: Don't just do something, stand there. As his critics observed, Bush promised little and we got what he promised.

Bush's public approval ratings were reasonably high in his first year and a half, yet commentators continued to be critical of Bush for showing too little vision, too little leadership, and too little passion. *Newsweek*'s Jonathan Alter wrote:

"Anyone can lead where people already want to go; true leaders take them where only their better selves are willing to tread. That's where the leader's own values come in. They must want to do something with their power, not just be powerful."[6]

Bush wanted his to be "a successful presidency," one prepared to handle the big surprises. If Carter had been preoccupied with management matters and Reagan with politics, Bush seemed addicted to procedure—to doing things in an orderly manner, to avoiding mistakes, and to carrying on with the proper functions of government. "I believe in the integrity of the process. I believe our institutions can still cope" and "I'm just not an emotional guy" were illustrative Bush responses to those looking for policy direction and passion.[7]

Even in his fourth year as president, finding much substance in Bush's domestic program was difficult. He did very little in his 1992 campaign to fill in the blanks—to outline how his second term would vary from his first. Bush kept saying the economy was going to improve soon and therefore nothing much was needed in the way of new domestic and economic programs. He and his advisors were philosophically opposed to Keynesian pump priming. Their opposition was reinforced by the huge federal deficit and the fact Bush had been a contributor to it. Both of these facts became campaign issues for which Bush was consistently attacked by Pat Buchanan, Paul Tsongas, and Ross Perot, as they vied for the presidency.

But was this the way to lead and govern in late-20th-century America? Was it a throwback to Calvin Coolidge–like presiding? If Bush's caution was central to his operational conduct of the presidency, it was the caution of a seasoned diplomat who wanted to do no harm or to do little and do it well, rather than engage in bold and possibly reckless ventures. Political scientist Bert A. Rockman offered this telling midterm appraisal:

"Unlike Richard Nixon, Bush's perspective as foreign-policymaker-in-chief was not shaped by a grand design or concept but by caution and temperamental conservatism. Like a well-honed bureaucrat, Bush has a high regard for the virtues of 'not doing.' In the midst of a historic transition in the Soviet Union, and under considerable criticism for failing to respond adequately to these changes, Bush proclaimed that he could best help move things along by 'avoid[ing] doing dumb things.' This is the response, not of a strategist, but of a foreign policy bureaucrat—the elevation of antiaction to modus operandi. If Bush is a man of few ideas, correspondingly few are disastrously bad."[8]

Bush was handicapped, too, by his inability to rouse the American public by rhetorical means. He had trouble talking in complete sentences; he mangled syntax and inspired the irreverent term "Bushisms" to describe his rambling prolixity and jumbled or inappropriate examples. Whereas Ronald Reagan could sometimes inspire and rally the American public, and therefore Congress, to go along with major initiatives like tax cuts, increased defense spending, and the Strategic Defense Initiative (Star Wars), President Bush could not. But, then again, if he had so little he wanted to achieve, oratory and rhetorical persuasion were skills he did not need. Still, observers were left wondering what was cause and what was effect. After all, how passionate and persuasive can you get about "doing no harm" and lowering expectations in a time of declining jobs and living standards?

President Bush's leadership efforts suffered for yet another reason. He followed Ronald Reagan, and the Reagan administration had already taken the lead on the three most prominent conservative Republican priorities: cutting personal taxes, doubling defense spending, and reducing or at least weakening the enforcement of the governmental regulations so disliked by American businesses. This is not to say there was nothing else to achieve, just to note that the central priorities of the Republican Party platform of 1980 had been addressed. This meant, especially in the absence of an authentically Bush-driven platform, that Bush inevitably ended up looking like a caretaker or at best a manager, rather than a true leader.

The Bush White House

It is often said that a president's effectiveness is only as good as the staff and the cabinet a president recruits. Equally important is how the president uses that staff and cabinet. Despite an apparent passivity, George Bush was more of a hands-on president than Ronald Reagan had ever been or ever wanted to be. Bush did not delegate responsibility nearly as much as had his predecessor. Yet to his credit, Bush also avoided the temptation of taking on problems and responsibilities that belonged in the departments headed by his cabinet officials. And he won great praise in 1990 and 1991, for example, for delegating authority to his secretary of defense and military chiefs for the conduct of the Gulf War, rather than trying to micromanage these efforts from the White House. He also believed strongly that the CIA director and secretary of state should run their own agencies and that the National Security Council was to serve as an advisory, not an operational, arm of the presidency.

Bush also won praise for many of his foreign and national security appointments. Dick Cheney, James Baker, Brent Scowcroft, and others were viewed as solid professional choices. But Bush also received severe criticism and suffered a major early political setback for his appointment of former Texas senator John Tower as secretary of defense. The Senate rejected Tower's nomination on the grounds of several character flaws and charges of conflict of interest, the first time a president's choice for a cabinet position had been rejected in 30 years.

President Bush made former New Hampshire governor John Sununu his White House chief of staff. The ideologically conservative Sununu soon became a forceful presence in the cabinet and in shaping Bush's political and policy decisions. He became Bush's hatchet man or tough cop, thus permitting Bush to take the high ground, to remain Mr. Nice Guy. But Sununu's arrogance became legendary and his gratuitous insults of White House aides, congressional leaders, cabinet members, and the press eventually created a backlash against Bush. Sununu developed a penchant for using U.S. military planes and White House–chauffeured limousines to make blatantly personal trips to ski resorts, football games, and even stamp shows in New York. The press soon termed it the "Air Sununu" flap. But Sununu's arrogance had other effects as well. White House aides and advisors were intimidated by him and his vindictiveness; he was known in some circles as "the Saddam Hussein of bureaucrats."

Sununu's political philosophy was generally more conservative than Bush's; moreover, he was given to overstatement in marked contrast to Bush's genial, conciliatory approach. For example, John Sununu told a late-1990 Conservative Leaders Conference that there was not another single piece of legislation that needed to be passed in the next two years of the Bush presidency. "In fact, if Congress [which had just been elected] wants to come together, adjourn and leave, it's all right with us. We don't need them."[9]

When later questioned about this "Sununuism" the president said Sununu could not possibly have said it. But he had. And this "style" and Sununu's subsequent dismissal of Republican Senator Trent Lott of Mississippi as "flat-out inconsequential" eventually doomed his usefulness to Bush. But the ever-loyal and cautious Bush kept Sununu on as chief of staff far too long. Ultimately, Bush would find himself in trouble over Sununu because of his own tendency to be decent, loyal, and gentle to his friends—even though his friend in this case had just the opposite disposition.

Sununu's profound conservatism also had consequences on the Bush presidency. The chief of staff made it hard for moderates such as William Reilly at the Environmental Protection Agency to get their views heard at the White House. And his opposition to policy initiatives dampened the climate for policy activists of the Jack Kemp school. Thus, President Bush got less useful policy advice than he would have had this self-styled "pit bull" not been at the top of the White House command.

George Bush had some excellent people in his cabinet—people like James Baker, Jack Kemp, Elizabeth Dole. But the longer his presidency went on, the more distant and uninterested he seemed in domestic issues and thus less available for working with the domestic, or "outer," cabinet. Housing and Urban Development Secretary Jack Kemp, brimming with new ideas, languished in his cabinet role for nearly all of the Bush presidency. Bush fired his Education and Veterans' Affairs secretaries, and others moved on of their own accord. Cabinet meetings, as in most presidencies, became infrequent—especially when Bush devoted most of his time to foreign affairs.

President Bush expanded various White House staffs. He provided more funds for the Council on Environmental Quality, he listened somewhat more than Reagan had to the Council of Economic Advisors, and, at least initially, he worked closely with his Office of National Drug Control Policy. He also worked effectively with his able Special Representative for Trade, Carla Hills.

But Bush's economic advisors, including his director of the Office of Management and Budget, his chair of the Council of Economic Advisors, and his secretary of the treasury, all faced considerable public criticism—from all kinds of partisan groups. In the end Bush turned on his economic advisors and said, during the heat of the 1992 campaign, that they would all be replaced if he were re-elected. This was a bizarre vote of no confidence in his own cabinet-level economic team.

The Bush Policy Legacy: Two Views

"I hope history will record that the Bush Administration has served Americans well. I am proud of my cabinet and staff. America has led the world through an age of global transition; we've made the world safer for our kids. And I believe the real fruits of our global victory are yet to be tasted."[10]

A case can be made that George Bush was often a good president. I will make that case here before arguing the counter-case later on that his was largely an ineffective and overly reactive presidency.

The case for Bush rests in large part on his foreign policy accomplishments, especially his effective handling of the Persian Gulf crisis in 1990. If the president and his advisors were caught by surprise by the Iraqi invasion of Kuwait, Bush's adroit diplomacy—his use of the United Nations and his ability to win widespread cooperation among not only our customary allies but also from the Soviets, Chinese, and Syrians—was a major triumph.

Bush also responded well to the breakup of the Soviet Union, and his skilled efforts led to the continuation of arms control negotiations. And he took the appropriate steps as Germany reunited, as NATO underwent a major shift in focus, and as the Somalia situation in late 1992 warranted United Nations and United States assistance.

Bush deserves credit for negotiating the North American Free Trade Agreement with Mexico in 1992. The United States enjoyed good relations with both Mexico and Canada, and Bush merits praise for his personal diplomacy in these cases. Bush fought the protectionist inclinations of conservatives and many trade unions. No one can be sure how these trade agreements with Mexico will work out and what consequences they will have for jobs and the overall economy. The optimistic estimate is that even though there will be job dislocations and losses in the short term, in the long term these agreements will prove beneficial to economic growth and expanded trade for the United States.

George Bush also won praise for working with Congress to disengage the United States from its prolonged involvement in Nicaragua. President Bush's intervention in Panama helped end short-term instability there, although it is unclear how that military venture will be viewed in the longer history of that faction-torn nation.

Bush and his advisors defended what critics called a slow conversion process from the Cold War to the post–Cold War military budgets. Bush

stated that the United States needed to be prepared to play a key role in shaping the future of regions and of nations where the United States had vital interests. But one of Bush's 1992 presidential-election rivals, Ross Perot, countered that our well-being in the 1990s and beyond depended less on military than on economic security, faulting Bush's downsizing of the military as too slow and unimaginative. Both Perot and Clinton called for troop reductions of at least 200,000 troops more than did Bush. Here again, history will have to judge. Perot's point is valid, but the United States has paid dearly on occasion for a too-rapid demobilization of its forces.

President Bush's national security team generally won praise. Its reliance on United Nations leadership in seeking a Middle East peace accord and its efforts in helping the former Soviet republics, while not flawless, were generally competent and well intentioned.

Bush's domestic policy record, as noted, is not extensive. Indeed, it is full of policy reversals and broken promises, yet there were accomplishments. For example, Bush:

- signed into law a much-needed increase in the minimum wage, even though he had vetoed one such bill;
- helped push and win approval for a landmark extension of the Clean Air Act of 1990;
- supported and helped win approval for the landmark Americans with Disabilities Act;
- encouraged and signed the Civil Rights Act of 1990, although he had vetoed one measure;
- appointed an environmentalist, William Reilly, to the Environmental Protection Agency and, for at least his first year or two in office, encouraged stronger enforcement of environmental regulations;

- pressed for better public schools and helped set standards by which we could judge progress in our schools. He also proposed various "voucher" plans and choice in schools—though these were never put in legislative proposals;
- signed into law a necessary tax increase, though he was faulted for doing so, especially by fellow Republicans for breaking his pledge not to raise taxes. His Budget Agreement of 1990 also had merit.

Others would argue too that Bush curbed the almost inevitable tendency for government to grow and spend. Of course, the government and the national debt did grow during his presidency—but the case can be made that it would have grown even more had Michael Dukakis been elected president.

Moreover, the Bush years could boast of some good economic news. Inflation dropped from nearly 5 percent to about 3 percent. Interest rates came down from almost 9 percent to about 7.5 percent. The stock market was trading at 2,235 when Bush became president, and it rose more than 30 percent to over 3,200 in late 1992. Bush, with Congress, also put together a reasonable savings and loan bailout program—responding to a problem that originated in the early 1980s.

These accomplishments led Bush supporters, such as his former boss Ronald Reagan, to conclude that George Bush "is a trustworthy and levelheaded leader who is respected around the world. His is a steady hand on the tiller through the choppy waters of the '90s, which is exactly what we need."[11]

Whereas historians are likely to credit Bush with a generally good record in foreign policy, they will fault him for neglecting America's economic problems. They will also criticize Bush for being insufficiently astute when it came to stating his case before Congress and the American people. Even when Bush did have initiatives, he was seldom effective before Congress. True, the Democrats controlled both houses in Congress, yet Bush could have fashioned more compromises between Democrats and Republicans. There were many areas such as election reform and health care and anticrime legislation where Bush could have worked with moderate Democrats to realize legislative victories. But in most cases, communication broke down and gridlock set in.

The same George Bush who enjoyed higher public approval ratings from the public in his first two and a half years in office than most of his predecessors lost touch with the American people in his last 18 months in office. "Bush averaged 68 percent approval during his first years, second only to Kennedy and tying with Eisenhower in overall support."[12]

Bush's high ratings are explained, in large part, by the national optimism associated with the end of the Cold War and in midterm by his handling of the Desert Storm victory. But when domestic and economic issues intruded in 1991 and 1992, Bush took the greatest free-fall in public support of any president since Gallup began polling in the mid-1930s. Bush's public approval rating fell from a high of 90 percent to a low of around 35 percent in mid-1992.

Bush was able to capture public attention and support when his administration emphasized foreign policy initiatives and when national press headlines focused mainly on the end of the Cold War and related events. But when attention became focused on the deficiencies and sluggishness of the American economy, Bush was largely unsuccessful in winning public support for his policies and leadership efforts, such as they were.

Bush had promised to be an "education president" and an "environmental president"—but he achieved little as either. He pledged to get our economic house in order after the binge of borrowing and spending during the Reagan years. But the deficit doubled and the national debt went from $2.6 trillion to over $4 trillion on Bush's watch. Moreover, the White House staff swelled and he encouraged pay raises for government officials while the wages of average Americans were going down.

Bush talked about the importance of family values yet vetoed a family and medical leave bill that would have encouraged parents to devote crucial time to the birth of their children and the early weeks of child rearing.

Indeed, George Bush used the veto a lot—46 times. And some vetoes were warranted. Yet the veto is largely a negative leadership tool. A president cannot veto a nation to greatness. Bush's use of the veto power became almost a metaphor for his leadership style: reactive rather than proactive. He seldom defined the legislative agenda for the nation. He abandoned this work, especially in his second two years, to Congress. It was not that his presidency was insincere or unserious. Most of the time there just seemed to be no policy compass steering it, almost as if he wanted little to happen, little legislation to get passed, and government to merely maintain the status quo.

Bush favored term limits for Congress, an item veto for the president, and the ending of political action committees. Thus, he did favor some reform yet was largely unable to say why these reforms would make America better. And in the end the reforms he advocated did not make sense, at least to informed observers of government.

Bush, and Congress, worried about rising health-care costs and the millions of Americans who are not covered by any insurance plan—but Bush never forced the issue by preparing serious legislation on this major concern to the American people. Doubtless, Bush was constrained on this issue since core Republican constituencies such as the insurance industry and small business owners were concerned about the high costs of compulsory insurance. Thus, Bush's lack of a health-care program can be explained by his ties to business as well as his own philosophical view that government should limit its role in the economic and social life of the nation.

President Bush will be remembered for appointing David Souter and Clarence Thomas to the Supreme Court. The Clarence Thomas nomination, which eventually won approval by a 52 to 48 Senate vote, bitterly divided the nation. Bush also appointed scores of conservative antiabortion judges to the lower federal courts.

Ultimately, Bush will be remembered for the prolonged recession of the early 1990s, for the slowest rate of economic growth since the Great Depression, and for presiding over a period of rising unemployment and lowered confidence in the American economy.

Bush and his staff tried to blame the deficit and the recession on Congress's failure to enact his programs and his budget. He talked of "gridlock" and urged Americans to vote Democrats out and Republicans in. Bush also tried to rally the American people to support a reduction in capital gains taxes.

George Bush was our 41st president. He won our 51st presidential election and lost the 52nd. How will George Bush's record be judged in 25, 50, or 100 years? He will get above-average grades for foreign policy and military successes. But his failed economic leadership and often discordant relations with Congress and the voters in 1992 will earn him a gentleman's C. Aside from the Gulf War, his will be viewed as a mostly caretaking, reactive, and cautious presidency, especially when compared with those of more dynamic leaders such as Woodrow Wilson, Franklin Roosevelt, Theodore Roosevelt, and Harry Truman. He will be viewed as an amiable, hardworking president who faced great problems but lacked both the policy and the political leadership the times demanded.

George Bush's Defeat in 1992

Political scientists hold it as axiomatic that voters reward incumbents when times are good and punish them when times are bad, no matter the reason for the good or bad times. The 1992 election was a national referendum on the weak economy and George Bush's handling of it. In the end, 62 percent of the voters in a record turnout on November 3, 1992, voted for change. Both Bill Clinton and Ross Perot had hammered on George Bush's failed leadership on economic matters. Perot relentlessly attacked Bush for the nation's soaring deficit and debt. Bush lamely agreed that the economy had been anemic. He kept saying things would get better, but he rarely got specific about what he might do, in a second term, to help revive the economy and slash the deficit.

Bush was in part the victim of his and his party's successes in foreign policy. The Cold War had ended. It had been exceedingly costly but, ultimately, it was a major victory for the United States. Ironically, the very arena in which Bush could claim experience and strength was one in which Americans were no longer interested. They now wanted their government to focus on reviving our economy and improving job, health, and educational opportunities at home. What was needed, most Americans felt, was a major conversion from a Cold War to a post–Cold War economy that stressed growth, jobs, and a higher standard of living.

Thus, George Bush was given "the order of the boot" just as Winston Churchill was after he had helped win World War II.

Voters seldom take a long view and they are often guided by the saying, "What have you done for me lately?" Only 20 months before the election a stunning 90 percent of adult Americans approved of George Bush's performance as president. But as the public saw how poorly the economy was performing, they increasingly blamed the White House. Bush's advisors kept telling him to ride things out, that the economy would improve itself without major intervention. But time ran out.

Bush hid his economic advisors at the Republican National Convention, and he failed to offer bold economic prescriptions during the campaign. In 1992 he relied once again, as he had in 1988, on a strategy of discrediting his chief opponent. But this time "going negative" did not work. Moreover, Bush fared poorly in the three presidential debates held in mid-October 1992. Bush had damaged Clinton by raising fears about his character and the likelihood of his rais-

ing taxes. But Bush had similar liabilities; he had said he would not raise taxes and then he did. And he had said he had not been involved with the arms for hostages deal with Iran in the mid-1980s, but former Secretary of Defense Caspar Weinberger's records (revealed in court proceedings right before the election) suggested Bush had lied.

George Bush campaigned vigorously, if not quite coherently, to the end. Even when many of his aides and advisors had given up any hope for victory, Bush held on. But on election day, even he realized that the weak economy, his own failure to project hope and to present programs and ideas that would earn him a second term, and an impressive Clinton campaign had doomed his chances for re-election. Voters told exit interviewers that the issues they cared most about were the economy and jobs, the deficit, and health care. These were issues George Bush had failed to address adequately in his presidency, and the voters were holding him accountable.

That only 38 percent of the public voted for him was a resounding vote of no confidence. Bush in defeat was, true to his upbringing, gracious. "When you win, your errors are obscured; when you lose, your errors are magnified," he said. "I expect history will take the edge off both interpretations."■[13]

2
THE PRESIDENT, CONGRESS, AND THE COURT:
THE PRESIDENT AND CONGRESS
THE SUPREME COURT

THE PRESIDENT AND CONGRESS

Leadership by veto

Glenn R. Simpson

Despite the widely perceived lack of an agenda, George Bush dominated Congress in matters both foreign and domestic between 1988 and 1992. In Supreme Court nominations, veto fights, separation-of-powers conflicts, and related war powers questions—standards by which we judge the power and effectiveness of our presidents—President Bush racked up an impressive record of victories over the Democrat-led Congress.

The most important reasons for this series of victories were the persistent inability of Democrats to unify their numerically superior ranks and the failure to craft legislation and parliamentary scenarios that would divide their Republican opponents. Remarkably, the Democrats' fractiousness worsened as Bush's term progressed because of a series of institutional scandals.

One of Bush's few major defeats in his contests with Congress—the 1990 budget agreement that resulted in the president breaking a major campaign promise by agreeing to raise taxes—is an exception that illustrates the prevailing dynamic. For this occasion was virtually the only major one when Bush's Republican allies abandoned him in significant numbers, forcing him into a humiliating agreement with Democrats that would ultimately exact a devastating political toll on him.

The most remarkable aspect of Bush's dominance of Congress was his record of sustaining his own vetoes, which remained unbroken well into the fourth year of his term, a record surpassing even that of his mentor Ronald Reagan. To override a presidential veto, both houses of Congress must pass resolutions to that effect by majorities of at least two-thirds; thus, to sustain a veto, a president must merely win the support of one-third of the members in either body, and not necessarily both.[1] Typically, Bush's necessary one-third vote to sustain a veto came from the Senate, where 44 of 100 members were Republican.

Apparently lacking the desire to pursue his own program, Bush, more than any other president in recent history, ruled by the veto, offering little legislation of his own while forcing Congress to modify its own initiatives to his liking. This tactic lends modern support for Professor (later, President) Woodrow Wilson's observation that "in his exercise of his power of veto, which is of course, beyond all comparison, his most formidable prerogative, the President acts not as the executive but as a third branch of the legislature."[2]

The statistics are remarkable. As of July 2, 1992, Bush was batting 1.000, having vetoed 29 bills without a single successful congressional override. By November 1992 Bush had vetoed 46 bills with one override. Among the measures Bush succeeded in blocking or modifying were a campaign finance reform act, bills to permit federal funding for abortions, trade sanctions against China for human rights violations, a law requiring employers to grant workers family and medical leave, a major civil rights bill, and legislation to protect domestic textile manufacturers from foreign competition.[3]

In light of this record, Bush's 1990 budget debacle is particularly instructive. The months-long, immensely complicated wrangle over the shape of the government's 1991 budget was costly to the standing of the entire Washington establishment.[4] The bipartisan reduction in incumbent re-election margins in 1990 was widely attributed, in part, to voter distaste with the budget and tax controversies. "Pundits Ponder" is a typical postelection analysis. The article quotes political scientist Gary Jacobsen's observation that "acting responsibly (i.e., raising taxes) became political poison."[4] But by 1992 the prevailing view was that Bush had suffered most. He had enraged conservatives by going back on his pledge not to raise taxes, his party had lost one Senate seat and eight House seats in the 1990 midterm elections, and the more conservative congressional Republicans, including Minority Whip Newt Gingrich of Georgia, launched a rebellion that severely disrupted the House GOP's alliance with Bush.[5]

What happened? In essence, Bush and the Republicans were "outnegotiated," as the top Republican on the House Budget Committee put it.[6] Democrats split the executive and the legislative wings of the GOP by exploiting their different needs. Bush, as president, felt forced to show he could govern and thus swallowed a tax increase to achieve that end, but Republicans in Congress, since they were in the minority, faced no similar imperative. Their imperative enjoined by ideology and the desire to be re-elected by conservative constituencies was to oppose all tax increases. Perhaps the best illustration of these divergent needs came when National Republican Campaign Committee strategist John Roberts advised House Republicans to run against the president's budget policy in the 1990 elections.[7]

Although a president's success is often judged by the success of domestic programs and policies, a lesson Bush learned all too well, other matters are perhaps of greater historical weight. The pivotal event in relations between the Bush White House and Congress between 1989 and 1993 was probably the legislature's handling of the 1991 war in the Persian Gulf.

Almost immediately following Iraq's seizure of Kuwait on August 2, 1990, U.S. preparations for war began, most noticeably with efforts to defend Saudi Arabia against Iraqi attack. Congress, despite much discussion, took no institutional action. Forty-five Congressmen did file a lawsuit in November 1990, claiming Bush had no authority to order an attack on Iraqi forces without congressional consent. Congressional leaders declined to provide legal backing, and the case was argued by the private Center for Constitutional Rights.[8] The suit was subsequently obviated.

When Congress did ultimately act, it did so reluctantly and with little effect, although with drama and revealing debate. On January 3, 1991, the 102d Congress convened, the 101st having failed to bring any war-making resolution to the floor in 1990, despite President Bush's January 15 deadline for Iraq's exit from Kuwait,

the massing of vast forces and materiel in Saudi Arabia, and the seeming clarity of the Constitution on this matter: "The Congress shall have the power…to declare war."[9]

Senator George J. Mitchell of Maine, the Majority Leader, sought consent from his colleagues to modify the traditional procedure of the Senate whereby the chamber opens for only minutes on January 3, and then recesses until January 23. Mitchell sought to keep the Senate in session *pro forma*—on standby in case something happened in the Persian Gulf. He made a vague promise that, during the week of January 7, Congress would "assess the situation…as to when would be the appropriate time to recall the Senate for a full session for consideration of that matter."[10]

Mitchell further proposed a rule that senators be prohibited from offering resolutions during the period without the consent of the Democratic leader (Mitchell) and the Republican leader (Robert Dole of Kansas). Though not directly foreclosing a war vote, the Mitchell proposals made such a vote extremely unlikely.

However, Senator Thomas Harkin of Iowa, a dovish, liberal Vietnam-era veteran, with one other ally, objected to Mitchell's plan. "These are not normal times," said Harkin. "It is the time when America is facing a war. We are assembled here. We have a deadline of January 15 facing us with American men and women who may be dying in combat. I believe it is time for the Senate to debate this issue, and more specifically, to debate whether the President of the United States, under the Constitution, must come to the Congress for the power before he can take offensive action."[11]

Harkin's objection effectively blocked Mitchell's

move to postpone action on the Gulf situation. It also forced Bush to recognize the inevitable and send letters to congressional leaders seeking support for possible military action. But Bush did not frame the request in constitutional terms—in fact, he made no reference to the Constitution. Instead, Bush indicated he sought not so much approval as moral support: "Mr. Speaker, I am determined to do whatever is necessary to protect America's security. I ask Congress to join me in this task. I can think of no better way than for Congress to express its support for the President at this critical time."[12]

Harkin got his debate. But in voting to authorize the use of force on January 12, Congress salvaged a mere scrap of its deeply eroded war-making power. Indeed, during the debate, House leaders additionally resolved that "any offensive action taken against Iraq must be explicitly approved by the Congress of the United States."[13]

Although House Speaker Thomas Foley maintained that the debate and vote "fulfills our constitutional responsibilities," it was not a task Congress undertook willingly or promptly.[14] Substantial doubt also exists as to whether a negative vote would have prevented the president from going to war. There is reason to believe that Congress, had the president ignored a negative vote and launched the attack anyway, would then have backed him *ex post facto*.[15] In the days after the war was launched January 16, the Senate unanimously passed a resolution in support of Bush. The House approved a similar measure 399 to 6. Bush was the clear winner in this momentous constitutional conflict.

It is difficult to imagine a separation-of-powers question rivaling the president's use of force in the Persian Gulf. But late in the term, a new matter emerged that would be of immense import in defining President Bush's relationship with Congress: the "check-bouncing" scandal.

The scandal centered on the defunct House Bank, a private operation that for decades provided representatives with unlimited, penalty-free overdrafts. The House Bank, which was closed December 31, 1991, was not funded with tax dollars and was not federally insured. Revelations about rampant abuse of the overdraft policy broke in fall 1991, but became a matter of concern to the executive branch in spring 1992, after the scandal became a political firestorm. Attorney General William Barr unexpectedly appointed a special counsel to investigate the House Bank. Barr named retired Judge Malcolm Wilkey, a jurist with a long record of criticizing congressional conduct and an extensive history of siding with the executive branch over Congress in separation-of-powers questions.[16]

The matter escalated into a constitutional conflict of the first magnitude in late April when Wilkey subpoenaed all records of the defunct bank. Speaker Thomas Foley described this legal move as "sweeping and unprecedented." Wilkey sought access to representatives' private financial records despite the lack of evidence of criminal conduct.[17]

Members of Congress and knowledgeable observers promptly questioned the constitutionality of the subpoenas, saying that, among other things, they violated the Fourth Amendment prohibition against unreasonable search and seizure.[18] One respected observer warned that compliance would "establish the most dangerous and sweeping precedent yet for executive-branch intervention into the affairs of the first branch of government."[19]

However, the House capitulated to Wilkey's demands, voting 347 to 64 on April 30 to turn over its records. Representatives freely acknowledged that while the Constitution and 200 years of American jurisprudence were on their side, politics was not. One observed that although opponents were "probably right on points of law, we are not now in a court of law. We are in a court of public opinion."[20]

Nonetheless, a small group of representatives carried the battle to court, arguing that the subpoenas violated their financial privacy rights and the separation of powers. "The chilling effect of these subpoenas on the legitimate activities of Members of the House cannot be overstated," argued Texas Congressman Henry B. Gonzalez, the chairman of the Banking Committee, who at that very moment was in the thick of a year-long effort to obtain executive branch documents relating to the Bush administration's pre–Gulf War aid to Iraq, including material relating to allegations of criminal conduct by U.S. officials.[21]

"The Members of the Committee have faced, on a regular basis, conflicts with the Executive Branch and negotiations with the Justice Department," he noted. "What will be the effect on the members if they know the Government holds the records of all of their financial transactions in its hands? Knows all the political affiliations, charitable contributions, or religious views each Member financially supports? Isn't that really the purpose and effect of these subpoenas?"

A federal court denied the motion to quash the subpoenas, and the Supreme Court declined to intervene. Although Chief U.S. District Court Judge John Garrett Penn denied the motion on its merits, many observers commented that the motion had been severely undermined by the

House's April 30 vote to turn the records over.[22]

Other scandals undermined Congress and enhanced the president's ability to dominate it. The nearly three-year-long "Keating Five" affair, the Senate Ethics Committee's much-criticized and inconclusive 1990–91 inquiry into the dealings of Republican Senator Alfonse D'Amato of New York, and the cocaine-dealing and theft allegations arising from a 1991–92 government probe into the House of Representatives Post Office are among these misdeeds. Neatly encapsulating Congress's problem was the 1988–89 scandal surrounding the Department of Housing and Urban Development. Congressional committees uncovered evidence of administration cronyism at HUD, but the inquiries were soon swamped by stories of similar behavior by congressmen. Congressional efforts to examine administration mismanagement and corruption in savings and loan regulation suffered a similar fate.

These are some of the events that will be remembered most clearly when we look back at President Bush's relations with Congress between 1989 and 1993, rather than any overt acts by the president himself.■

That the Grammy-winning pop group Milli Vanilli built a career on lip-synching to someone else's music created a major flap in American popular culture. We had been the victims of fraud. We've begun to see the political establishment in much the same light. Both Congress and the president posed, postured, and danced about, but neither had a real tune to offer. Congress accused Bush of failing to lead; Bush blamed Congress for refusing to follow. In the end, the public got political constipation. Nothing moved.

MILLI VANILLI

We believe in majority rule, but the president's veto power can make him a one-man majority. The threat of a veto can be a creative use of presidential power. It can tailor legislation so that, although neither the president nor Congress get all that they want, the public gets something. A successful veto produces nothing. It may indicate presidential power, but it also demonstrates ineptness and a lack of political sophistication. A veto is like the Heimlich maneuver; it works but it would have been better to trim the morsel in the first place.

WE'VE COME TO A FORK IN THE ROAD.

George Bush was more weathervane than signpost. There are two ways to be a leader. You can choose a direction and persuade the public to follow. Or you can find out where the parade is going and get in front. President Bush attempted to do the latter, but the winds keep changing. Having spent the Reagan decade shouting, "Every man for himself," he had trouble getting much public response to "follow me."

Many presidents are associated in the public's mind with some dramatic phrase or slogan. "Read my lips" aside (and Bush ended up wishing it was), "I hate broccoli" may be this president's quotable legacy. Many commentators believed he felt the same way about the nagging domestic problems we face. And with the budget crisis you don't even get cheese sauce.

About 20 years ago, Congress set limits on the size of individual political campaign contributions while opening the door to the formation of Political Action Committees. PACs are allowed to channel the contributions of their members to members of Congress likely to support their cause. Incumbents need money to defeat, or scare off, challengers. Interest groups need access to, and influence with, Congress. PACs are the conduit and money is the language. If "money is the mother's milk of politics," Congress has found itself a bountiful wet nurse and become addicted.

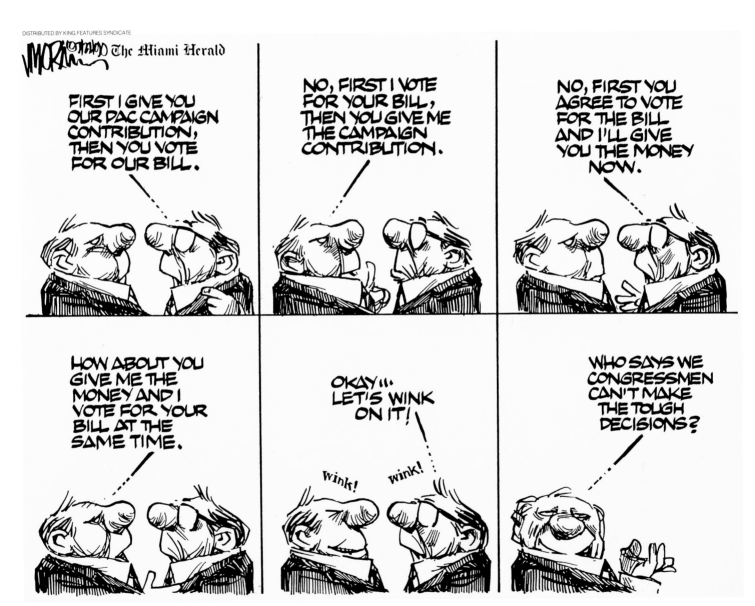

Like most politicians, George Bush found it easy and rewarding to speak of "values" and unpalatable to produce "policies." The difference between the two is that policies cost money. Unwilling or unable to significantly reduce spending or generate new revenues, American politicians have chosen to run on a platform of character, values, and vision. If the public got all of that and a nickel, it would have five cents.

Every four years, during the presidential primary season, Republican candidates charge to the right and Democrats gallop to the left. George Bush, faced with an all-Republican electorate in the 1992 primaries, twanged the heart strings of the far right. The successful Democrat had to sound like Franklin D. Roosevelt reincarnated. Once nominated, both candidates scrambled back to the middle and stood four-square behind moderation. The electorate never gets exactly what it bargained for. Leopards can't; politicians do.

REST EASY AMERICA, JESSE IS ON THE JOB.

Though it is not clear how or why he visited an art exhibit, or spoke to anyone who did, Senator Jesse Helms discovered in a touring exhibition of photographs sponsored by the National Endowment for the Arts a threat to American morals. In the end, Congress refused to defend freedom of expression for fear of appearing to defend pornography. The National Endowment for the Arts accepted a pruned-down version of the First Amendment in order to ensure continued funding. And the American public was defended from its museums.

The National Rifle Association may well be the country's most successful interest group. The NRA has a narrow focus, deep pockets, and a long memory. In short, it scares hell out of politicians. It has successfully resisted the most mild and innocuous limitations on the types and availability of firearms in America. Restricting the sale of automatic assault weapons would somehow turn Miss Liberty into the Venus de Milo. In the unlikely event that Congress had passed a comprehensive firearms control act, it would doubtless have been "Bush whacked" by George, who rides tall in the saddle up Kennebunkport way.

The Republican Party captured the flag in 1860 when southern Democrats seceded to create the Confederacy. Since then, the Republicans have made massive use of the symbols of patriotism at every opportunity. Modern Democrats, as the party of change, have faced the necessity of criticizing the existing situation. They have yet to find a way to find fault and wave the flag at the same time. In the battle of bumper stickers, Democrats must cope with "America—Love It or Leave It." They might try "America—Fix It or Lose It."

America has found that it was much easier to end slavery and segregation than it has been to incorporate African Americans into our society on an equal basis. Indeed, the earlier process was primarily one of making the South be nice. Ironically, the problem, along with a majority of the African American population, has shifted from the South to the North and from rural areas to urban ones. Social transformation is always painful, and "the ball is now in our court."

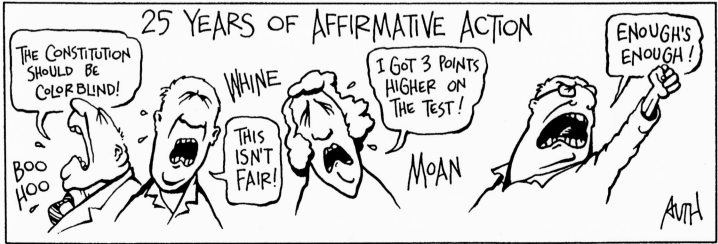

9-20-91 THE PHILADELPHIA INQUIRER. UNIVERSAL PRESS SYNDICATE.

The Reagan administration pulled off a political coup when it offered the American public massive tax cuts and a budget that was to be balanced by "cutting the fat out of government." A decade of living with a constricted budget has seen Congress render much of the fat out of our political carcass. And still the budget is unbalanced. The Democratic Party confounded President Bush by agreeing with him. No new taxes. But George had a country to run and he needed money to do it. So who is going to bell the cat?

During the 1980 primaries, George Bush labeled opponent Ronald Reagan's economic plan "voodoo economics." Then, as Reagan's vice president, he was part of the process in which Congress and the administration tried to paper over our growing deficit problem. It was called "creative accounting." Hilariously inaccurate "projections" and "anticipated" revenues were combined to produce budgets that should have been stamped MADE IN OZ. Once Bush was president, additional cuts had to come from large and adamantly defended entitlement programs like Social Security. Washington faced the painful truth. No more placebos.

Presidential appointments require the "advise and consent" of the Senate. A failure to get appointees confirmed is seen as presidential weakness, and many presidents have stubbornly supported candidates who are seriously flawed. Media coverage of hearings has encouraged the most sensational kinds of exposures. Most candidates try to prove they have the knowledge and experience to do the job, but a couple of decades of CIA scandals forced CIA veteran Robert Gates to prove how little he knew and how ignored he had been in planning. Alice would feel right at home in Washington.

CIA NOMINEE GATES REVEALS ALMOST ALL

THE SUPREME COURT

The coveted fifth vote   Stephanie Saul

What President Ronald Reagan began with the appointments of Sandra Day O'Connor, Antonin Scalia, and Anthony Kennedy to the U.S. Supreme Court, President George Bush attempted to finish. By the end of his fourth year in office, the Supreme Court's 1973 decision legalizing abortion, *Roe v. Wade,* was hanging by a thread, with the Court upholding abortion rights by a fragile 5 to 4 vote. The Court had shifted decidedly right on other issues as well—from civil rights to free speech to the death penalty.

Not since President Franklin Delano Roosevelt's conscious effort to revamp the federal judiciary, which had resisted his efforts at New Deal reform, had the executive branch so successfully moved to reshape the courts. Reagan and Bush had not only named five Supreme Court justices, they had also appointed 538 of 815 federal district and appeals court judges across the country. Just as the liberal activism of the Warren Court had caused vast changes in the lives of citizens in that era, no American was untouched by the conservative backlash.

The transformation of the federal judiciary had begun under Reagan, pressed on by conservatives to reverse what it considered a decline in morality in the past few decades, and Bush signed on wholeheartedly. The president had previously been identified with the Republican Party's moderate wing. But he was determined to preserve the administration's backing from conservatives.

Bush's desire to please the conservatives, and particularly the Christian right, led to one of the biggest debacles of his administration—the nomination to the Court of Clarence Thomas, former director of the Equal Employment Opportunity Commission (EEOC). Allegations that Thomas had sexually harassed a former EEOC aide, Oklahoma law professor Anita Hill, led to sordid, nationally televised hearings in which Hill described Thomas's alleged behavior in graphic detail. It was the worst scandal involving the Court since Abe Fortas's resignation in 1969 under threat of impeachment. Fortas had accepted money and agreed to perform services for a foundation controlled by a convicted stock manipulator.

Liberal opposition to Thomas, although formidable, was neutralized by the fact that he is African American. And aided by a well-financed lobbying campaign led by the moral right, Thomas was confirmed. He quickly joined the Court's most conservative faction, staking out a position to the right of Justice David Souter, a former New Hampshire attorney general and Bush's other nominee. In 1992, Thomas cast a fourth vote to overturn *Roe v. Wade,* leaving abortion opponents one vote short. "I fear for the darkness as four Justices anxiously await the single vote necessary to extinguish the light," wrote Justice Harry A. Blackmun, who authored the *Roe* decision. "I am 83 years old. I cannot remain on this court forever."[1]

The campaign that had turned the Court almost 180 degrees in 20 years really began in the 1950s, following the Court's decisions on school prayer, rights for criminal defendants, and women and minorities.

The decisions triggered a conservative campaign that gained new impetus in the 1980s, with Reagan's election boosted by the "Moral Majority." The Court had become a lightning rod for conservatives. The Republican Party's platform in 1980 carried a plank urging the selection of "family values" judges. The Reaganites wanted a counterrevolution, a return to the morals of the old days, before civil rights, women's rights, and gay rights.

High on their agenda was a reversal of the decisions handed down by the Court during the years of Chief Justice Earl Warren. And much of their campaign had sympathy from broad portions of the public, who were angered by many judicial decisions, such as those promoting racial and gender quotas in hiring, school busing, and the rights of criminal defendants.

Ironically, the conservatives railed against judicial activism, but wanted judicial activism with a conservative bent—justices who would legislate from the bench, who would interpret the Constitution to effectively change the meaning of laws imposed by a Congress they saw as increasingly liberal.

President Reagan obliged, sending up a slew of federal district, appeals, and Supreme Court nominees with conservative pedigrees. Members of the Senate Judiciary Committee, the panel charged with reviewing judicial nominees, were at a loss to prevent the transformation of the courts. The senators grilled nominees on their position on *stare decisis,* the legal principle that court decisions are to be based on precedent. One by one, the nominees assured the lawmakers that judicial activism was anathema.

On his elevation to Chief Justice in 1986, William H. Rehnquist told the panel, "I think that the Chief Justice can exercise a certain amount of leadership on the Court, but I do not think it is apt to be in a philosophical direction."[2] And during his confirmation hearings in 1987, Anthony M. Kennedy said, "Judges are not to make laws, they are to enforce the laws."[3]

Despite such protestations at their confirmation hearings, once the appointees donned their robes, their combined actions smacked of activism. With Kennedy's nomination, the conservatives were firmly in control of the Rehnquist Court. No precedent was sacrosanct, it appeared. The notion troubled legal scholars, jurists, and practicing lawyers, who depend on the foundations established by the Supreme Court and hoped that changes, if they came, would come slowly.

By 1988, Kennedy's first year on the bench, the Court had announced its intention to review a statute that had been interpreted to allow monetary damages to victims of employment discrimination. A chill went through the civil rights community.

The next year, the Court issued five key rulings that narrowed the redress available to victims of employment discrimination.[4] Blackmun opined, "One wonders whether the majority still believes that race discrimination, or more accurately race discrimination against non-whites, is a problem in our society, or even remembers that it ever was."[5]

The Court's shift to the right had already introduced a partisan tone to the normally noncontroversial selection and confirmation of district and appeals court judges, with the Senate Judiciary Committee giving greater scrutiny to the lower court judges. Now, the divisiveness was about to enter a broader legislative arena—the debate over actual legislation.

As a result of the Court's controversial decisions on employment discrimination law, Congress began almost immediately to prepare a bill designed to reverse the Supreme Court's actions. It led to one of the Bush administration's most rancorous splits with Congress, with the administration labeling the legislation a "quota bill" that would require employers to fill numerical quotas in hiring. Attorney General Dick Thornburgh, never a favorite of Congress, attacked the legislation in particularly harsh tones, and the Bush administration's posture prompted the Leadership Council on Civil Rights, an umbrella group of civil rights, labor, and liberal organizations, to accuse the administration of bowing to the right wing of the Republican Party. Bush vetoed the lawmakers' efforts, and an override attempt failed by one vote. The next year, with Bush's stature in the civil rights community, particularly with women, diminished over the Hill-Thomas affair, the White House relented. Bush signed a modified version of the bill, which became the Civil Rights Act of 1991.

Bush, meanwhile, had made his first Supreme Court appointment—Justice David Souter. Anxious to avoid the controversial confirmation battles of the Reagan years, such as the defeat of Robert Bork, Bush chose the enigmatic Souter. Despite an extensive record, including two years as New Hampshire attorney general, seven years as a state supreme court justice, and a brief stint on a federal appeals court, there was little to indicate how Souter would vote on such highly charged issues as abortion.

Once Souter was nominated, White House Chief of Staff John Sununu, former governor of New Hampshire, quietly began assuring conservatives that Souter was in their camp. But Senate staffers reviewing the record found little evidence of how he would vote on the Court. Souter carefully declined to express his personal views. Senator Edward M. Kennedy (Democrat, Massachusetts) protested that the Senate could not confirm a blank slate, but Souter's nomination was approved easily. Another conservative had been named to the Court, this time replacing its most outspoken champion for individual rights, Justice William J. Brennan, Jr.

Bolstered by Souter's appointment, the Rehnquist Court began issuing even more sweeping opinions on a broad variety of topics. Figuratively stepping out of his judicial robes and taking on his role as spokesman for the judicial branch, Rehnquist urged Congress to bring under control the number of lawsuits by habeas corpus petitioners—state prisoners seeking release from prison in federal court.

When Congress failed to oblige, Rehnquist used his considerable power, leading the Court to place limits on such appeals. In *McCleskey v. Zant,* the Court ruled 6 to 3 that, except in rare cases, a prisoner may file only one habeas petition in federal court.

In another 6 to 3 opinion, *Coleman v. Thomp-*

son, the Court said a death row inmate may not file a habeas petition if he or she violated state court procedural rules. Rehnquist, who historically had favored the rights of government over the rights of individuals, also directed a retrenchment in other law governing criminal defendants.

The Court ruled that coerced confessions did not necessarily require that convictions be thrown out in *Arizona v. Fulminante*. In *Harmelin v. Michigan,* the Court said that states could sentence first-time drug offenders to life in prison without parole without violating the Eighth Amendment to the Constitution, which prohibits cruel and unusual punishment. In another case, *Riverside County, Calif. v. McLaughlin,* the Court said police could hold a person for 48 hours without a hearing. In still another decision, the Court ruled that the impact of a crime on a victim's family could be introduced in hearings to determine whether defendants should be put to death (*Payne v. Tennessee*).

With the interpretation of the Bill of Rights vastly changed in criminal law, the Court also revamped First Amendment rights, although not to as great a degree. The Court decided that states may bar nude dancing (*Barnes v. Glen Theatre*), and it sided with the Bush administration on an abortion "gag rule," which prohibited health-care workers at federally funded clinics from giving their patients information about abortion (*Rust v. Sullivan*). The Court also said that the First Amendment does not shield news organizations from lawsuits if they break their promises of confidentiality to their sources (*Cohen v. Cowles Media*).

To many watchers of the Court, the *Payne* decision on victim's impact was particularly bothersome because it reversed decisions the Court had made in 1987 and 1989. Writing on the doctrine of *stare decisis,* Rehnquist said that adherence to precedent was preferred, but not an inexorable command. Justice Thurgood Marshall, in what was to be the final dissent of his 24 years on the Court, predicted that the *Payne* decision foreshadowed a dreary future for the nation's downtrodden.

"Cast aside today are those condemned to face society's ultimate penalty," wrote the aged warrior of the civil rights movement. "Tomorrow's victims may be minorities, women, or the indigent. Inevitably, this campaign…will squander the authority and the legitimacy of this Court as a protector of the powerless."[6]

With the selection of Thomas to replace Marshall, Bush solidified the conservative majority on the Court. But several decisions of the Court's 1992 term must have reminded Bush of the lessons learned by one of his Republican predecessors, Richard M. Nixon. Although Nixon had promised to give the Court a more conservative tilt, one of his nominees had been Harry A. Blackmun, who has become one of the Court's liberal members. Court packing was indeed an uncertain endeavor.

The conservative Court, for example, dealt a blow to the religious right by ruling that even nondenominational prayer could not be allowed at high school graduation ceremonies. Kennedy and Souter surprised many conservatives by adopting positions against school prayer. And in its most controversial decision of 1992, the Court approved Pennsylvania's abortion restrictions, but upheld a woman's basic right to have an abortion. In what appeared to be an emerging centrist bloc on the Court, Reagan appointees O'Connor and Kennedy joined Bush appointee Souter to make up part of the 5 to 4 majority.

And, ironically, Souter used the opportunity to voice what appeared to be criticism of the Bush administration's politicization of abortion. With the spectre of the Thomas hearings haunting the Court, one wondered whether Souter feared its public standing was evaporating.

Explaining why *stare decisis* is so important, Souter wrote, "The Court must take care to speak and act in ways that allow people to accept its decisions…as grounded truly in principle, not as compromises with social and political pressures having, as such, no bearing on the principle choices that the Court is obliged to make.

"To overrule under fire in the absence of the most compelling reason to re-examine a watershed decision would subvert the Court's legitimacy beyond any serious question."[7] ■

The Constitution makes no mention of qualifications for appointment to the Supreme Court. That gives both the president and the U.S. Senate license to establish standards of their own. The motivation behind nearly every presidential appointment is intensely political. The president wants his general political philosophy imprinted on the Court. The Senate is aware of that and has usually acquiesced. But both Reagan and Bush had a specific policy in mind, the reversal of ROE V. WADE. That opened the door for Senate liberals to apply a test in kind, and an appointee admitting an antiabortion stance would not be confirmed. Souter kept his opinions to himself.

It is probably inevitable that presidents, given the opportunity, will attempt to "pack" the court with justices who share their ideology. Modern presidents establish a committee within the White House to identify and screen prospective appointees. Careful selection allows a president to have an affect on national policy long after he leaves office, in some instances, long after he's dead. That situation frequently produces tension between the public and the Court. American public opinion alternates between periods of more liberal attitudes followed by a more conservative cycle. Elected officials reflect that cycle rather quickly; the Court lags behind.

"...AND THEN,... THERE WERE THREE!!"

The Constitution, in its brevity, is subject to multiple interpretations. It is that flexibility that has allowed it to function more or less effectively throughout our history. Every time the Court is called upon to make a major decision, it is establishing as law something that is not in the document. If it were there, any lower court judge would already be applying it. Thus the basic amendments remain as they were originally written, but are variously interpreted. We change what they mean when we change those who interpret them. And we do that by electing presidents such as Ronald Reagan and George Bush. If you don't like what the Court does, be more careful when you vote.

THE RISE AND FALL OF THE AMERICAN UMPIRE

We define the Court as "strict constructionist" when it is inclined to hew rather closely to the express wording of the Constitution. The Court is "broad constructionist" when it demonstrates a willingness to extend the meaning of the document to meet a social need or protect a group of people. An "activist" Court aggressively seeks out cases that allow it to move in the direction it wishes to go. The present Court is a strict constructionist one where social issues are concerned. Its members refuse to stretch the Constitution to defend civil or human rights. But it is also an activist Court, quick to seek out cases that allow it to shrink interpretations of the Constitution.

The U.S. Supreme Court is faced with the frustrating task of trying to balance the sometimes contradictory values of the American people. We praise freedom but want order; we believe in individual rights but also in the public welfare. We tend to emphasize one or another of these values for a time and then decide we've gone too far. The Reagan-Bush Court reflects the belief of many Americans that order and the public welfare have been sacrificed for the sake of individual rights and freedoms.

WHEN YOU'RE NOT PERRY MASON, YOU NEED A CONFESSION.

America's police are fundamentally keepers of order, not solvers of crime. They generally have neither the budget, the time, nor the training to do the latter. They have traditionally depended upon eyewitnesses or confessions to apprehend and convict criminals. The MIRANDA warning (reading a suspected criminal his or her rights at the time of arrest) seriously reduced the number of confessions admissible in court. Since the MIRANDA decision, the lower courts have extended the meaning of that decision in ways that the Reagan-Bush Supreme Court believes have unduly limited the actions of police. They will not reverse the MIRANDA decision, but they will reverse some of the interpretations of that decision that resulted in the exclusion of otherwise reasonable and probative evidence.

American police have a frustrating, depressing, and often dangerous job. They deal with the most twisted and degraded of our citizens on a daily basis. They serve a court system weakened by plea bargaining and inhabited, in part, by attorneys seeking every imaginable loophole to frustrate justice. None of that can be allowed to excuse brutality or condone racism. For the good of the police themselves, the brutes and racists within their ranks must be weeded out. Liberals are quick to point out that crime is the product of social conditions as well as individual decisions. It seems likely that the same is true of police brutality.

A DEMOCRATIC RIDDLE: WHAT CAN YOU KEEP ONLY IF YOU'RE WILLING TO GIVE IT TO OTHERS? ANSWER: YOUR CIVIL RIGHTS.

A fascinating aspect of our Bill of Rights is that most of us will never really use it. We don't say inflammatory things; we don't need to protect ourselves from self-incrimination; nobody cares what we have stashed in our homes. But we are frustrated by the criminals who use our civil rights to protect themselves from the legitimate operation of the law. It's tempting to prune back those rights to streamline our law enforcement system. We must hope the Supreme Court acts with caution, because even we may one day need that Bill of Rights in all its interpreted and embellished glory.

AND YOU INSIST, MR. PRESIDENT, THAT THE FACT THAT MR. THOMAS WAS A HIGHLY CONSERVATIVE, YOUNG, BLACK, REPUBLICAN LAWYER OPPOSED TO ABORTION HAD NOTHING TO DO WITH YOUR CHOICE?

Clarence Thomas must have looked like manna from heaven to George Bush. The president was under pressure to replace the retiring Thurgood Marshall with another minority jurist. Bush was also anxious that his appointee be conservative and antiabortion. The conservative wing of his own party demanded as much. Thomas's appointment looked like a coup. His race would disarm liberals and his youth meant he would provide a conservative voice for decades. Then along came Anita Hill.

Supreme Court Justice Thomas is clearly the product of the civil rights reforms and affirmative action programs that came out of the liberal crusade of the 1960s. Doors were opened for him and assistance granted him that would have been unavailable without those liberal programs. Paradoxically, he came to see such programs as ill-advised and assumed a philosophical stance diametrically opposed to the movement that created him.

This nation discovered that removing most of the economic barriers confronting racial and religious minorities, and women, left the economic structure that created those barriers unchanged. At issue is how to make those changes. Liberals and the excluded groups are anxious to use governmental policies and laws to expedite change. That probably means some kind of "percentage goals" for hiring. Conservatives damn such "quotas." Perhaps a more fruitful approach would be to rise above the semantic shootout and decide what really is the fairest and most effective way to produce economic equity.

Liberals in America were faced with a riddle that would have flustered the Sphinx. How do you produce a society that does not discriminate on the basis of race (color blind) and at the same time produce policies that are cognizant of the need to move that race forward (color conscious)? The phrase adopted for such policies was "affirmative action." But in a society where there is stiff competition for good jobs, one person's gain is another person's loss. A liberal Court would accept some discomfort to whites and males in the corrective process. The Bush Court would not.

At regular intervals some Americans express shock at finding the Supreme Court involved in politics. They apparently believe the justices should be above the fray and finding within our omniscient Constitution a way to mete out truth and justice for all. Not quite. Justices are appointed because they reflect a particular political point of view. They have had most of a lifetime to arrive at a political ideology, and they do not take some kind of intellectual physic to purge themselves of that before they are sworn in. We can hope that they will not be overtly partisan, but they most certainly will be political.

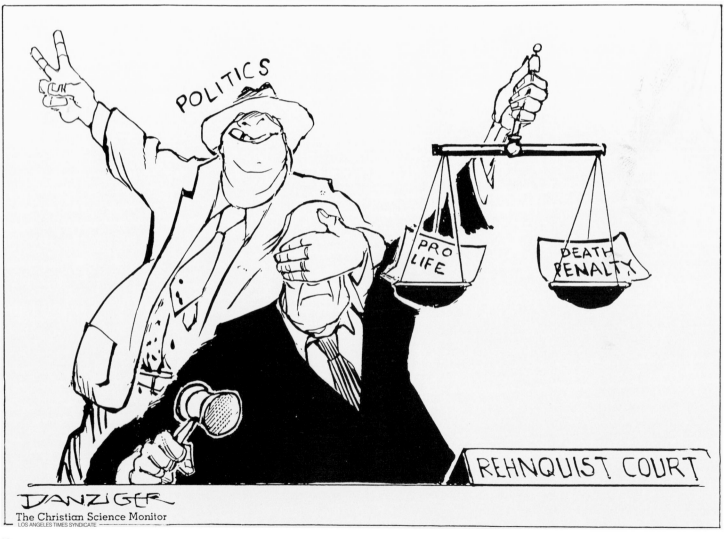

Unfortunately, "justice" is a relative thing. In a democracy, it is generally what the majority thinks is right or fair. The polls indicate a comfortable majority of our population is essentially pro-choice. There are several mechanisms whereby that majority could have given their interpretation of justice the protection of the law. Congress could have been forced to enact legislation guaranteeing the right to choose. A constitutional amendment could have been pushed through (although the Constitution allows a minority to block the will of the majority in this process). And the majority could have elected pro-choice presidents.

The Supreme Court establishes precedents that, under our system of stare decisis, *the lower courts must enforce as the law of the land. The process gives us predictability and protects us against a capricious interpretation of the law by a lower court judge. But it also depersonalizes the application of the law. Clearly it would be easier to decide that the generic "woman" must carry a fetus to full term regardless of the circumstances of conception or the situation of the mother, than it would be to deal with a terrified and inept teenager trapped in an unwanted pregnancy.*

3

THE CHANGING WORLD ORDER: FOREIGN POLICY MILITARY SPENDING

FOREIGN POLICY

New world, old vision

John B. Judis

In the wake of the Cold War's end and America's stunning defeat of Iraqi dictator Saddam Hussein's forces in Kuwait, George Bush repeatedly conjured up the image of an America straddling the globe triumphant. He boasted of "winning the Cold War"; he pledged to create a "next American century" in which America would continue to dominate the world. "We can't right all wrong, but neither can any nation lead like ours," he told graduating Air Force Academy cadets in May 1991.[1]

But less than a year after American tanks rumbled across the desert, another image of America gained ground. In January 1992, Bush led a delegation to Tokyo of American corporate executives seeking trade concessions from the Japanese. On the eve of the visit, Japanese Prime Minister Kiichi Miyazawa urged that the Americans, who were suffering from a long recession, be treated with "compassion." At dinner with Miyazawa, Bush suddenly lurched toward the prime minister and vomited. When the president, ill with a violent stomach virus, collapsed to the floor, Miyazawa cradled his head in his arms. One Japanese official said later, "It's so symbolic. The superpower America is tired, and everyone around it has to take care of it."[2]

Was this the same president who promised a "next American century"? And was this "tired superpower" the same America that had been portrayed only a few months earlier as the unchallenged world leader? The chasm separating these two visions of America reflected the confusion that lay at the heart of the Bush administration's foreign policy. The United States had triumphed over both the Soviet Union and Iraq, but had emerged from these conflicts into a world no longer defined primarily by military strength and by a quasi-religious battle against an "evil empire." Instead, power in the world was increasingly based on economic strength. And here, the United States—plagued by soaring budget deficits and an eroding industrial base—was at a growing disadvantage.

The transition from a bipolar world rooted in military and ideological conflict to a multipolar world based primarily on economic competition took place over several decades. But these germinating changes burst forth during the Bush administration, making it appear that 30 years of history had been compressed into 4 years. Bush had to deal first with the turbulence of the Cold War's end and then with the novel challenges of the post–Cold War world. Bush proved an able leader during the transition out of the Cold War that occupied the first two years of his presidency. With Secretary of State James Baker's help, he resolved Cold War–era conflicts in Nicaragua, El Salvador, and southern Africa and worked to ensure a bloodless transition from Communism in Eastern Europe. In his third year as president, Bush took advantage of the Cold War's end to forge an unprecedented coalition against the Iraqi invasion of Kuwait.

But faced with America's declining economic position, Bush stumbled. Instead of leading America into the new post–Cold War world, he perpetuated the assumptions of the old—from its alliance systems to its trading arrangements. As a result, at the end of Bush's first term, Americans found themselves bewildered about their country's role in the world.

In the 20th century, there have been two competing, but sometimes complementary, traditions of American foreign policy. One tradition, called "idealistic" or "evangelical," envisages America as having a moral or religious mission to transform the world according to its own image. Idealists like Woodrow Wilson, Jimmy Carter, and Ronald Reagan have portrayed foreign policy as a struggle of good against evil. At their best, idealists have furthered America's democratic aspirations. At their worst, they have plunged the country into holy wars.

The other tradition, called "realistic," has conceived of foreign policy as a struggle for power and stability rather than for democracy and virtue. Realists like George Kennan and Henry Kissinger have downplayed the role of political ideology in conflicts among nations. They have urged Americans to act according to their own national interest and to eschew attempts to convert the world to Christianity or democracy. They see the goal of foreign policy as establishing order or stability through creating a balance of power.[3]

Bush, who learned diplomacy under Kissinger in the Nixon and Ford administrations, was a practitioner of realism, and he filled his administration with other disciples of Kissinger's realism —National Security Advisor Brent Scowcroft, Baker, and Baker's Deputy Secretary of State Lawrence Eagleburger. Nixon and Kissinger themselves became important administration advisors, particularly on U.S. relations with China and the Soviet Union.

But Bush's realism was not so much a philosophy that could be adapted to different periods as a pattern of learned behavior that he extrapolated from the 1970s to the 1990s. Bush often acted as though the challenges the United States faced in 1991 were the same as those the Nixon administration faced in 1971. Where the periods were similar, Bush was at his best. But when dissimilarities reigned, he and the country floundered.

Bush's realism proved most useful in winding down the Cold War. Bush and Baker had no interest in prolonging the anti-Communist rebellions that the Reagan administration had funded in Central America and Africa. Bush was also far more cautious than the Reagan conservatives about encouraging, in the name of freedom, the breakup of the Soviet Union. In winter 1990, Bush prudently rejected urgings from both conservatives and liberals in Congress to send an American ambassador to the Baltic states. To have done so might have precipitated a civil war or a military coup before the Soviet reform opposition could assume power.

But even in ending the Cold War, Bush's realism at times failed him. Although Reagan had raged against the Soviet "evil empire," he had intuitively sensed Soviet President Mikhail Gorbachev's commitment to ending the Cold War, and had hurtled the United States toward drastic arms reductions. As a Kissingerian realist, Bush doubted internal change could seriously affect Soviet foreign policy; and in his first year, Bush and Scowcroft rejected Gorbachev's overtures for arms cuts, charging they were a ruse to divide the United States from Western Europe. Only after Bush saw Gorbachev encourage the fall of East German and Czech Communists did he realize the Soviet leader meant to end the Cold War. He then pressed ahead with agreements.

Bush also shared Nixon and Kissinger's skepticism about democracy outside the industrialized West. When China's rulers brutally repressed a student reform demonstration at Tiananmen Square in June 1989, Bush refused to throw American support to the students. Instead, while offering token protests, he secretly sent Scowcroft and Eagleburger on two missions to assure the Chinese rulers of American friendship. Bush wisely rejected extreme measures proposed in Congress to close off China's trade to the United States by revoking most-favored nation status, a euphemism for reinstating a prohibitive tariff, but he vetoed mild congressional efforts to grant asylum to Chinese students in the United States.

In his policy toward China, Bush revealed just how literally he was committed to Nixon and Kissinger's foreign policy realism. Just as Nixon had not allowed the Chinese Cultural Revolution to deter him from opening relations with China, Bush refused to allow events in Tiananmen Square to endanger Sino-American relations. "It was the same logic," Scowcroft explained. Yet as Bush's critics pointed out, in 1971 the United States needed China's friendship to balance the power of the Soviet Union; by June 1989 the Soviet threat had disappeared. The United States had little to lose by mildly rebuking China's brutal gerontocracy.[4]

Bush also had difficulty redefining or withdrawing from historic Cold War institutions and commitments. He continued to prop up NATO. When the French and Germans organized their own 50,000-person defense force in summer 1991, Bush loudly protested, even though NATO had been originally devised as a stopgap until the Western Europeans could defend themselves. Bush also persisted in spending as much as $60 billion a year defending Japan and South Korea from communist attack. And he ignored Japanese wishes to have a greater role in international decision making—spurning proposals to grant Japan and Germany permanent seats on the U.N. Security Council.

Despite growing budget deficits, Bush sustained high levels of foreign aid and military spending—about 5 percent of national income and proportionately double what America's economic competitors were spending. Bush did so partly out of inertia—the gigantic American military establishment could not be dismantled overnight—but also because he continued to adhere to a Cold War model of American leadership that rested upon its military superiority. By midterm in his presidency, this model of American foreign policy had become dangerously obsolete. But for Bush, its relevance was confirmed by America's military success in the Persian Gulf.

Bush correctly saw Iraq's invasion of Kuwait in August 1990 as a threat to international stability —because Iraq's control of the oil-rich country would give it a greater role in determining oil prices and because Iraq's conquest might embolden Saddam Hussein later, when armed with nuclear weapons, to precipitate an even larger war. To oust the Iraqis, Bush and Baker assembled a post–Cold War coalition that included the Soviet Union and that enjoyed the support of Israel and Syria. Afterward, Bush and Baker used the coalition's victory to score a diplomatic coup—bringing the Israelis, Palestinians, and neighboring Arab nations together for the first time in negotiations.

Yet Bush saw in America's Gulf War triumph not simply a successful application of post–Cold War containment, but also confirmation for his view of the country's global role. Bush claimed to have achieved a "new world order"—a phrase used by Woodrow Wilson in 1919. Bush did not use the term, however, as Wilson had. Wilson had wanted to create a new international organization so that America's economic strength would not be drained in military expenditures and adventures, but Bush was not interested in ceding American power to the United Nations or to a new world alliance. Instead, he saw the war in the Gulf as affirming America's military leadership in a post–Cold War world, where the main threat to order would come from unruly dictators like Hussein. For Bush, what was new about the world order was that the United States now lacked any rivals. In speeches after the Gulf War, Bush proclaimed the onset of a "next American century."

Bush's new world order was literally, and figuratively, built on sand. Because of the U.S. deficit, the American war effort in the Gulf had to be financed almost entirely by Japan, Germany, and Saudi Arabia. Both the Japanese and the Germans emerged from the war determined to take a more independent course in foreign relations. And Iraq's challenge, while formidable, was certainly atypical. Most of the national conflicts unleashed by the collapse of Communism—whether in Yugoslavia or the old Soviet Union—have not been susceptible to U.S. military intervention. Instead, their resolution requires multilateral diplomacy through international bodies.

Most important of all, Bush's concept of a new world order ignored the growing role of economics in international relations. Like Kissinger, Bush saw international relations primarily in terms of military rather than economic power. (When Secretary of Commerce Peter Peterson asked Kissinger in 1972 about granting most-favored nation status to the Soviets, Kissinger responded, "That's just a minor economic consideration." Two years later, detente collapsed when Congress linked most-favored nation status to Jewish emigration from the Soviet Union.[5] Bush assumed, if anything, that the United States could use its military predominance to ensure its continuing economic strength. In his general conception of foreign policy, as in his particular applications, Bush showed that like many acolytes, he could mimic his masters but could not adapt their principles to an entirely new situation.

As the precipitous decline of the Soviet Union demonstrated, nations that neglect their domestic economy to pursue global military power will eventually suffer not only internal decay, but loss of international influence, regardless of military strength. And in the long run, military strength itself will also erode as such nations fall behind technologically. When Bush took office in 1989, the United States was entering an economic decline that threatened not only its standard of living but also its position in the world.

Bush' policies accelerated rather than halted this decline. Bush allowed the deficit to balloon —to a record $400 billion in his fourth year in office. He shut down or cut the funding of government programs designed to promote American high technology. And he resisted shifting resources from Cold War military expenditures to civilian production.

During Bush's term, American industry continued to suffer severe internal woes—the result of contentious labor-management relations, a structure of corporate decision making that discourages long-term planning, and a decaying national infrastructure. Instead of addressing these ills, Bush assumed that the country's flagging economic performance could be remedied externally—by ensuring cheap raw material imports and opening new markets. Bush's international economic strategy was designed to make any significant domestic intervention unnecessary.

In developing an energy policy, for instance, Bush, a former oilman, rejected conservation and the development of alternative fuels in favor of using America's military in the Mideast to ensure cheap imported oil. The short-run benefits to the consumer were largely illusory. The costs of maintaining the U.S. military in the Mideast, wrote political scientist Alan Tonelson, "push up the real price paid by American taxpayers for Gulf oil by factors of three and four even in peacetime—to levels higher than estimates for many available alternative fuel sources currently dismissed as uneconomical."[6]

Bush sought to revive American manufacturing by getting other countries to open their markets to U.S. goods. He undertook fruitless negotiations—dubbed the Structural Impediment Initiatives—to convince Japan to change its fiscal policy to encourage more imports. He agitated for a new General Agreement on Tariffs and Trade (GATT) and initialed a Mexican Free Trade Agreement. But he did nothing to pressure or encourage American manufacturers to make goods that could compete in foreign or in America's own markets. Bush's trip to Japan in January 1992 epitomized almost everything wrong with his approach to the new post–Cold War world.

The trip was initially supposed to concern security matters, but Bush, facing voter unpopularity because of the recession, decided to devote it to winning trade concessions from the Japanese. He did not encourage Japan to take a larger security role in its own region, which might have freed up American resources at home. Instead, he tried to use the leverage of the American nuclear and military umbrella to pry open Japanese markets to American autos and auto parts. He gained some token concessions, but they were essentially meaningless. The American auto industry's principal problem was not its failure to sell its cars overseas, but its inability to compete at home. To improve American industrial performance at home, however, would have required Bush to undertake new domestic initiatives.

In its foreign economic policy, the Bush administration set a disastrous example for the future. If the United States persists in a strategy of using military predominance to exact trade and debt concessions, while ignoring domestic economic reform, the nation's economy will continue to decline; its debt will spiral; and the conflict between the United States and its former allies over debt repayments and trade barriers could grow fierce. International relations could return to the parlous condition before World War I when countries used force to increase their share of world markets.

Bush appeared oblivious to these dangers. Faced with an election challenge centered on the sinking economy at home, Bush boasted of his administration's foreign policy accomplishments. But if the trends encouraged by his post–Cold War policy continue, future generations, looking back on his administration, will declare that both the Soviet Union and the United States lost the Cold War. And they will see the Bush years not as the foundation of a "next American Century," but as the last dismal years of this one.■

George Bush, in the 1988 presidential campaign, emphasized heavily his skills and experience in foreign policy. By 1992, for many Americans, those skills seemed irrelevant. The doubts arose from two circumstances. First, most post–Cold War Americans were convinced that our domestic problems and, most importantly, our economic problems, ranked first on the national agenda. And many other Americans wondered whether Bush, who had been trained in an era of saber-rattling foreign policy, was really flexible or creative enough to deal with a new and complex set of international problems.

IF YOU'RE GOING TO HAVE A RACE, WHY NOT CHOOSE ONE WHERE YOU GET SOMETHING NICE WHEN YOU WIN.

Russia and the U.S. allowed themselves to be ensnared in an arms race. The trouble with that kind of competition is the fact that nobody ever really wins. The fundamental difference in their two ideologies was economic, and in this arena, they should have competed. The citizens of both societies would have been better off. To test that hypothesis, look at Germany and Japan. They lost the arms race of the 1940s and were excluded from the next one. Now they move and shake the world economy.

A map is artificial and arbitrary, representing power relationships at an instant in time. Many areas of the world have repeatedly seen their populations redefined and relabeled. Left behind is a tangled mass of ethnic identities. Communism was an ideology superimposed upon a collection of residual ethnicities. The Communists hoped to build loyalty to a broader nationalism. In retrospect, it didn't work. Ethnic ambitions and animosities were released with the collapse of Communism. If the process of division along ethnic lines continues, Liechtenstein may one day be a European superstate.

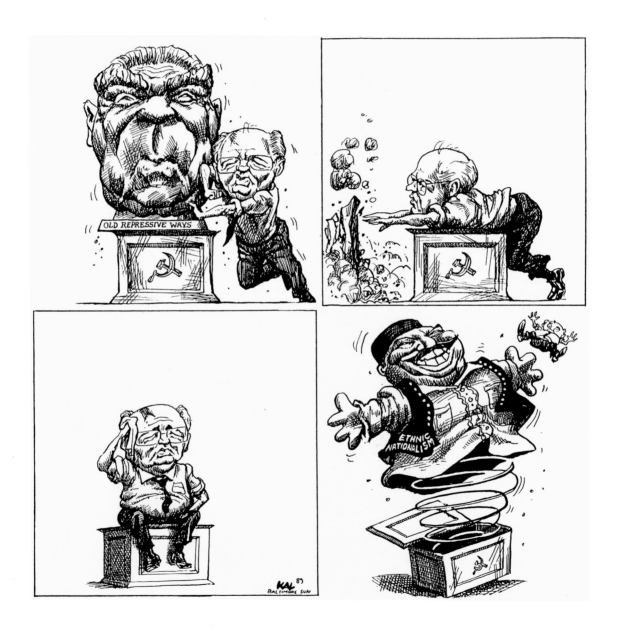

Early in the Cold War Nikita Khrushchev announced, "We will bury you." Both sides to the conflict assumed victory would go to the nation with the biggest bombs and the best missiles. As it turned out, Communism fell because Russia couldn't make a good pair of jeans or an adequate supply of toilet tissue. Mikhail Gorbachev faced a terrible paradox. He couldn't improve life for Soviet consumers while the economy was hemorrhaging with Cold War expenditures. But it was only the Cold War which made endurable the domestic inefficiencies of the communist system.

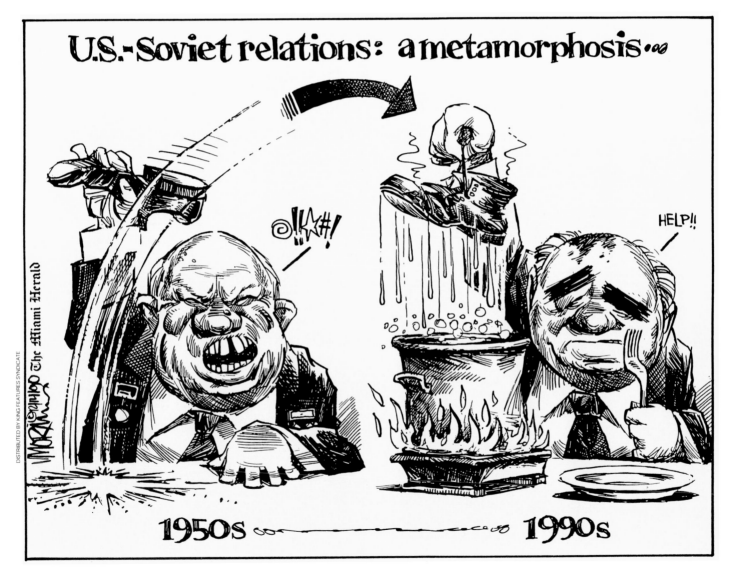

We avoided Armageddon and the "Evil Empire" fell of its own weight. But 40 years of Cold War commitment and tension had taken its toll in the United States as well. For too long the U.S. government had to concentrate attention and resources upon our rivalry with Russia, resources that might otherwise have been expended upon domestic problems. Idealism and faith were squandered on a fruitless war in Vietnam. By 1990 we were a tired and jaded nation coming off of a decade-long, self-indulgent binge. The fragile new democracies in Eastern Europe found no strong shoulder to lean on.

The North Atlantic Treaty Organization arose from the Cold War. The single issue member nations agreed upon was the need to deter Communist aggression. The question now is whether NATO can or should exist in a world where that particular threat no longer exists. The concept of a multinational military force to be deployed against aggressors is attractive. How often, though, will the member nations be able to reach consensus on the next generation of international crises? NATO's response to the Yugoslav problem was not a hopeful sign.

Neither Ronald Reagan nor George Bush felt particularly comfortable with the international human rights movement. Their response to Nelson Mandela and the racial situation in South Africa illustrates their acceptance of the traditional limitations of foreign policy. Foreign policy concerned problems among nations, not within them. Sovereignty included the right of nations to arrange their domestic affairs free of outside interference. Throughout history, nations have accorded that right to others in order to claim it for themselves. John F. Kennedy once said, "We must resist the temptation to believe we can right every wrong or reverse every adversity." Still, it would be nice to stand up for our principles.

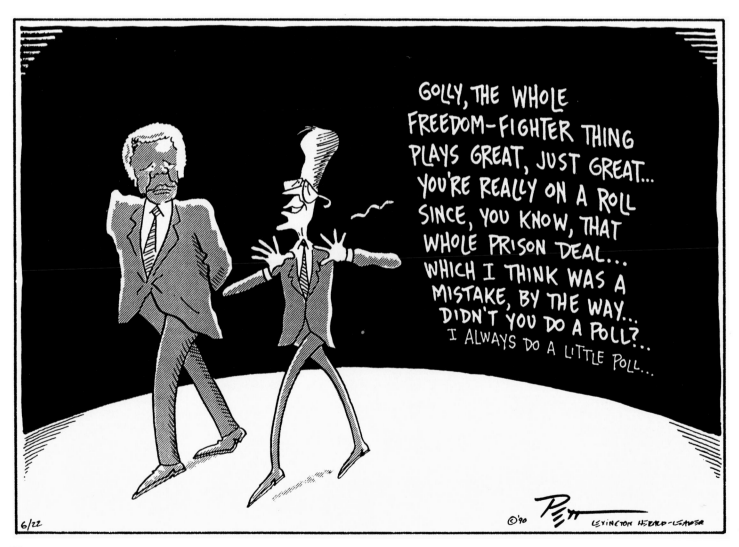

And history was on George Bush's side here as well. We have meddled in Latin American nations continually since before the turn of the century. Our willingness to intervene in some situations and our sanctimonious refusal to do so in others is undeniably linked to rewards we expect in return for our efforts. In Latin America, intervention props up compliant regimes and often protects U.S. business interests and provides access to natural resources. In human rights situations, intervention produces only a sense of moral satisfaction.

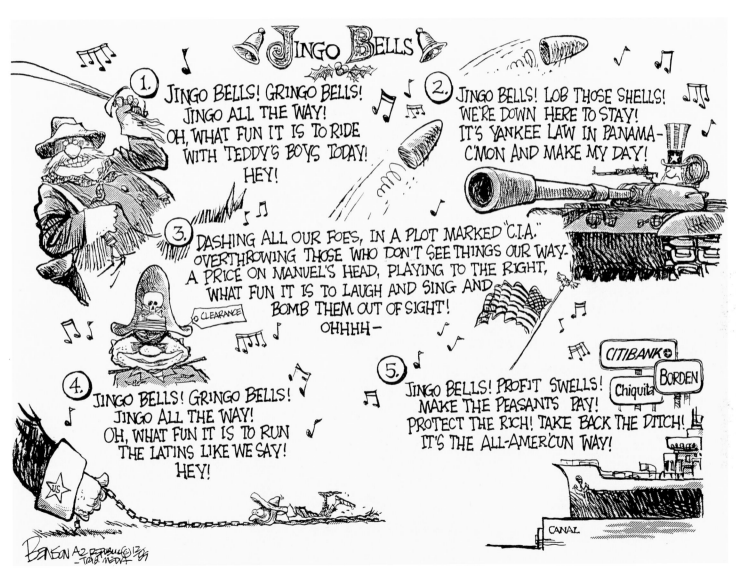

57

While we sponsored a bloody insurgency in Nicaragua, we poured even greater resources into stopping one in neighboring El Salvador. For most of a decade, the United States propped up the repressive regime in that small country. U.S. support, based initially on unwillingness to "lose" another nation to Communism, continued despite increasingly warm relations with Russia and the disintegration of the Communist bloc in Eastern Europe. Somehow we felt compelled to stop a threat that was no longer threatening. A radical regime in minuscule El Salvador in fact endangered nobody but the country's own landed oligarchy.

EL SALVADOR

The United States had a perpetual semantic problem during the Cold War. We divided the world into two camps. Defining the enemy was easy. They were godless Communists. We were freedom-loving democrats. American presidents had the embarrassing task of making the actions of some thoroughly vicious regimes fit under the umbrella of our elevated phraseology. Henry taught Eliza to sing,"The Rain in Spain." George Bush's lyrics ran, "I swear to God there's no murder squad." Still, the bodies kept showing up.

Ever since the Hessian affair (remember George Washington in the rowboat), Americans have detested mercenaries. But U.S. presidents, when a declaration of war and the use of American troops was inconvenient, have found ways to arm and bankroll insurgents seeking to overthrow governments unacceptable to us. The Nicaraguan affair differed in the degree to which we "manufactured" the insurgency. The CIA identified, recruited, trained, and directed the Contras. They were salaried agents of the U.S. government and were quickly abandoned when the Daniel Ortega regime surprised us with free elections and a peaceful transfer of power to its opponents.

Every party to the continual tensions in the Middle East agrees the issues must be settled by negotiation. And just as unanimous are these countries in insisting that their major demands are nonnegotiable. The Bush administration hoped that the changed situation in that region following the defeat of Iraq might offer some flexibility to the negotiations. The U.S. had clout enough to get these countries to the table in Madrid, but not enough to wring concessions from them that could lead to new and stabilizing agreements. While they spoke to one another, their real audiences were their constituents back home.

A LOT OF BULL IN MADRID

It is not necessary to deny the importance of Middle Eastern oil to insist that the United States has other important reasons to work for stability in the region. One of which is the U.S. commitment to Israel's welfare. Those who interpret American Middle Eastern policy as driven solely by our insatiable appetite for petroleum must explain away our support for Israel when abandoning Israel would endear us to the oil-producing Muslim states. The peace process requires not just changed attitudes among Middle Easterners, but a more sophisticated understanding of the area by the American public.

Ours is an ambiguous response to China. Its huge population is enough to make American business salivate. But that same population makes China a potential military superpower. China has recently moved from being an international pariah to a growing force in the world economy. Unfortunately, improvements in international deportment have not been matched by changes in domestic conduct. American pragmatists (and Bush is one of them) feel we must deal with the world as it is. American idealists believe we must try to make it better. It's not clear the Chinese give a damn what we believe.

The suppression of Chinese dissidents in Tiananmen Square disturbed American citizens. The elderly bureaucrats who govern China obviously felt threatened by rapid change. George Bush preached that evolutionary change could be promoted in a China that wouldn't accept revolutionary change. He argued that trade would bring that evolution about, and we must renew our Most Favored Nation agreement with them. American liberals favor using the threat of a trade cutoff to pry domestic reforms out of the Chinese. But perhaps the larger issue is whether they will buy our Levis or just sell us cheaper copies.

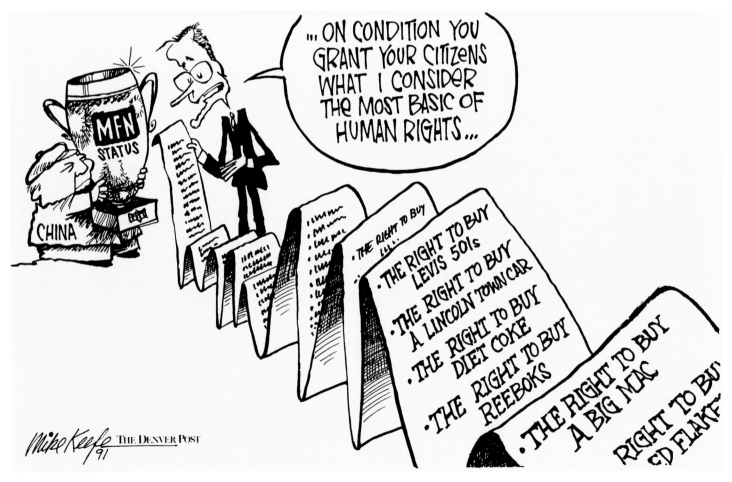

Our continued trade imbalance with Japan has become an explosive political issue. George Bush had to appear to be fighting aggressive and unfair trade policies. But he carried some major liabilities into the talks in 1992 with Japanese Prime Minister Nakasone. One was his own oft-stated opposition to restrictions on international trade. A second was that the Japanese presence in the U.S. bond market and on Wall Street left the United States vulnerable to serious counterattack for any trade restrictions we might threaten. Unfortunately, we appeared to be pleading for favors, not demanding fair play.

George Bush obviously let his political instincts cloud his economic vision. Because the Japanese autos have outsold American-made cars and are one cause of higher American unemployment and frightened American workers, Bush included prominent representatives of the U.S. auto industry in his entourage to the trade talks with Japan. The gesture backfired. Bush never intended to restrict Japanese auto imports, and he could hardly expect the Japanese to buy American-made cars that Americans weren't buying. A poor decision, as it was over other trade issues that serious progress might have been made.

" OF COURSE, ALL OF OUR NEW AMERICAN CARS COME EQUIPPED WITH AN *AIRBAG!*"

On three separate occasions, this nation has made the transition from the world's greatest military power to the most prosperous and rapidly growing economy on earth. Following the Civil War and both World Wars, we rapidly disarmed and turned the enormous energies of this nation to the business of building a bigger and better America. We are blessed with amazing diversity of resources, prodigious accumulations of capital, an ambitious and talented workforce, and an educational and transportation infrastructure that has been neglected but is still the envy of the world. Only a bankruptcy of ideas and shoddy political and economic leadership can prevent us from doing so again.

MILITARY SPENDING

In the absence of enemies

Rear Admiral Eugene J. Carroll, Jr. (Ret.)

George Bush is a long-standing and dedicated supporter of a strong U.S. military. Coming from a family with a distinguished history of public service, he volunteered for combat duty as a naval aviator during World War II. Presumably, his later experience as director of the Central Intelligence Agency in 1976–77 strengthened his conviction that America requires a powerful military as the key element of national security.

No doubt, his thinking has also been shaped by two significant assignments in the diplomatic corps. As chief of the U.S. Liaison Office to the People's Republic of China in 1974–75 he saw firsthand the potential threat to U.S. security posed by the world's most populous nation. His tour as U.S. ambassador to the United Nations in 1971–72, when the Security Council was largely paralyzed by Cold War confrontations, clearly left him doubtful about relying on the United Nations for leadership or protection. Even after the United Nations authorized the United States to take the military lead against Iraq in 1990–91, his commitment to the United Nations remained tenuous. In August 1991 he pledged to pay up all United States arrears to United Nations agencies by 1995![1]

This background partially explained his unswerving commitment to a large military establishment and continued military budgets at near–Cold War levels. Practical political factors have also shaped his position. The influence of a conservative and powerful military-industrial complex that lobbies persistently for large Pentagon budgets, and is generous with campaign contributions, is undeniable. On a more personal level, President Bush prospered in the oil industry and unfailingly supported political and economic policies favorable to big oil. Five oil companies rank among the top 100 U.S. military contractors.[2]

Given these personal and political predispositions, it is not surprising that on September 27, 1991, he declared, "The peace dividend I seek is not measured in dollars but in greater security. In the near term, some of these steps may even cost money."[3] This statement revealed his fundamental commitment to continue spending for the military at Cold War levels although the Cold War was over.

The question then is how he justified his support for large military forces and budgets to the American public once the Cold War was over. The answer is: with great skill and a willingness to color the facts. For example, in the same address that discounted a peace dividend, Bush referred to a proposal "to reduce defense spending by 25 percent."

The fact is that he proposed a military budget that dipped 2.8 percent to $281 billion for 1993 and then would rise every year thereafter, reaching $291 billion in 1997. His five-year total is $1,424 trillion. Bush's request was only 4 percent below the all-time record spending level set at the height of the Cold War. As Senator Jim Sas-ser, chairman of the Senate Budget Committee, pointed out, "The administration's latest proposal for defense spending gradually approaches the average Cold War peace-time level."[4] Bush described this 4 percent reduction as a 25 percent reduction because of the effect of inflation on military purchasing power. Unfortunately, taxes and borrowing are not indexed to inflation, and high military spending continues to contribute heavily to the growing burden of a $4 trillion national debt.

Bush matched creative claims of reduced defense spending with imaginative definitions of the new threats America faced once the Soviet Union had disappeared. In an August 1991 statement entitled "National Security Strategy of the United States," President Bush referred to "obstacles and uncertainties before us," "the turmoils and dangers in the developing world," "a dangerous world of ethnic antagonisms, national rivalries, spreading weaponry."

He accented the theme of uncertainty and instability to justify the need to be prepared for global military action. As commander-in-chief, George Bush stated: "There is no substitute for American leadership. Our responsibility, even in a new era, is pivotal and inescapable." This assumption of a primary U.S. responsibility to maintain world order was the fundamental reason President Bush sought to uphold America as the world's only military superpower. He stated openly that it was military strength that enabled America "to call the shots" in regional confrontations.

The continuance of old patterns of American hegemony and military intervention conflict with the need for dramatic change. The Carnegie Endowment National Commission on America and the New World recently observed that "this is the time for us to change the way we think about the world and the way we conduct our affairs at home and abroad."[5]

Yet despite such domestic and international proposals for change, military power was consistently a central element of Mr. Bush's foreign policy and was embodied in what his administration called the Base Force. According to the Bush plan, the Base Force will be achieved in 1997, by which time America's active military forces will number only 1,626,000, down about 15 percent from the current 1,907,000. Reserve forces and civilian employees of the Department of Defense will be comparably reduced. These reductions will necessitate a significant restructuring of present combat forces. For example, the Army will have four fewer active divisions; the Air Force, seven fewer active Tactical Fighter Wings and a smaller bomber force; and the Navy, 88 fewer ships.

But though these appear to be major changes in defense capabilities, no fundamental change in Cold War strategy will result. John Steinbruner, director of foreign policy studies at the Brookings Institution, has observed that the "United States defense effort is still being designed to sustain active military confrontation."[6] The Base Force is sized and shaped to continue all tasks previously justified as necessary for "containment of the Soviet Union."

Only the threat changed, according to General Colin Powell, chairman of the Joint Chiefs of Staff, who echoed the language that Bush used in the National Security Strategy. "The real threat we now face is the threat of the unknown, the uncertain. The threat is instability and being unprepared to handle a crisis or war that no one predicted or expected…. As the only nation with the military capability to influence events globally, we must remain capable of responding effectively if the United States is to successfully promote the stability required for global progress and prosperity."[7]

Based on this perceived global role, General Powell goes on to prescribe four broad missions for the Base Force.

1. *Strategic Deterrence and Defense.* Unchanged from Cold War days, this mission requires the United States to maintain nuclear offensive forces, and to continue development of a limited missile defense system for the United States and tactical missile defense systems for deployed U.S. forces and our allies.

2. *Forward Presence.* Forward deployment of major U.S. forces around the world on a network of 395 military bases, the backbone of the Cold War containment, will continue. The network will shrink, but the Base Force will continuously deploy approximately 250,000 troops in Europe, Korea, and Japan to defend U.S. interests against the new enemies, "the unknown," and "the uncertain."

3. *Crisis Response.* During the Cold War it was assumed that crises would inevitably arise as part of the continuing East-West confrontation. Now, General Powell states: "Regional contingencies we might face are many and varied, and could arise on very short notice. U.S. forces must therefore be able to respond rapidly to deter and, if necessary, to fight unilaterally or as part of a combined effort." This new world policeman role is much bigger than the one that protected Western nations from Communist aggression. Now the United States is to protect everybody, everywhere, from "many and varied" threats.

4. *Reconstitution.* This vaguely defined task is a direct carryover from the Cold War. In the past it was always assumed that the United States might have to rebuild its military following a nuclear attack by the USSR. The task now is to reconstitute our forces and industrial base to forestall any potential adversary from competing militarily with the United States.

This brief account of the current budget and near-term plans for the Department of Defense makes it clear that President Bush saw a strong continuing role for military power in the conduct of foreign affairs. Indeed, his presidency was distinguished by a willingness to order American troops into action. While in office, President Bush authorized involvement of U.S. military forces in foreign nations on five separate occasions.

First, he continued to authorize U.S. military personnel to assist El Salvadoran forces during operations against Farabundo Marti National Liberation Front (FMLN) insurgents in 1989. Second, in September 1989, he put U.S. military advisors into the field in Colombia as part of a drug interdiction effort. Third, U.S. fighter aircraft provided air cover in the Philippines as a show of support for President Aquino in December 1989 when right-wing dissidents attempted a military coup.

Then, on December 20, 1989, he sent U.S. forces into Panama to depose Manuel Noriega, a task quickly accomplished by 27,000 U.S. troops with few American casualties. However, heavy damage was inflicted on Panamanian civilian and military facilities, and hundreds of Panamanians were killed or wounded in the assault. The action in Panama was widely supported in the United States but roundly condemned around the world.

Little was actually accomplished by the Panamanian invasion. Drug trafficking and associated money laundering are still rampant in Panama. The Panamanian government became more respectful to President Bush but remains far from democratic; its economy remains in a shambles; and its damaged infrastructure is largely unrepaired. Manuel Noriega is in a U.S. jail.

If Bush's decision to use military force in Panama was questionable, even greater questions arise around Operation Desert Storm. These were not questions about Bush's performance as a global leader, which can only be called brilliant in forging a strong international consensus for this action.

It is clear from the massive buildup of offensive U.S. forces that President Bush had decided as early as September 1990 to use military force to expel Saddam Hussein's forces from Kuwait. No effort or U.S. offer was ever made to negotiate an Iraqi withdrawal from Kuwait. Instead, President Bush built support for U.S. military preparations by focusing on the United Nations.

Step by step the world community came together to impose an impressive series of political, economic, and military sanctions on Iraq. While many authoritative voices, at home and abroad, called for patience to give these sanctions time to work, the U.S. military buildup proceeded inexorably. By January 1991, 540,000 Americans were in the Persian Gulf, and war

was inevitable. Military victory quickly followed.

The confrontation in Iraq between Saddam Hussein and U.N. inspectors in July 1992 was further proof that the Middle East remains in turmoil. Nevertheless, President Bush's first action once again was to order additional U.S. military forces into the region.

Although Desert Storm was a war organized and led by the United States, President Bush did involve the United Nations in ways that demonstrated an increasing potential for effective U.N. leadership in international crises. And plausibly, Bush's reticence to commit U.S. forces in Yugoslavia in summer 1992 reflected some sense that U.N. leadership might offer a greater chance for a successful outcome than direct U.S. military involvement.

At the end of George Bush's first term, a compelling picture of a president prone to use military force as a prime instrument of foreign policy had emerged. Each military action he ordered was undertaken in a situation involving enduring political and economic issues that could not possibly have been resolved by military force alone.

The underlying motive for much of this pattern of crisis response is perhaps best revealed in the relationship of the president, the armed services, and Congress. All shared a strong drive to sustain high levels of military spending and troop strength. The president satisfied his powerful conservative constituents in the defense industry; the military preserved its perquisites and promotions; and Congress continued to deliver jobs and profits to voters at home. To justify these costs to American taxpayers, uses had to be found for the U.S. military.

The role of commander-in-chief was a good

fit for President George Bush. His two peaks of popularity followed the commitment of U.S. forces in Panama and Iraq. And because he made little progress on domestic issues, he found it rewarding personally and politically to divert attention to external threats to U.S. security.

There may be a high price for such diversions. David Calleo, political scientist at Johns Hopkins University, fears that the United States "will end up clinging to military power because it is economically weak…. Failure and decline at home will have to be masked more and more by vigorous assertions of economic and military power abroad."[8]

History is always slow to reveal itself in truth. The jury is still out on the Bush administration's national security policies and programs. Certainly, political rhetoric and media "spin control" exercised to put his actions in the best possible light color current efforts to evaluate his successes and failures.

Nevertheless, the "new world order" to which he often referred seems very much like the old world order. U.S. military superiority is required to support U.S. foreign policy and sustain a global intervention capability by U.S. forces deployed worldwide. The Pentagon spent $12 trillion to win the Cold War, and President Bush proposed to fund the military at the same level until at least the year 1997, although the United States is without any identified enemies except instability, uncertainty, and unpredictability.■

Presidents select their own advisers. Understandably, they select people who share their point of view. Consciously or unconsciously, the president conveys what he wants to hear from those appointees. If he isn't careful, he won't get advice; he'll get an echo. When the agency involved is the CIA, the situation can be truly dangerous. Throughout the 1980s the White House wanted to hear that the Soviet Union presented an imminent threat to the U.S. and that the U.S. was falling behind in the arms race. Until the U.S.S.R. actually collapsed, that is exactly the information the CIA provided.

Some Americans have a fanatical faith in science and technology. A record of past "miracles" leads many of us to accept as possible almost anything the mind of man can conceive. To keep an open mind is a virtue, but most of us wouldn't follow that with an open purse. The Reagan-Bush administrations accepted as "possible" what was essentially only "conceivable" and sold it to the public as "doable." The Strategic Defense Initiative would have led to a whole new arms race to produce both the new defense system and then a new offensive system to circumvent that. Americans in general, and George Bush in particular, should thank Gorbachev for saving us from our own folly.

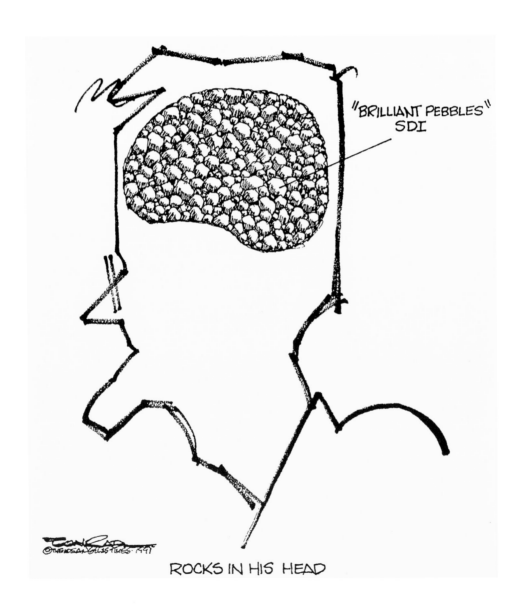

"BRILLIANT PEBBLES" SDI

ROCKS IN HIS HEAD

George Bush may have wished our educational system were healthier. He may even have wished it were better funded. But he decided Americans would not pay the taxes to achieve that. So, he paid lip service to the need for technological excellence and warned Americans they must prepare to compete in a global economy. To show a commitment to technological advances, he pressed for the construction of a space station. What Bush would not support was an investment in education anything like what our international competitors are willing to commit. Oh well, maybe the kids can pick it up watching "Star Trek."

THE SOVIET UNION DISINTEGRATED EVEN AS IT MAINTAINED AN IMPRESSIVE SPACE PROGRAM AND AN ENORMOUS MILITARY MACHINE BECAUSE IT NEGLECTED ITS CITIZENS.

There must be a lesson somewhere in the collapse of the U.S.S.R. Most observers seem convinced that the international "battleground" for the foreseeable future will be economic competition. The soldiers in that struggle will be workers, technicians, scientists, and entrepreneurs. The weapons will be schools, transportation systems, worker health, public commitment, and innovative leadership. The Bush administration seemed to be preparing for the wrong war.

AND I BELIEVE THAT EVERY SOLDIER NEEDS AN ELECTRIC TOOTHBRUSH.

Our military responds to some kind of "technological imperative." As soon as a technical breakthrough is seen to have possible military applicability, it is transformed into a military necessity. Economists speak of something called marginal utility. It is an effort to measure whether the next input of money or effort will produce commensurate improvements in performance. The Pentagon tends to ignore such questions. The results are weapons systems which gain efficiency arithmetically but increase in cost geometrically. The Bush administration refused to ask the generals the hard questions.

Modern man suffers any number of debilitating addictions. Heads of state are afflicted with a virulent form of "weapons dependency." They get hooked on "guns." They excuse their excesses as necessary for national security. But experience demonstrates that new weapons bring not security but an arms race. After each escalation, everyone is a bit less secure than before. Presidents must learn moderation. A little restraint might leave more revenue for developing human resources. And that might genuinely promote national security.

" HEY BUDDY!...CAN YOU SPARE $100 BILLION...TO GET ME BACK ON MY FEET?"

We must take care that the American military doesn't become like Listerine—a medicine in search of a disease. The world situation was dramatically altered with the collapse of a more or less unified Communist bloc. The American military establishment is now without a qualified challenger. Still, Americans will be persuaded to maintain an effective military presence to meet inevitable, but as yet unidentified, dangers. But our present military is an overfed behemoth. What we will need for the future is something quicker, leaner, and cheaper. What we don't need is a military or political effort to identify or manufacture a major new threat.

"WHADDAYA MEAN 'IT'S EXTINCT!'?!"

We will never know for sure whether our atomic arsenal ever truly deterred anything. Perhaps we're better off believing it did, otherwise we might come to feel we wasted a lot of money. Then again, it may have helped to bring about the collapse of Communism by forcing the Soviet Union to spend equivalent amounts that they could afford even less than we. Regardless of their efficacy as deterrents or as agents of bankruptcy, those systems have no role in the post–Cold War world. As our war with Iraq demonstrated, you don't kill fleas with a jackhammer.

During the Cold War, defense contractors, the Pentagon, and members of Congress became ever more sophisticated about the relationship between weapons, money, and votes. Companies peddling major weapons systems took great care to develop a web of subcontracts and production facilities spread through as many congressional districts as possible. The Pentagon did the same with bases and facilities. Congresspersons who voted "correctly" could crow to the folks at home that they had brought a payroll into the district. Gee, maybe we can use the B-2 to fight forest fires or the Stealth bomber to shuttle government officials around the country.

George Bush sensed the end of the Cold War marked a turning point in world history. It was an opportunity to establish a cooperative rather than confrontational response to the problems among nations. On the one hand, Bush was anxious to lead and to establish the terms of this new approach. On the other hand, many American arms producers depended heavily on foreign sales. And the United States defense establishment had a surfeit of "nearly new" equipment. Bush never did get the hang of that "vision thing." You can't have much order if disorderly governments have surface-to-air missiles.

THE FOUR HORSEMEN OF THE 'NEW WORLD ORDER'

One scenario for international chaos envisions nuclear weapons in the hands of megalomaniacs like Saddam Hussein and Momar Khaddaffi. And almost as chilling is the thought of such devices in the possession of terrorist groups like the Irish Republican Army. The United States and those states in the former Soviet Union in possession of nuclear arms must cooperate to ensure that such a scenario does not happen and agree to jointly nullify the threat if it arises. Could we offer to buy all the bombs now held by the Russians, Ukrainians, and other ethnic states of the old Soviet Union? They probably need the money.

AFTER WORLD WAR I, THEY CALLED THEM "MERCHANTS OF DEATH"; NOW THEY'RE KNOWN AS BLUE-CHIP INVESTMENTS.

An item's cost is directly related to the volume produced. The research and development costs of U.S. weapons are picked up by the American government. The per unit costs are reduced when large numbers of weapons are sold by the firm. It is, then, in the interest of the American government to promote the sale of sophisticated weapons to "friendly" and "responsible" nations. Our ability to distinguish such traits can be seen in our enthusiastic sales to Iraq.

If you're a thoughtful citizen of some underdeveloped nation, you've just got to be terrified that the United States and the various pieces of the defunct Communist bloc are going to hold a "surplus sale" (in our case) or a "going out of business sale" (in their case) to try to recoup Cold War costs. After all, that makes better business sense than just "mothballing" the damned stuff. If we can interest one party in each dispute to buy some of our surplus hardware, the other will have to respond in kind. And as nations break up into new nations, the market expands! It's enough to make a salesman salivate.

It would have taken some enormously careful and creative planning to bring about a "peace dividend" without also creating damaging dislocations in our already troubled economy. Massive layoffs in our defense industry and disbanding our standing military are hardly a prescription for economic recovery. The industries and people in question could have been helped to move to new and useful activities, but activating the mechanisms to do that was beyond the capacities of our bickering political leadership. We'd better consider staying on the job as our peace dividend, the other kind just ain't in the cards.

Among the explanations for the reluctance of the Bush administration to reduce our military capacities following the end of the Cold War is the thesis that the U.S. government had become accustomed to its role as "leader of the free world" and didn't care to be just "one among equals." We have a tendency toward self-righteousness that could lead us to try to impose our notion of stability and order on the rest of the world. A little disarmament might induce some healthy modesty in our view of our international role.

4

THE NATION AND DOMESTIC ISSUES:
THE ECONOMY
THE CITIES
THE ENVIRONMENT
EDUCATION
HEALTH CARE
ABORTION
WAR ON DRUGS

THE BUSH ECONOMY

How voodoo economics came back to haunt Bush   Barry Bluestone

In the spring of 1980, what was to become known as Reaganomics was savaged as "voodoo" economics by George Bush in his unsuccessful bid for the Republican presidential nomination. Only months later, when he joined the Republican ticket as the vice-presidential nominee, the same George Bush performed a magnificent political pirouette, embracing all the tenets of Reagan's supply-side nostrum: deep tax cuts, unbridled defense spending, and government deregulation. Joining the stampede to what economists called the "supply-side" seemed at the time the wise thing to do.

Yet the voodoo of Reaganomics came back to haunt George Bush with a vengeance. It left a legacy of recession and slow economic growth during his presidency unequaled in the post-World War II era. More important, it left the federal government with few tools to reverse the economic slide. Under Bush's stewardship, overall growth in U.S. output, in the number of jobs, in weekly wages, and in family income, was lower than during any presidency since the Great Depression. The next worst economic performance occurred during the second Eisenhower administration (1957–60)—a prelude to the election of John F. Kennedy. Indeed, economic growth during Bush's tenure was only one-third as strong as during that ill-fated term of President Eisenhower.[1]

The economic agenda practiced by Ronald Reagan served his administration well. But just as Reagan's tenure in the White House came to an end, the voodoo of supply-side economics began to unleash its inevitable consequences on his protégé. In less than two years' time, the weak state of America's economy catapulted George Bush from the pinnacle of voter approval during the Gulf War to deep disfavor even within his own party.

Supply-side economics had been developed for Ronald Reagan by a small band of policymakers far from the mainstream, including Arthur Laffer, Jude Wanniski, and George Gilder. The theory rests on a credible premise: to regain its global competitive advantage and to reverse the nation's moribund standard of living, American enterprise must unleash greater productivity, build higher-quality products, and surpass the Japanese and European proclivity for innovation. What turned out to be unreasonable about the Reagan brand of supply-side theory was the proffered mechanism for achieving these goals. Suggesting that nearly all of America's economic and social problems could be traced to high taxes and government red tape, Reagan's advisers had little trouble convincing the new president that sharp cuts in taxes would encourage people to work harder and save more, in the process boosting output and aggregate tax revenue despite the lower tax rates. Cuts in industry regulation would encourage business to rebuild America.

The early "success" of the supply-side nostrums followed on the heels of the economic debacle that befell Jimmy Carter. With the so-called misery index—the arithmetic sum of the unemployment and inflation rates—surging past 20 percent just before the 1980 election, Mr. Carter was virtually doomed at the polls.[2] That home mortgage rates reached nearly 13 percent did not help his re-election bid, nor did the unresolved Iran hostage crisis. Mr. Reagan came to the White House promising a "new morning" for America. His colleague in this quest was Paul Volcker, chairman of the Federal Reserve Board. Under Volcker, the Fed choked off the money supply, sending interest rates through the roof. Within two years, double-digit inflation rates were curbed in the old-fashioned way—through a deep and painful recession.

Then Mr. Reagan's supply-side economics took hold. Personal income tax rates were slashed, especially for wealthy families, corporate tax rates were cut, and environmental and labor regulations were weakened by "pro-growth" appointees to Reagan's cabinet. Meanwhile, the Pentagon was entirely refurbished. The military budget skyrocketed from $131 billion in 1980 to $282 billion in 1988.

The combination of sharp tax cuts and lavish federal spending for the military put Americans back to work by the millions. With more money in the pay envelope and a new middle- and upper-class attitude of entitlement—some called it greed—families spent their entire incomes and often more in the process, fueling a consumer boom. Supply-side seemed to be working. What we now know is that it was not working according to supply-side predictions. Although tax revenue increased as unemployed workers found jobs, the increase in employment and earnings was nowhere near enough to provide the federal revenue necessary to fund the defense buildup in the face of declining tax rates. Federal tax receipts rose 65 percent during the Reagan years. Unfortunately, total outlays (excluding "off-budget" items like Social Security) grew by 81 percent with the Department of Defense budget up by 115 percent. As such, supply-side economics was actually working according to the older "demand-side" dynamic pioneered by John Maynard Keynes and implemented by Franklin Roosevelt during the 1930s. Reaganomics pulled the country out of recession via deficit spending just as President Kennedy had ended the 1961 recession with a tax cut that stimulated consumption.

The big difference was that as the 1981–82 recession ended, the tax cuts were not rescinded, the spending spree was not curtailed, and the deficits continued to skyrocket. What the government did, consumers and businesses did too; they spent well beyond their means.

A few statistics reveal just how indebted the nation became. Outstanding personal installment credit liability more than doubled from $326 billion in 1982 to $664 billion in 1988, rising twice as fast as total personal income. The merger and acquisition boom that highlighted business strategy during the Reagan years was also a product of debt, much of it of the junk-bond variety. It took 13 years, from 1970 to 1983, for the corporate debt-to-equity ratio to rise from

under 2 to just below 4. Yet in just three years, from 1983 to 1986, the ratio doubled again. For its part, the federal government under Reagan spent $1.6 trillion more than it received in taxes and other government receipts. As a result of this debt, close to one-third of the nation's increased total economic consumption during the 1980s was paid for by funds borrowed from the future or borrowed from foreigners, rather than paid for out of current production. Essentially, the United States mortgaged its future. By the end of the 1980s, the bill for voodoo economics was coming due—and Mr. Bush, now president, was in no position to pay it.

Whatever else it has done, supply-side economics has not repealed the business cycle, the ups and downs of the economy occasioned by speedups and slowdowns in consumption and investment. Inevitably, the protracted boom of the 1980s had to end or at least slow down. During Reagan's years, the overall economy grew by a respectable 2.9 percent a year. During Bush's first three years, the economy expanded at only 0.9 percent a year. When Reagan left office, the unemployment rate was 5.2 percent. During Bush's re-election campaign, it averaged over 7.5 percent. Corporate profits in 1991 were 11 percent below 1988 levels. Net farm income was down over the same period by 8 percent. New housing starts in 1991 were one-third below the 1988 figure; construction of commercial and industrial buildings was down 44 percent.

Overall, America's standard of living stopped growing during the Bush presidency. Inflation-adjusted personal consumption spending was lower in 1991 than in 1988. Voters invariably blame the president when the economy performs so poorly.

The fact is, having embraced the supply-side, Mr. Bush was left with little control over the economy, less so perhaps than any president since Herbert Hoover.

Before Reaganomics, the White House and Congress could counteract a recession by using fiscal policy—cutting taxes and/or boosting government spending to prime the economic pump. For all practical purposes, the government used up fiscal policy during the 1980s. By running massive federal deficits during the boom years, the debt burden became so great that there was little capacity left for further deficit finance as an economic stimulus. After all, in 1980 the existing federal debt accumulated since the nation's founding two centuries ago was less than $1 trillion. To pay the annual interest on that debt took the equivalent of 21 percent of all the personal income tax paid to the IRS that year. Only twelve years later, the debt was $3.6 trillion. As a consequence, in 1992, it took 40 percent of all the federal personal income tax collected to service the debt. With the fiscal year 1992 budget deficit nearing $300 billion without a major antirecession spending program, and the fiscal 1993 budget scheduled to be out of balance by as much as $400 billion, no politician has been willing to sponsor programs that would send the deficit much higher. Not surprisingly, Mr. Bush opposed spending more money on unemployment insurance as the number of jobless climbed, and he opposed all but a trivial amount of federal aid to cities in the aftermath of the most deadly urban riot of the 20th century.

The remaining traditional tool for counteracting recession is monetary policy—the manipulation of interest rates through active intervention by the Federal Reserve Board. In the past, the

Fed could quickly stimulate a moribund economy by lowering interest rates. At lower rates, consumers normally buy cars and new homes, and businesses invest in new plants and equipment. But the debt-financed spending spree of the 1980s compromised this economic tool as well. With existing debt burdens, neither families nor corporations were comfortable taking out additional loans even if they could get them at bargain-basement interest rates. The result at the end of the 1980s was a "balance sheet" recession. Businesses and families refused to risk bankruptcy by borrowing more, and presumably will not do so until they retire a good part of the excess debt they have already accumulated.

What adds to the problem is that Reaganomics, as practiced by both presidents Reagan and Bush, did not mend what is fundamentally wrong with America's economy—the nation's weak performance in global markets and the growing disparity between the rich and the poor at home. The first saps our standard of living; the second, our civility. Productivity growth, the best measure of the efficiency of the economy, averaged 1.4 percent a year during the 1980s, far below the rate Japan achieved and significantly worse than most of our major trading partners. Low productivity growth means that over time it is difficult to remain price competitive relative to other countries without driving down our own wages and therefore our standard of living. Under Reagan the trade deficit reached $160 billion even though businesses cut average inflation-adjusted weekly earnings by 7 percent between 1984 and 1991.

Moreover, cuts in wages and family incomes have been unevenly distributed in the extreme. The latest statistics show a discouraging growth in inequality, particularly during the years when supply-side economics was practiced with abandon. Adjusting for family size, between 1977 and 1989, the top 1 percent of all families enjoyed 44 percent of the total growth in after-tax income. In contrast, the bottom 60 percent of all families were 4 percent poorer after the spending spree of the 1980s.[3] Nowhere is this more evident than in the major cities where a Beverly Hills seems a galaxy away from a poverty-ridden south central Los Angeles, in reality located only a few miles down the freeway.

In conclusion, it now seems clear that Mr. Bush's initial reaction to Reaganomics was savvy indeed. Voodoo economics did not fundamentally repair a weak economy; it created a growing chasm between the haves and the have-nots. And it left Washington policymakers with few tools to deal with what historians will call the "Bush recession." Inevitably, the voodoo pins that Reagan thrust into the economy in the 1980s, with George Bush's full acquiescence, landed in George Bush in 1992.■

Ronald Reagan was less the leader of this nation than a mirror image of it. His handlers spent years analyzing what Americans wanted to hear and believe. Surveys, polls, and audience analyses produced a message that was carefully honed to reflect our aspirations, biases, fears, and weaknesses. That message was then artfully presented, and it mesmerized the public, like hearing a tape of oneself for the first time. What he did was glossed over by what he said. George Bush was less successful because Reagan's unscrutinized actions changed public attitudes and Bush couldn't meet those expectations.

Typically, the government goes into debt during a war, a recession, or for a program of capital improvements. The next generation inherits a debt, but, for example, it bought them "world safe for democracy," the "Four Freedoms," or public works projects like the Tennessee Valley Authority (TVA) system. The burgeoning debt of the 1980s will bring the next generation the cold comfort of knowing that they are paying for Ronald Reagan's re-election in 1984, the election of Bush in 1988, and the perpetuation in office of nearly 535 congressmen who refused to risk their re-election by acting responsibly.

The decision to borrow money can be a healthy thing, as most businesses and homeowners can testify. American governments have at times resorted to borrowing when a crisis arose that would merit the burden of debt. During the Reagan-Bush era, we abandoned that tradition and borrowed out of political expediency. The president first reduced taxes and later refused to restore them. The Congress refused to cut programs. They compromised by borrowing the money. Everybody won but the future. The ship of state now carries an obese passenger that slows it down, reduces maneuverability, and threatens to swamp it.

THE SHIP IS FOUNDERING AND THEY'RE DRILLING A HOLE TO LET THE WATER OUT.

The deficit is the amount we are adding to the national debt this year, and servicing it has become a perilous process. The government must print and sell new bonds in addition to the mountains of them that must be sold to fund the existing debt. We need Japanese and other foreign buyers for these bonds. Foreign policy choices are narrowed when you borrow money from the people with whom you negotiate foreign policy issues. In some recessions, even very low interest rates will not produce sufficient private spending to bring about recovery. Government can ordinarily borrow and spend to make up the difference, but not when it's already borrowing with both hands.

DISTRIBUTED BY KING FEATURES SYNDICATE

The Miami Herald

Every president is isolated from "average" Americans. It goes with the job. Perhaps more than most, George Bush seemed callous about the victims of America's "deindustrialization" (the exportation of American jobs and business bankruptcies caused by foreign imports) and the recession. His opposition to an extension of unemployment benefits, while pushing for a reduction in capital gains taxes, was seen as an example of class bias. Most Americans had accepted that some kind of sacrifice was probably necessary to get this nation back on its feet. But they also believe the burden should be broadly shared. President Bush left the impression that it would be quicker just to toss some citizens overboard. Okay, so who wants to be Jonah?

In their efforts to sell their economic theories to the American people, both liberals and conservatives have developed a whole arsenal of jargon, catch-phrases, slogans, and hype. Formal economics is not the stuff out of which one can design a political campaign. The voters tend to accept or ignore these oversimplifications when times are good. During hard times the phrases don't cut it. During the Reagan administration we lived on credit, and the trickle-down theory of economics seemed more or less palatable. The obvious failure of Reaganomics rendered the slogans increasingly indigestible for the electorate George Bush faced in re-election.

Confidence is one of the factors that fuels the American economy. With enough of it, "wishing will make it so." A president who forecasts gloom and doom might well find himself with a self-fulfilling prophecy. Still, a president must not continue to chortle optimistically through prolonged hard times for fear of appearing callous, unrealistic, or dishonest. If there is too great a gap between verbiage and reality, the public just tunes him out. They are particularly quick to do so when they know he views the economy through electioneering glasses. Such a president can come to seem irrelevant.

During the last 30 years, the Federal government has inserted literally hundreds of thermometers into the American economy. From these we receive a vast array of statistics purporting to show the health of the system. The statistics are probably accurate, but are useless without interpretation. George Bush and his advisers trumpeted recovery and ignored contrary evidence. Apparently, the state of the economy depends on the economist you talk to. George chose those with happy faces. The unemployed wanted jobs not statistics.

Americans have never felt particularly comfortable with the provision of welfare services. Our self-help ethic gets in the way, so we have never established a comprehensive plan for the unavoidable delivery of such services. Ours is a jerry-built structure of ad hoc decisions reluctantly made and minimal steps hesitantly taken. As a result, our social programs are spread through every level of government and financial responsibility, often poorly defined. In hard times, government agencies treat the issue like a hot potato, juggling and tossing it to the next level. Nobody loves you when you're down and out.

For more than a decade American consumers were damned as profligate because they made excessive use of credit and, in a sense, mortgaged the future. As the bills came due from that prolonged credit binge, neither the United States government nor the private sector had much discretionary income. We had an attack of consumer anxiety and business expectations were low despite the fact interest rates were at their lowest in years. George Bush, prepared to be a cheerleader for prosperity, was ill-equipped to lead a nation in recession. Play now and pay later was the watchword of the 1980s. George Bush arrived later.

Most economists agree that the key to recovery from a recession is increased investment by business in plants and machinery and increased residential construction. But during the 1991–1992 recession, reduced interest rates proved surprisingly slow in prompting a recovery. American business was reluctant to expand production in the face of limited consumer demand. But for more than a decade Americans have watched their jobs shifted overseas, their real income reduced or stagnant, their fringe benefits squeezed or eliminated, and the cost of government services shifted from tax revenues to fees. Perhaps those at the top should recognize that you rattle the cage long enough and you will change the animal's behavior.

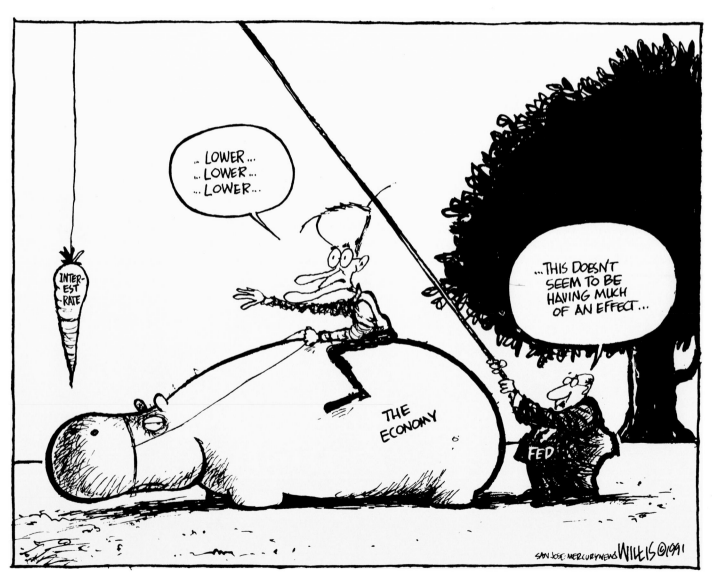

There was something clever, almost Machiavellian, in George Bush's insistence on no new taxes. The consequences were clear: deterioration of our parks, highways, educational system, military preparedness, and social welfare programs on the one hand, or continued deficit financing and a debilitating national debt on the other. Bush obviously intended to wait until the situation had deteriorated so far that constituent discontent would force Congress to bite the bullet. He would then reluctantly give in and damn them as spendthrift liberals. In the meanwhile, he remained the hero of his monied constituents and of the millions of other Americans who want government services but don't want to pay for them.

It worked for Ronald Reagan but not for George Bush. Perhaps the American working class is brighter than they are given credit for, or at least capable of learning through experience. Reagan's across-the-board percentage tax cuts resulted in tax savings of nickels for the working class and millions for the economic elite. The public was told the windfall for the rich would result in investment and jobs. Instead, the tax cuts resulted in an inflated stock market, a rash of mergers, and extensive investments overseas. When Bush offered another tax reduction with identical promises, the public indicated they weren't buying it.

"NO, SEE, THIS HELPS EVERYBODY........ WHEN YOU SELL THIS HOME YOUR TAX LIABILITY TOPS OUT AT 19.6%....."

The auto industry is almost a caricature of what went wrong with some elements of the American economy. It had become arrogant, complacent, and inflexible. It substituted advertising for quality and cosmetic changes for engineering improvements. To keep profits high, it refused to invest in new technologies. It proved first unwilling, and then unable, to compete in the economy car market and then watched the small cars grow bigger. Frustrated by their own mismanagement, auto executives bought foreign-made parts and marketed foreign-made cars. Finally, they laid off workers by the thousands, closed plants, and ruined towns. Now they have to regain the confidence of the very market that made them what they are today.

" YOU'LL BE PLEASED TO KNOW THAT *PART* WAS MADE IN THE *U.S.A.!*"

When American corporate leaders finally got around to devising a response to foreign competition, they adopted a strategy that called for the quickest short-term fix with the least possible sacrifice on their part. The goal was to make American business "lean and mean." As applied, that meant investing in foreign nations with low labor costs, the elimination of hundreds of thousands of jobs up through middle management, and reductions in worker health benefits and pension plans. What it did not do was reduce dividends to stockholders or cap the obscene salaries and perks of upper management.

The American political and economic system is essentially a reactive one. It responds to problems after they arise and applies remedies that are ad hoc and short term. Planning is seen as restriction on free choice, an inhibition on creativity. Environmental constraints warn us that we must reduce consumption of finite resources, consume less energy, produce less waste, and, in short, limit growth. On the other hand, the remedies we have on hand for the current recession require that we increase production, accelerate consumption of energy, and, inevitably, produce more waste. With the possible exception of cancer, nature imposes limits on growth. Current policies may well be carcinogenic.

THE CITIES

Once the holder of the dream

Yvonne Scruggs

Cities have been a challenge to every American president from the first administration of Franklin D. Roosevelt in 1932. Beginning with the economic recovery programs of the Great Depression, through the urban renewal and city revitalization programs of the post–World War II era, to the social engineering programs of the Great Society and the place-rather-than-people-oriented National Urban Policy of the late 1970s, ever stronger links were forged between cities, especially big cities, and the federal government.

The interdependence between cities and the federal government chained them to an enduring, if not endearing, alliance. This alliance was not created for appearance' sake or for political convenience. Given the seriousness of urban problems, the alliance has been essential to survival.

Large cities have been burdened with especially difficult challenges. Today, they have the nation's oldest housing stock and the highest rate of unemployment, which in some cities is higher than levels recorded during the peak of the Great Depression. Fewer students complete high school in these cities than was the case 20 years ago. More babies are born to single mothers in cities than elsewhere, heavily loading the odds for economic survival against these urban children. Industry has abandoned cities for nonurban locations at an alarming rate. Drug abuse and associated social disorganization, along with steadily increasing incidents of violent crime

against persons and property, characterize these communities.

Yet despite these bleak demographics, cities are almost always the first stop for newly arrived immigrants, the majority of whom are now Spanish-speaking nonwhites, followed closely in numbers by Asians. Between 1980 and 1990, immigrants accounted for 37 percent of America's total population growth. They represent a population increase of 11.5 percent in the nation's 10 largest cities.[1] Cities are also the primary residence for three out of four African Americans, in whose eyes cities still promise escape from poverty into the American mainstream.

Some observers feel that it is artificial to distinguish the Bush years from the Reagan years when discussing federal urban policy during the last decade. Both administrations succeeded in cutting the umbilical cord that, some said, stretched from the White House directly into city halls across the country. Under Reagan and Bush, federal assistance programs and economic aid to cities and their residents were dismantled. Between a high point in 1978 and 10 years later when President Bush began his term in office, direct aid to cities fell by almost one-third: from 28 percent of the total aid distributed in 1978, to 17 percent of the 1988 total. Conversely, overall aid from the federal government to states and noncity localities (counties, suburbs, and rural districts) increased roughly 65 percent: from $69 billion to over $114 billion.[2]

The Reagan-Bush team, moreover, owed substantial ideological debts to their supporters, who were mostly suburban or rural, and in the main, conservatives and self-made "New Federalists." They believed the best government was one that governed least. And President Reagan's antiurban attitudes found a place in the Bush presidency. Ronald Reagan danced with the mainly nonurban constituents who brought him to the presidency. George Bush, Reagan's vice president for two terms and successor, inherited Reagan's dance card and continued to fill it out.

At the beginning of the Bush presidency, a survey of nearly 600 local officials gave the Reagan-Bush administration "a lousy report card" on how it had handled six important urban issues: illegal drugs, housing, disposal of hazardous materials, unemployment, poverty, and the federal deficit.[3] Further, a bipartisan panel of mayors from such large cities as Newark, Indianapolis, Dallas, Hartford, and New York called for an urban agenda for the 1990s, stating that "education, housing, drugs, AIDS, transportation and the elderly are problems from which the Federal government cannot continue to distance itself."[4] They challenged President Bush to create a national council of urban advisers to handle urban issues. He did.

Bush's 1988 campaign had promised "a kinder, gentler nation." But the president rejected proposals by an interagency task force that he had appointed to study poverty and come up with new strategies for cities. His administration decided to do as Reagan had advised: just make things work better. One administration official with a rather bizarre and callous sense of humor stated that "it was fun to think about" things that might "do something about poverty," but that there was no money to fund them. So "fun" or not, nothing was recommended.[5]

This is not to say that the entire Bush administration was totally silent on the subject of cities. In the first year of Bush's presidency, Secretary of Housing and Urban Development Jack F. Kemp, a former congressman, advanced his perennial (since 1980) solution to urban decline: enterprise zones. Issued as a HUD Report in 1989, *Enterprise Zones In America: A Selected Resource Guide II,* Kemp's proposal was designed as an alternative to direct budgeting of federal dollars for urban economic development.

Enterprise zones (EZs) were intended to attract private investments and new small businesses to the inner city. Tax relief was the primary inducement to invest, while reduction of government regulations, replacement of abandoned commercial spaces with new businesses, and an increase in jobs for local residents were added attractions. However, no tax incentives were funded in the EZ legislation, because the Bush administration was unable to agree with Congress on how to fully implement federal EZs. In late 1991 a HUD proposal was issued that promised to "chart a new course for our Nation's urban policy based on growth and opportunity for those in need."[6] Instead, a conglomeration of existing programs and value-laden pronouncements about fair housing, drug-free public housing, and homelessness was the sum and substance of the offerings.

The push for creation of Kemp's EZs intensified after the urban explosion in south central Los Angeles in April and May 1992 that followed the verdict exonerating the four Los Angeles policemen who beat Rodney King. Frustrated by their poverty and joblessness, a mob of south central Angelenos, made up largely of Hispanics and African Americans and some whites and Asians, burned and looted the inner city. Looting and outbreaks of violence simultaneously broke out in a number of U.S. cities in the wake of the King verdict and the unrest in Los Angeles.

Democrats in Congress and urban advocates outside argued that the Republican obsession with controlling taxes contributed significantly to these events. Dollar shortages for federally funded urban programs had interfered with the development of new urban and poverty strategies. Urbanists described the grim conditions in south central Los Angeles as typical of those found in every other major urban center in the country. Those who had been watching George Bush's lips, as he had so instructed them to do during his 1988 presidential campaign, finally saw him whisper "urban policy."

Meanwhile, Bush's traditional dancing partners, those who "brought him" to the presidency, were outraged over the riots in Los Angeles. Said one Republican congressman from California:

"There's resentment from the rural areas... that the administration was about to send the wrong message that urban terrorism brings federal largesse."[7] And Vice President Dan Quayle, emerging just before the 1992 Republican National Convention as the administration's ideological stalking-horse, charged the Democrats with promoting inertia with their past welfare-state, tax-and-spend urban solutions.

Under attack from both liberals and conservatives, and beleaguered by Democratic and third-party presidential opponents due to his nonexistent "urban policy," George Bush came late, and comparatively ill prepared, to the dilemma that has confronted every other president since FDR—how to help the cities and their residents stay alive and have a decent quality of life.

The estimated $5 billion price tag for the Los Angeles destruction finally forced the Bush administration to review the issue of urban aid. For the first time since he took office, Bush issued a formal statement on urban policy, a news release captioned "President Bush's Initiatives for Strengthening Urban Areas." The "initiatives" came mainly from Secretary Kemp's HUD budget request of 1991, with minor augmentation from other federal departments with urban constituents. The Bush initiatives prompted one reporter from National Public Radio (NPR) to comment: "Bush has finally discovered his urban policy. It has been hiding in Jack Kemp's drawer."

Highlights of the initiatives were:

Weed and Seed: $500 million to "weed out" the criminals and drug dealers from the streets and to "seed" social programs and assistance, to reduce crime and drug use.

Home Ownership for People Everywhere (HOPE): a $1 billion program to help 100,000 families living in public housing and other government-owned properties to purchase their housing units.

Enterprise Zones: Jack Kemp's urban disinvestment response.

America 2000: largely noncash incentives for educational reform based on a set of proposals that grew out of a summit conference Bush called with the nation's governors early in his presidency (including the controversial proposal for parental choice of private, religious, or public schools).

Welfare Reform: a call for greater flexibility in welfare administration that proposes to relax various welfare restrictions at both state and federal levels.

Youth Jobs: urges congressional passage of a jobs and training program, long supported by urban and poverty activists.

President Bush's options were further narrowed by sustained assaults from the civil rights community, which saw racial bias as a factor in his attitude toward the cities and the people who live there. African Americans especially felt that his positions on civil rights and urban relief were ambivalent and insubstantial at best, mean spirited at worst. Given what Congresswoman Maxine Waters, of Los Angeles, described as the "knock-down, drag-out battle" to get Bush to sign the 1991 Civil Rights Bill, African Americans were pessimistic about the value of any urban policy Bush might advance. Mayor Emanuel Cleaver of Kansas City, Missouri, stated that he lived in fear that President Bush would declare himself the "urban president," because of the destructive consequences, to African Americans and to poor people, that his declaring himself the "education president" produced.

After the Republican National Convention, Bush made the expected effort to convert his renomination into an electoral mandate in November 1992. But the window for a meaningful urban policy for Los Angeles and the other urban time bombs narrowed in direct relationship to the oncoming presidential election. And the conservatives, small-towners, and suburbanites who brought him to the presidential dance last time—and who he hoped would bring him again

—had become strident and adamant about their positions on his dance card. They told him, "George, the band is playing our song. Shall we dance?"■

America's cities' most recent economic bind is, in part, a side effect of unrestricted private enterprise. George Bush hoped that unassisted private enterprise would ease this ongoing economic deterioration. It is plausible that, given enough time, that might happen. But the history of the 1980s suggests it won't. During a decade of what was called "sustained growth," most of the nation's cities declined. If there is such a thing as a private enterprise escalator, it doesn't reach the urban floor.

The history of America's African-American population is one of multiple tragedies, missed opportunities, and just plain bad luck. Until World War II, most African Americans lived in the South, the poorest and most backward part of the nation. They endured racism and all the attendant woes that go with economic stagnation and limited governmental resources. In the period that followed, one of the largest internal migrations in our history occurred as African Americans moved to major cities. They arrived just in time to join the great urban spiral downward. They watched in frustration as the jobs moved to the very areas they fled.

The real gap between America's suburban middle class and its urban poor has been unintentionally brought into relief by the women's movement. Affluent white women saw employment and single parenthood as exciting escapes from the boredom of home and conventional marriage. Poor urban women were already there. White middle-class women were affirming they could "have it all"; women in the ghetto had it all and wanted help!

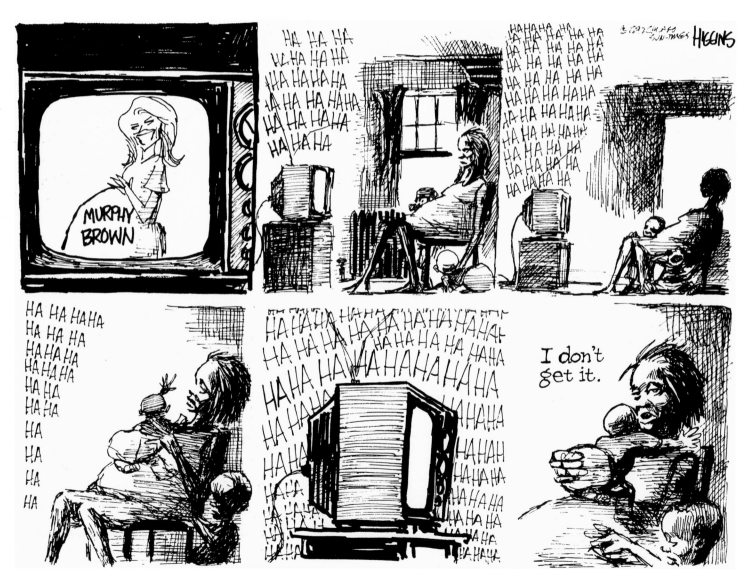

Most Americans will testify to the greatness of Martin Luther King, Jr., and will credit him with almost single-handedly bringing the nation to long-overdue racial reform. But the same people find it much more difficult to accept his guiding philosophy of nonviolence. Without that unifying theme and the moral high ground King secured for it, the Civil Rights movement suffered schism and atrophied. The brutality and counterbrutality we witnessed in the Los Angeles riots in 1992 suggest that we need another leader who will make us believe we truly can have love, peace, and brotherhood.

It does seem strange that we can take such strides in technology and remain so stagnant socially. Perhaps the answer lies in America's passionate commitment to individuality. Economic and technical progress can be achieved individually and its rewards are individual as well. Urban problems must be attacked collectively, and the rewards and costs shared by all. There is apparently a lot more nourishment and energy in the profit motive than in "the milk of human kindness."

The eruption in Los Angeles in 1992 looked disturbingly like the Watts riot of 1965. Everybody agreed that the causes were the same. After Watts, there was brave talk about urban renewal, but little was achieved as the nation shifted its attention to the Vietnam War. Simultaneously, the country exploded in student protests and the advent of the drug culture, and gradually began a national shift to the political right. Jimmy Carter was an ineffectual parenthesis between conservatives. Reagan became president, having earlier won the governorship of California riding the law-and-order reaction to Watts. During the entire period, nobody found a profit, economic or political, in attacking our urban problems.

Though violence may earn a "quick fix" response on the part of government, it does not engender a long-term commitment or empathy among the population in general. Our urban ills require major societal changes and an enormous injection of public monies. You may frighten the general public into a short-term effort, but some other approach must be adopted if a sustained and sincere concern for the plight of the urban poor is to occur. As policy, "Burn, Baby, Burn" is quite likely to evoke "then stew in your own juice" as a response.

It is only in the last couple of generations that the public decided that the national government should have any direct involvement with the cities at all. Once the federal government evidenced a willingness to be involved, state and local governments divested themselves of burdensome fiscal responsibilities with both hands. The regeneration of the cities will take more than policies. It will take money. That money must inevitably come from the taxpayers, but state and local governments are reluctant to shoulder such burdens. Let Uncle Sam take the rap for collecting it.

LOS ANGELES TIMES SYNDICATE

WHETHER YOU'RE COOKING A "REVOLT" OR A "RIOT," THE INGREDIENTS ARE ABOUT THE SAME.

The American left was quick to label the eruption in Los Angeles a "protest" or a "revolt" and to read a political statement into it. The conservative right saw it as a "riot" and the participants as criminal opportunists. It probably doesn't make a lot of difference what you call it, the causes are the same and indisputable. But responding to it is somewhat more difficult. Los Angeles is no more needy than a hundred other cities, and just because its citizens were enraged enough to trash the place hardly entitles them to special treatment. The fundamental solutions to urban problems are the creation of a more vibrant and "fairer" economy, combined with a renewed commitment of Americans to each other.

The priorities of the Bush administration and to a large extent the Democrat-controlled Congress were evident in the way they handled the U.S. budget crisis. The Savings and Loan bailout was justified because to do otherwise would bring misery to millions of depositors. And continuation of weapons procurement programs was adopted because "deserving" constituents would otherwise be injured. The beneficiaries of this tender concern were generally white and middle class. Then, the money "gone," we slashed programs for education, health, and the cities. The beneficiaries there are not white and middle class.

It's not how much you steal, or how much damage you do, but rather the way you do it that distinguishes rioting from the business practices of the 1980s. Corporate raiders move in, destroy whole industries, loot pension funds, and ruin communities. They get their names in print all right, but it's on the "Big Board" of the New York Stock Exchange. Given what this nation's working class has seen of this nation's political and business leaders during the last decade, it's unlikely that there are very many with a guilty conscience in Los Angeles.

Timing is everything. We opened the door a bit for this nation's African-American citizens just as the economic elevator began to stall. Blue-collar jobs were the traditional economic entry point for immigrant and minority groups. But African Americans joined the race just as these jobs began to be lost by the hundreds of thousands. Replacement jobs were either high-tech or in service occupations that paid poorly and offered no advancement. African Americans were finally allowed into unions in the midst of major union decline and got into public employment just as a "taxpayer revolt" resulted in austerity budgets and no promotions. As they say in the ghetto, "stuff happens."

The deindustrialization of America has been particularly hard on the cities. They have become service centers in which the dominant economic activities are banking, insurance, wholesale marketing, legal firms, and the like. Those businesses require employees with adequate general education and considerable specialized training. In time, and with a renaissance of urban public education, this new urban economic mix will provide first-rate employment for African Americans, Hispanics, and Asian immigrants. But right now, the blue-collar jobs are gone, and these minorities are not qualified for the new white-collar opportunities. What's left are dead-end jobs, and a treadmill to poverty.

Urbanologists discuss something called the "pathology" of poverty. In that environment, the moral niceties are sloughed off. What's left are neighborhoods where anarchy, brutality, and exploitation are the realities of everyday existence. Most of the ensuing violence stays insulated in those enclaves of misery. The denizens of America's urban pestholes prey upon one another, which has allowed middle-class America to overlook the rotten circumstances which produced that poverty and degradation.

George Bush was fundamentally uncomfortable with what the modern presidency had become. Indeed, he seemed aghast at what the federal government had become. NONE of the issues listed in this cartoon were considered within the province of the federal government earlier in this century. Bush did act with some decisiveness in matters of foreign policy. But those acts fit his image of the office. The great social issues of our time found him hesitant and quick to retreat behind the budget problem. At heart, Bush believed those problems are best handled by local governments or the private sector.

There are 250 million Americans, all of whom resent paying taxes. For the last 30 years, conservatives sought to persuade citizens that they were overtaxed. And they succeeded. During that same 30 years, liberals persuaded the nation that all our citizens deserved health care, a decent education, and an environment fit to live in. The public accepted both messages but not the connection between them. Governments, trying to match policy to the public's impossible expectations, responded by borrowing money or shifting responsibilities. Clearly, this isn't utopia.

The seminal cause of America's urban problem is poverty—the paucity of jobs offering a decent wage to working-class families. The loss of those jobs is the product of a thousand decisions by private enterprise to locate elsewhere. In short, business saw advantages in operating somewhere else. Bush offered as an urban policy a program to invite business back into urban areas that have declined precipitously since business left them in the first place. The idea might even work, but it will take a hell of a lot more enticement than the Bush administration was willing to offer.

THE ENVIRONMENT

Missed opportunities   David Weir

In 1987, the year before George Bush was elected president, a commission put together by the United Nations released a report, little noted in this country, called *Our Common Future*. The report argued that a new model of sustainable development was necessary to help the world's people better themselves without destroying the biodiversity needed to support life on earth.

Unlike similar studies, *Our Common Future* struck a somewhat hopeful tone, pointing out that only in the past quarter century had we come to possess indisputable visual proof (photographs taken of earth from outer space) that our planet is a "fragile ball dominated not by human activity and edifice but by a pattern of clouds, oceans, greenery and soils."[1] The report speculated that the widespread distribution of these photos had precipitated a turning point in the evolution of human thought.

It was in this context that George Bush assumed the presidency of the country that is the world's biggest polluter and biggest consumer of natural resources, and home to the world's most-entrenched environmental movement. With only 5 percent of the world's population, the United States consumes 25 percent of the world's energy and emits 22 percent of all carbon dioxide. Modern American environmentalism had emerged roughly at the moment those first spectacular space photos were released, and by the late 1980s, Americans in record numbers

had gotten the message that the planet is indeed fragile.

In 1989, just as Bush came to power, a number of events made the environment front page news. Scientists, for example, were just accumulating the first concrete data about the hole in the earth's ozone layer, as well as disturbing evidence that theories about global warming might prove accurate.

And these events came on the heels of the eco-scare headlines of 1988 such as: medical waste washing up on East Coast beaches; unwanted garbage barges wandering the seas like Flying Dutchmen; and potential global climate changes posing danger for American farmers. The summer of 1988 had also been the hottest ever recorded in United States. Whether the summer heat was related to real or imagined environmental changes, it helped give environmental issues added credibility with the public and with policymakers.

The stage was set for an ambitious political response. Recognizing the opportunity, Bush promised to be the "environmental president."

Over the next four years, he did act to justify that claim. He signed a cornerstone piece of U.S. environmental legislation—a reauthorization of the Clean Air Act. He declared a moratorium on offshore oil drilling along some of the U.S. coastline. He appointed a career environmentalist, William Reilly, to head the Environmental Protection Agency (EPA)—a first for any president.

But by 1992, any assessment of Bush's environmental record had to be judged less on what he did than on what he did not do. Among the many urgent items he had ignored were the need for government-sponsored mass transit systems, incentives for energy conservation, development of alternative energy sources, and support for recycling. Bush angered many by announcing an energy bill that envisioned constructing 600 oil, coal, and nuclear power plants over the next 40 years, and neglected conservation and renewable technologies altogether. Senator Paul Wellstone (Democrat, Minnesota) said, "The administration's energy bill is basically a giant Christmas tree of goodies for big energy corporations."[2]

Other critics have charged that, despite numerous polls documenting high levels of public concern for environmental issues, big business was the main beneficiary of Bush's policies, and that those interests that needed to be regulated if environmental goals were to be met were, in fact, controlling the regulators.

Among recent presidents, Richard Nixon, a Republican with substantial business backing at a time when public outrage over pollution was peaking, perhaps best compares with Bush. Nixon signed the original Clean Air Act in 1970 and also the law establishing the EPA. At that time, though environmentalists were smaller in numbers, these initiatives enjoyed broad public support.

By the late 1980s and early 1990s, growing awareness of the serious threats to the earth's ecological integrity led to a global consensus that people had to cooperate across national borders and act now to reverse the trends. Spurred by grass-roots pressure from many parts of the world, U.N. agencies directed a concerted effort to create a new, sustainable plan for economic development in poorer countries, whose desperate populations were razing tropical rain forests, hunting game to extinction, and using as fuel anything they could lay their hands on. Scientists estimated that these countries would destroy 10 to 20 percent of all plant and animal species by the year 2020.

In the United States, public support for a strong new environmental consciousness reached a crescendo on Earth Day 1990. Massive celebrations around the country (and overseas) demonstrated to politicians the need for decisive leadership on the environment. But throughout these historic developments, Bush seemed out of touch with both the American public's concern and the rest of the world's commitment to action. Citing a responsibility to preserve American jobs and economic competitiveness, he established a council to review (and essentially gut) any new environmental regulations. This antiregulatory unit, called the Council on Competitiveness and headed by Vice President Dan Quayle, gave business leaders with a vested interest in slowing down environmental reforms what amounted to a veto at the highest level of the Bush administration.

The council was involved in many controversies, including a plan to allow development of half the nation's endangered wetlands (which in 1988 Bush had pledged to preserve), logging in the few remaining old-growth forests, and development of the national forests and wildlife parks by private industry. It overturned an EPA requirement that waste incinerator operators must recycle 25 percent of their waste, and altered a Clean Air Act rule to permit 30 percent higher sulfur dioxide emissions. By 1992 the Sierra Club was calling for the Quayle council to be abolished.

Overseas, the United States under Bush forced a severe weakening of an international treaty to reduce the use of greenhouse chemicals before agreeing to sign it. Because the United States is the largest emitter of these substances, this action sent a dangerous message to developing countries like China, which has the potential to inflict even greater insults to the earth's atmosphere by unrestrained development than anything yet seen. After the collapse of the Soviet Union and its hegemony in Eastern Europe, which occurred during his tenure, Bush was handed an unprecedented opportunity to exert global leadership on the environment; but instead he responded by undermining the fragile coalition intended to reduce the use of greenhouse contributing chemicals.

The ultimate litmus test for Bush's environmental leadership came as the United Nations prepared its first-ever Earth Summit in Rio de Janeiro, Brazil, in June 1992. Despite Bush's mixed record, the rest of the world still looked to the United States for environmental leadership —largely because of earlier actions taken during the Nixon and Carter presidencies that included bans on dangerous pesticides, stronger automobile emissions standards, occupational safety and health initiatives, and regulation of hazardous waste dumping.

Furthermore, a growing portion of the U.S. and international business community recognized the growth potential in "green" industries and "green" exports, dismissing the notion that environmental reforms were bad for business. Nevertheless, Bush seemed captive to outmoded assumptions that equated government regulation to lower profits for business. Despite pressure from EPA chief Reilly and others inside his administration, Bush strongly resisted participating in the summit, stating a focus on domestic concerns was a more important use of his time. He reluctantly agreed to join other world leaders in Rio, only after he had succeeded in undermining the draft treaties on global warming and biodiversity that had been painstakingly negotiated in the months before the conference.

By reasserting that his primary goal was not to protect the planet's ecology but American jobs, President Bush pitted himself and the United States against the rest of the world. This perception was strengthened by the revelation that Bush's opposition to the biodiversity agreement had been engineered by U.S. biotechnology corporations through the Council on Competitiveness.[3] He was denounced in Rio, but he held firm, believing his position would play well with his political constituency in an election year.

The gamble Bush was taking was that the environment would not be a major issue in the fall election, because if it was, he could be in trouble with a significant portion of the electorate. The public believed broadly that the legislative solutions for pollution problems were working, and had little awareness of how the Quayle group was undermining that process. Environmental organizations saw what was happening, however, and near the end of Bush's term, some of them issued "report cards" on his performance.

The evaluations were uniformly low. The nonpartisan League of Conservation Voters cited the "failure of President Bush to deliver on the promises of candidate Bush," and gave him a D.[4] Peter Dykstra of Greenpeace stated that "the Grand Canyon is the only place big enough to hold all of his broken promises."[5] The consensus among environmentalists was that halfway through his term, Bush had abandoned his earlier environmental commitments and sided with those interests that felt threatened by further government intervention, thereby bringing the reform process to a standstill.

Given what might have occurred in Rio, it was easy to understand environmentalists' disappointment with the Bush presidency. Bush had failed to seize an opportunity to build an unprecedented global unity on environmental issues and avert what many believe to be impending ecological catastrophe. A president with vision could have led the world into a new era. He might have reversed the colonial-like relationship the United States maintained with many Third World countries, in which the United States exploited their natural resources, exhorted them not to destroy their rain forests, and yet promoted consumption at home. Instead, America seemed to be going back in time. Those worried about the planet's future—and there seemed to be more of them every day—could only dream of what might have been at Rio, and hope that a critical moment for action had not been irretrievably lost.■

Congress created the Environmental Protection Agency to protect our environment. Unfortunately, a major threat to our environment is the traditional U.S. economy. Both Reagan and Bush came to office as avowed champions of that economic process, and with the support of those who dominate it. Conflict with a strong EPA was inevitable. Reagan solved the problem by appointing bureaucrats hostile to EPA goals. Bush starved the agency with inadequate funding, refused to support its initiatives, and gave "aid and comfort" to its enemies. Neither president chose to kill the agency, they just worked to make it ineffectual.

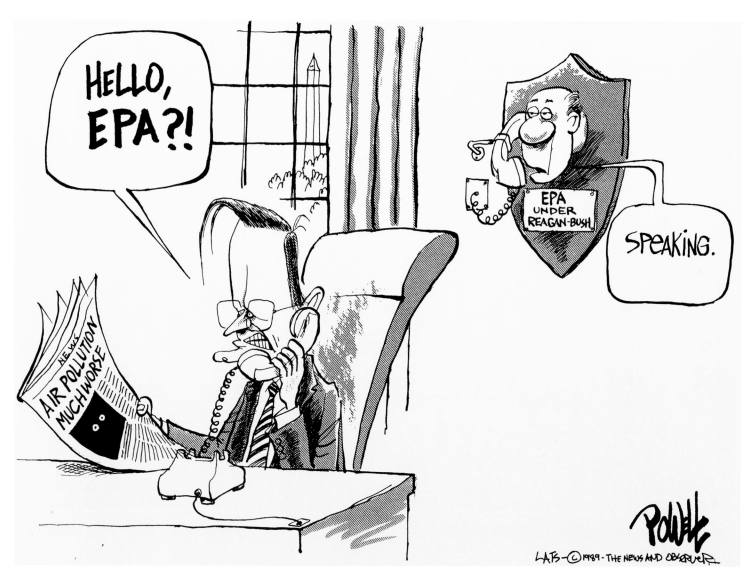

There are perhaps three major areas of assault on the environment. Oversimplified, these are production, consumption, and technology, exactly the areas in which the U.S. economy leads or excels. They are also thoroughly interconnected. Changing one will inevitably require changes in the others. Solutions for the environmental problems we face will require committed and informed leadership from the president, courageous and continued support from Congress, and patience and a willingness to sacrifice on the part of business and the public. That time has not yet come.

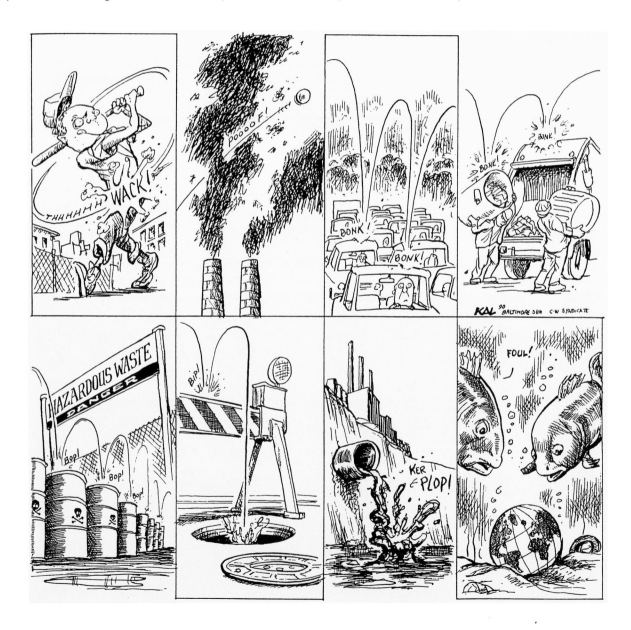

It would be hard to find an environmentalist enthusiastic about Bush's energy policy. Bush saw the goal as provision of adequate energy supplies with minimal dislocation to the economy. Environmentalists saw the same goal as conservation changes in patterns of production and consumption. The president's time frame was short term and his goals immediate. He wanted a burgeoning economy to ensure re-election. Environmentalists have a longer-term point of view. They have to live here long after Bush doesn't live in the White House.

131

Consensus has it that the high standard of living in industrialized nations is based upon prolific, even exuberant, use of fossil fuels. Reserves of such materials are finite, but we don't have to deal with that right now. Meaningful conservation efforts will require more than remembering to shut off the light in the bathroom. We will have to change products, production methods, and patterns of consumption. That will probably require legislation of rules, standards, and regulation. President Bush found regulation about as palatable as broccoli.

AS POGO ONCE OBSERVED, "WE HAVE MET THE ENEMY, AND HE IS US."

Most Americans make profligate use of energy in one way or another. Indeed, one measure of success in our society is the number and cost of the "toys" you can afford—and who wants tiny toys? George Bush and Ross Perot apparently get a kick out of owning and operating power boats. But then, damned few Americans have willingly switched to gas-sipping mini-compacts. We'll become environmentalists when it's unavoidable. That time may be fast approaching.

The fates seem to have a delicious sense of irony. Economic success for any society has always been based upon that society's ability to use and manipulate the earth's natural resources. Living standards are the product of how much and how fast raw materials are pushed through that process and the results consumed. Ah, but physics has set a trap for us. Both the production and consumption phases produce heat, pollution, and waste. Our goose lays more than golden eggs. We need more than a president; we need an alchemist.

ALL THESE SCIENTISTS DO IS COMPLAIN ABOUT THE OZONE LAYER. LOOK OUT THERE, SMITHSON, DO YOU SEE A HOLE?

WHAT IS IT THAT YOU CANNOT SEE, NEED A LOT, AND MAY SOON NOT BE THERE?

Give up? The earth is constantly bombarded by various damaging rays coming from space. We are protected by an invisible ozone shield that is now being eroded by fluorocarbons and other substances produced by industrialized nations. Our pollution problems seem to be taking on cosmic dimensions, and George Bush was no Captain Kirk. While we have a global problem, Bush showed a parochial point of view—protecting the ozone layer might injure the air-conditioning industry.

There is something mind-boggling, perhaps inconceivable, about the concept of global warming. The scope of the problem is so grand, and the consequences so dire, that politicians have a dreadful time dealing with it. George Bush was no exception. He was much more comfortable in the other environments with which he deals, the environment of the polling booth, of the boardroom, and of the fund-raiser. He reflected the ideas and world view of those with whom he associated. There were not many ecologists or "tree huggers" there.

Not many years ago Third World countries were enormously enthusiastic about something called the Green Revolution. Massive inputs of chemicals (pesticides, herbicides, and fertilizers) would let them escape from the trap of growing populations and limited agricultural productivity. As we are now finding, these same chemicals created a whole new set of problems. The more highly processed a substance is, the less biodegradable it turns out to be. We can now buy gorgeous green lettuce with nary a hole in it. But soon we may not be able to wash it in the carcinogenic water that comes from the tap.

The petroleum industry is a marvel of efficiency. We can buy gasoline made from Arabian oil shipped halfway round the world and run through an enormously complex refining process more cheaply than we can buy milk produced by a cow on a farm 10 miles away. But when the Exxon tanker VALDEZ fouled the waters off Alaska, we had driven home a lesson that haunts us still. Accidents are unavoidable, and yet we must continue to produce and ship frightening amounts of terribly toxic materials. Where is the preparation for the next INEVITABLE disaster?

Congress and state legislatures tend to hold private property rights sacrosanct, and because of the strength of lumber, mining, and development interests within those bodies, strong environmental legislation is seldom passed. They have, though, occasionally enacted laws that seemed unthreatening at the time. One of those was the Endangered Species Act. The Bush administration's animosity toward the Endangered Species Act had much more to do with protecting profits than it did with defending jobs. Jobs would be better protected by enacting inhibitions to the shipment of raw logs and the movement of processing plants out of the country. For their part, environmentalists used the strengths of that act because it was all that was available to interrupt current logging practices. Still, much more than the owl is at stake. The struggle is over the last virgin forests, threatened watersheds, public control of public lands, and long-term employment in the lumber industry.

Americans have long seen bogs, marshes, and swamps as wastelands, not as the vital wildlife incubators and refuges they are. We raced across the continent draining and filling such areas to the point where they are now in dangerously short supply. When other flatland is thoroughly developed, developers turn to the wetlands. They tell us jobs and private property rights are at stake. The Endangered Species Act provides a means by which such development, where harmful, can be halted. But environmentalists are then stuck with defending the rights of salamanders while, at the same time, knowing that many more-vital factors are at stake. The Bush administration came down on the side of the developers. The general public isn't very interested and salamanders don't vote.

"Developed" means changed and prosperous. Underdeveloped means less changed and poor. Those nations in the second category absolutely see that correlation. Now environmentalists from developed countries see the need to leave part of the earth unchanged. The trick, of course, is to break the connection between unchanged and poverty. Until we can do that, our conservation preaching to Third World nations is blatant hypocrisy. When we refuse to protect the tiny remnants of our own heritage of virgin forests, that hypocrisy is doubly evident. Physician, heal thyself.

Here was the problem. They were holding an environmental summit meeting in Rio. They appeared willing to make some economic sacrifices to protect the ecological future of the world. But in the United States it was an election year, the economy was shaky, and the business community was in no mood for sacrifices. Bush's solution: avoid responsibility by refusing to go personally, propose to send a delegate you can later repudiate, instruct him to water down everything he can and refuse to sign anything he can't, then, at the last moment, change the plan and attend the meeting, while offering an alternative plan to confuse the issue but look like you're trying. Bingo.

Possibly, in some more economically stable period, the Bush administration would have taken a more positive approach to the environment. The president might have been more supportive of parks or hazardous waste cleanup. But it was unrealistic, regardless of the economy, to expect him to embrace effective industrial regulation or any program that would reduce business freedom or limit the prerogatives of private property owners. The values and philosophy of George Bush just do not mesh with those of environmentalists. He campaigned as the executor of the Reagan legacy, and that's what he was.

EDUCATION

Our weakest subject

David L. Kirp

Summit conferences almost always involve heads of state, but George Bush had a different idea. Nine months after his 1988 election, he called all the nation's governors together in Charlottesville, Virginia. Not since Franklin Delano Roosevelt had an American president convened a domestic summit. FDR's agenda was the New Deal, Bush's was education. It seemed the candidate who had promised to be the republic's first "Education President" was about to fulfill that promise.

The problems with American schooling are real and complex, but none of them saw the light of day in Charlottesville. Instead there were press conferences, sound bites, and photo ops—along with what William Bennett, Ronald Reagan's combative secretary of education, described as "pap and things that rhyme with pap." By the year 2000, the president and the governors pronounced, the lives of the young would be radically different. Every American child would start school "sound in body and sound in mind." Every American school would be drug-free, American students would be the best in the world in math and science, and so forth, six such goals in all.

Unfortunately, the bold statement of these goals carried the pious ring of New Year's resolutions. Without concrete proposals for how to reform schools—and the dollars to implement them—these goals became so many political artifacts offering appearances but no real solutions. And a president who confessed to being bored by domestic affairs soon changed the subject, from pedagogy to Panama.

Even so, the "Education President" had voiced in his campaign the concern of most Americans: something had to be done about education. About that there was widespread agreement at the outset of the Bush administration. Historically, education policies had been entirely set by states and localities. Local control was the byword, "The Battle Hymn of the Republic," as one school official called it.

To be sure, there had been previous periods of intense federal activity in education. The post–Civil War Morrill Act encouraged the establishment of land grant universities. After World War II, the GI Bill paid millions of veterans' college bills. Segregation had been largely undone, at least in the South, through federal intervention. Beginning in the 1960s, federal funds were provided to equalize the life chances of the "educationally disadvantaged" and, later, the handicapped.

Republicans, historically fearful of an excessive federal presence in the schools, had resisted many of these measures. Indeed, during the 1980 presidential campaign, Ronald Reagan promised to abolish the Department of Education and turn over all responsibility for education to the states. But the appeal of this hands-off approach was short-lived. With schooling increasingly regarded as a national concern because of the purported tie between educational achieve-

ment and America's place in the world economic market, Washington became a logical locus of policy-making.

Alarms about falling national test scores were sounded in a bookshelf's-worth of reports written during the 1980s. Education Secretary William Bennett became one of Ronald Reagan's most visible and polarizing cabinet members. Whereas previous administrations, Republican and Democratic, had emphasized providing equal educational opportunity and eliminating segregation, Bennett crusaded for excellence, which he contrasted with equality. He promoted the "three Cs"—more content in the curriculum, greater family choice among both public and private schools, and schools that explicitly molded character—and in the process lambasted everyone, from the teachers' unions to Harvard University, that he saw as antagonistic to his views.

Meanwhile, the real action around education was taking place in the states. During the 1980s, most states boosted educational standards by toughening teacher certification requirements and student graduation requirements. Longer school days and school years were adopted. States also increased school spending by 23 percent during the decade. Yet the results proved disappointing. Test scores measuring basic literacy and numeracy did rise during the 1980s, but SAT scores slipped. Scores on national high school exams that demanded reasoning rather than regurgitation of facts also declined.

In this context, it made sense for George Bush to situate himself as the "Education President," yet his administration was either not prepared or was unwilling to proceed with a program for education. After the Charlottesville summit, the White House went silent on the subject of education. Lauro Cavazos, a onetime university administrator from Texas, presided fitfully over a dozing Education Department. But as criticism mounted —in 1990, *U.S. News & World Report,* normally friendly to the administration, labeled education "the President's worst subject"—Cavazos and his top aides were dumped.

In their place, the Bush administration recruited the ablest leadership the Education Department had ever seen. The new secretary, Lamar Alexander, had made school reform his top priority as governor of Tennessee. David Kearns gave up his job as CEO of Xerox to become Alexander's deputy, and whip-sharp Columbia University historian Diane Ravitch took over responsibility for research.

The America 2000 report that Alexander unveiled in April 1991, while perhaps glib and certainly incomplete, is nonetheless a remarkable document. It represents the most probing official thinking about what the federal government might do to accomplish school reform since the Great Society days of President Lyndon Johnson.

The America 2000 report emphasized that correcting the failures in American education would mean more than mere tinkering with the system. A key proposal is the creation of 535 experimental "New American Schools." There are already many interesting experiments in education going on, some of which the document acknowledged, such as accelerated and enriched programs focusing on slow students. But, to date, the America 2000 reform effort remains fragmentary. Yet, as the report suggests, sparking new ideas and helping others learn from success is an important job, one conceivably within Washington's grasp.

America 2000 proposed new nationwide tests in five core subjects, based on "world standards" for what students at various levels should know, tests that would give students a sense of what they need to learn—and would give communities a report card on their schools. The announced intention is to move away from the standard multiple-choice model of testing, toward the essay format that other industrialized nations rely on. This proposal makes sense— provided that the costs of such a major shift to an essay test doesn't scare off the bureaucrats. Emphasizing thinking rather than content would also encourage many fresh approaches to teaching, and kids who fail would get help, not just bad news.

Finally, the America 2000 plan urges that public dollars support greater family choice among schools. *Choice* is a vague term, and the plan is ambiguous about what it means. The plan can be read as focusing on options within the public school system—a fine idea, and one that most states already promote. However, red flags are hoisted if, under this scheme, private schools would also get public dollars: concerns arise about government underwriting church institutions as well as concern that such choice could effectively kill off the public schools, and further widen the gap in educational opportunities already existing along racial and economic lines in this country.

The changes America 2000 proposes are major, and implementing them would necessarily cost money. American students, whose performance has slipped well below the levels set by other developed nations, won't suddenly move to the head of the world class without more and better instruction, but the only new dollars in the administration's plan would go to the experimental schools.

Moreover, the proposals contain no recognition that America's cultural and ethnic diversity complicates the issue. Nor is there much acknowledgment that schools have to be concerned with more than academics, that schools in poor communities also must provide hot meals and warm clothes, a safe place for after-school hours, health care, and teaching about sex and drugs: the public equivalent of parental love.

None of this should have been news—and none of it is necessarily inconsistent with the America 2000 blueprint. An activist White House, riding the crest of its post–Gulf War popularity, could have negotiated an education bill with Congress that included real support for experimentation and accountability as well as attention to diversity and equity.

Instead, President Bush dithered. In the months following release of the America 2000 report, his few remarks about education emphasized how this new approach would help private schools—an unpopular idea that aroused broader political suspicions about the entire scheme. He devoted just seven sentences of his hour-long 1992 State of the Union Address to education. When Michigan Congressman William Ford, chairman of the House Education and Labor Committee, was asked what President Bush had personally done to help his cause, he replied, "Zilch."

Not until 1992, as Congress was debating its

own education bill, did Bush—now derided as "The Part-Time Education President" by the *New York Times*—again talk about schooling, but it was too little, too late. Polls revealed popular disappointment. Less than half the American public approved of how Bush had handled education issues and a 46 percent to 31 percent plurality thought the Democrats would do better.

Bush's famed inarticulateness did not help his cause. The *New Republic* quoted the President, at a Q-and-A session with schoolchildren in Marietta, Georgia, as describing his education agenda this way: "We are going to keep pushing, because I think the six goals are sound—math and science, and nobody is too old to learn…. Tests—volunteer, but nevertheless standard, so a parent can tell how his or her kid adds up to others across the country. And these are good."

The bill that Congress eventually sent to the White House provided modest new dollars for existing programs, coupled with the barest start on national testing and experimental schools. "The time has come for Congress to get on board or to get out of the way," the president complained. He then signed the measure.

In April 1992, in the midst of a campaign trip, George Bush spoke at a high school assembly in Allentown, Pennsylvania. He stood beside a large papier-mâché apple, hurriedly made by an art teacher at the White House's request. Above his head hung an oversized yellow pencil with the inscription "Welcome 'Education President,' George Bush." This appearance was really just another photo op—accompanied by Bush's solemn promise that he would make education his "top domestic priority" during his second term.■

Our founding fathers adopted the system we call federalism. Its unique concept is that the states should retain powers outside the jurisdiction of the national government. Assigned to the states were governmental functions closest to the people's everyday lives. These included law and order and education. Federalism encouraged diversity and permitted local control. If we are to retain those characteristics, the national government's major role then becomes funding assistance. Another is to offer advice. George Bush emphasized the latter—it's free.

Pundits, politicians, and parents have embraced the phrase "the failure of our schools." To some extent, that's like blaming the police for a rising crime rate. Americans seem to feel the public schools can be a panacea for all societal ills as well as a magic cauldron in which we can brew satisfaction for all our societal aspirations. That kind of faith is a mixed blessing. Failure is inevitable. Just as the schools are only part of the problem, they can be only part of the solution.

START WITH FRESH, EAGER FACES

ADD POVERTY

BEAT IN BROKEN HOMES (REMOVE ROLE MODELS)

SMOTHER WITH VIOLENCE, DRUGS, AND APATHY

DUMP ON PRE-BURDENED SCHOOLS. ALLOW TO FESTER ON BACK BURNER, BOILING OVER OCCASIONALLY

MAKES MILLIONS OF BITE-SIZE TRAGEDIES, OR ONE SO BIG YOU CAN'T STOMACH IT

Only after World War II did the American public begin to look to Washington for financial assistance for education. The Cold War apparently placed our public schools on the front line in our confrontation with the Soviet Union. Congress legislated some financial assistance for math, science, and foreign language (Soviet schoolchildren performed better in those areas). Subsequent federal wars on prejudice and poverty saw the government intervene with rules or money for public education. In each instance the programs were small and the financial commitment modest. If the schools are indeed the front line in our battle for a better future, it is difficult to fathom why the teachers we've sent to do battle are underpaid, poorly equipped, and generally denigrated.

"...SO IT ISN'T JUST THE CLUTCH.....?"

George Bush's problems with education were in the nature of a self-inflicted wound. Had he stuck to the Reagan line of states' rights and local responsibility, he would have charmed conservatives, maintained ideological consistency, and saved himself a great deal of embarrassment. A bit of self-examination and a close look at the situation should have shown him that being the "education president" would raise expectations he was unwilling to meet. What education needed was money. Bush didn't have it and, in a nation of lip-readers, he wouldn't ask for it.

Each generation of education professors (and each "commission on education") faces the reality that the system needs money not manipulation. It takes money to attract and pay better teachers, to reduce class size, to provide better equipment and adequate buildings. Because they know that significant funding increases are unlikely, and because they want to do something, they fiddle with words, creating slogans, catch phrases, euphemisms, and gimmicks. They shuffle programs, regroup students, and add administrators. And in the classroom, reality remains unaltered.

There is something attractive in the Ivory Tower concept. It suggests a place where students are safe and secure enough to explore the world of ideas and the possibilities of life. But that "ain't" the way it is in most urban schools. The nation's most intractable social and economic problems seem concentrated and magnified there. Drugs, crime, unemployment, ethnic diversity and animosities are the backdrop for learning. You may keep these disturbing images out of the Ivory Tower, but not out of Franklin Junior High.

For those who accuse the schools of failing to educate our children and who damn the curriculum, the methods, and the teachers, there is an unsettling conundrum. Why do some students succeed? Perhaps we spend too much time studying why students fail. A more fertile field for investigation might be why some win. The interesting aspect of this whole situation is that it suggests that much of the problem lies OUTSIDE the schools. It may not be the books kids take home but the attitudes they arrive with that make the difference between success and failure. The schools should do better; so should we all.

How in hell did he learn that game when he can't master his multiplication tables? How can so many others, who wouldn't know an adjective if it ran over them, learn the complex mental and manual gymnastics required to operate an automobile? All children are not meant to be brain surgeons, but all of them bring to this world a great deal more capacity than we are developing and using. The most positive aspect of the last 200 years of world history is that one disparaged and denigrated group after another has become productive in ways never previously imagined.

Every president knows that his "image" affects his ability to lead the nation and deal with Congress. The trap is that he may concentrate on manufacturing a favorable public image and fail to follow through on the promises. George Bush announced some truly admirable (and voter-pleasing) educational goals. But goals set, and not worked for, are at best platitudes and at worst lies. Nobody could expect George Bush to solve the myriad problems of our public schools. But he gave us the right to expect him to seriously try.

The Bush administration proposed the creation of 535 experimental schools. (What a coincidence, that's how many congressional districts we have.) In theory these schools would develop new strategies and methods that could be used in the public schools throughout the rest of the country. Few experimental schools materialized and, even if they had, their effect would have been marginal. Innovations cost money. Actually, the schools are already innovative. They hold cake sales to get books for their library and auctions to raise money for art classes or to buy a new computer.

BUSH TO THE U.S. GOVERNORS, "I AM GIVING YOU THE OPPORTUNITY TO SOLVE YOUR OWN PROBLEMS."

During the 1960s and 1970s, Congress initiated grant programs and revenue sharing to help economically hard-pressed states. In the 1970s and 1980s it shifted responsibility for implementing many social programs from Washington to state governments, with a promise of funding assistance. Under the Bush administration, Congress has had to reduce revenue sharing and slash assistance. But the federally mandated programs remain an albatross around the neck of the state governments. As the "education president," Bush could have picked up the tab for social welfare and thereby allowed the states to expend scarce dollars on schools.

Advocates of public education see the "push for private" as another manifestation of the "white flight" that followed efforts to bring racial balance to U.S. schools. Whatever the motivation, the effects would probably be the same: concentration of most of our educational problems into urban public schools and an elite private education for those who could afford it. Under a voucher system, parents would receive from the state "their share" of public education monies, to supplement with as much of their own funds as they chose, and enroll Johnny in a place "po folk" couldn't go.

The Constitution divided responsibilities and resources between the states and the national government. As the federal government had very few functions, the states retained the two primary sources of tax revenue—property and sales taxes. These taxes became inflexible and, in the case of property tax, unfair. In competition to attract and hold businesses, states now hesitate to increase sales, property, or even state income taxes. The citizen-led tax rebellion of the 1980s exacerbated the situation, and the recent recession has reduced revenues even at current levels of taxation. But the kids keep showing up at school.

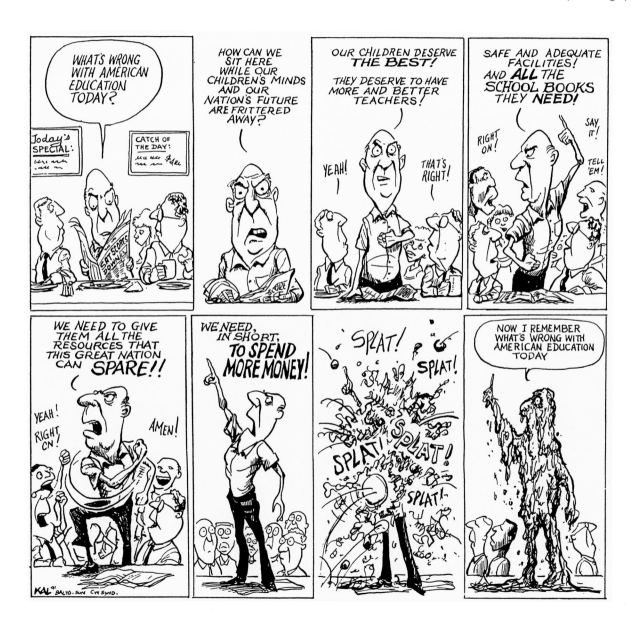

HEALTH CARE

A basic right?

Constance Matthiessen

During a meeting at the White House, according to a story making the rounds in health-policy circles, a health expert had 15 minutes to talk to President George Bush about health-care reform. After the expert had been talking for a minute and a half, the president's eyes glazed over. After a few more minutes, the president spoke. "We have to move forward," he said with conviction. "We have to build on what we have, because we have the best education system in the world."

Whether or not this story is apocryphal, the perilous state of the U.S. health-care system made it impossible for President Bush to ignore the matter altogether. For if the condition of a nation's health system indicates its overall well-being, the United States is in big trouble. The Employee Benefits Research Institute (EBRI) calculated that in 1990, approximately 35.7 million Americans, or 17 percent of the population, had no health coverage at all and that 85 percent of the uninsured lived in families headed by workers.[1] The Children's Defense Fund reported that in 1990, 40 percent of American children had no health coverage provided by their parents' employers.[2] And growing numbers of elderly Americans have been forced to "spend down" into poverty to afford long-term care.

The United States is the only industrialized country except South Africa that does not provide public health care for its citizens, yet the U.S. system costs more than any other. In 1989,

for example, 11.8 percent, roughly $600 billion, of the U.S. gross domestic product went for health care, compared with 8.7 percent in Canada and 6.7 percent in Japan.[3] The 1992 U.S. health-care bill is expected to reach $800 billion, over 13 percent of the gross national product. At that rate, according to a recent government study, health care will consume nearly one-third of the GNP by the year 2020.[4]

Health economists attribute these enormous costs to a variety of factors, including an aging population, expensive technologies and treatments, ballooning administrative costs, unnecessary medical interventions, and the emphasis on acute rather than primary care—which results in people seeking help when their problems are more expensive to take care of. AIDS has also contributed to the bill: the lifetime cost of treating a person with AIDS reached $102,000 in 1992.[5]

But this hefty price tag has not meant more or better care for Americans. A 1992 report by the National Commission to Prevent Infant Mortality found that, compared to other countries, the United States ranked 22nd in the number of babies who die in the first year of life. Japan's rate, the best in the world, was less than half that of the United States.[6]

By the late 1980s, health care had become a solidly middle-class concern. Since World War II, American workers were accustomed to receiving health benefits as part of their employment package. When health insurance was relatively

inexpensive, many employers were happy to provide it since doing so contributed to worker productivity and goodwill. By the late 1980s, however, health coverage was no longer a fringe benefit, but the source of bitter labor-management disputes. Employee health plans had become a drain on profits. Between 1970 and 1989, the cost to employers of providing health benefits increased 163 percent.[7]

The health-care crisis escalated, creating a growing momentum during Bush's four years in office for health reform. On the one hand, Congress was awash in health-reform proposals from labor unions, seniors, and consumer groups. While on the other, business leaders demanded relief from the escalating employee health costs. Numerous commissions were formed to examine the health-care problem and recommend action. Even the American Medical Association (AMA) and the health-insurance industry offered prescriptions for change.

By 1992, seventy percent of Americans believed the health-care system needed fundamental reform. But studies, such as one by the New York–based Public Agenda Foundation, found that few citizens understood the complex causes of the health-care crisis, and large numbers had never heard about many of the reform proposals being debated in Washington.[8]

Reform ideas ranged from making health insurance more affordable for small businesses to proposals for a complete structural overhaul that would provide universal health coverage under a system modeled on Canada's. But no comprehensive proposals won enough support to win passage: the only consensus seemed to be about the need for change.

How did President Bush respond to the increasing drumbeat for health reform? From the beginning, he seemed to want to avoid taking it on. One of his few major health-reform statements came during the 1990 State of the Union address when he announced that he had requested Louis Sullivan, secretary of Health and Human Services, to review the "quality, accessibility, and cost" of U.S. health care.

Sullivan, in turn, appointed the Advisory Council on Social Security and gave it the task of examining the entire health-care system and recommending potential reforms. The 13-member panel included representatives from business, organized labor, academia, and the AMA. Deborah Steelman, a Bush health advisor during the 1988 presidential campaign, chaired the panel. Steelman was also a lobbyist for major health-industry interests, including the Pharmaceutical Manufacturers Association and Aetna Life & Casualty.

Having given Sullivan his marching orders, Bush retreated from the issue. Whenever members of the Bush administration were asked what the president planned to do about the health crisis, they said he was waiting for Sullivan's report to formulate his final reform proposal. The waiting stretched out through most of his term.

In lieu of any official plan, Secretary Sullivan tackled other issues. He took a strong stand against the tobacco industry for targeting sales to minority communities. He was also an energetic spokesperson for the importance of in-dividual responsibility for staying healthy. In numerous speeches, Sullivan blamed damaging "behaviors and lifestyles" for the bloated U.S. health-care budget. In 1990, when he issued "Healthy People 2000," a blueprint to improve personal health, critics reacted angrily.[9] "From one side of its mouth, the Bush administration issues goals for better health for Americans," said Congressman Henry Waxman (Democrat, California), a key congressional health-reform advocate, "but from the other side of its mouth, the same Bush administration opposes paying for the health programs that would make these goals real. That's not health policy. That's kinder and gentler hypocrisy."[10]

The Bush administration's approach to health care was far better at rhetoric than results. When the Advisory Council issued its 12-volume report in December 1991, after two years of deliberation, it proved to be exhaustively researched and ultimately inconclusive.

In fact, the council could not agree on a single reform plan. "A majority of the council concludes that, at this time, there is no one right choice," the report stated. "The national consensus so essential to the successful systemic reform the council believes necessary has clearly not developed."[11] Instead, the council recommended various incremental reforms and study projects, including school-based health-care programs, medical malpractice reforms, and public education to promote healthier lifestyles.

But four council members, including two labor union representatives, a Harvard professor, and former Commissioner of Social Security Robert Ball, blasted the majority report, arguing "[the panel has] failed in its major mission… [it] urges us to buy some new furniture for a house that is on the verge of collapse. The more urgent task, we suggest, is to rebuild the house."[12]

An exasperated Ball told *Modern Healthcare,* "I don't get a sense of urgency in reading these recommendations. It's written as if it were calculated to delay."[13]

Many Washington observers believed President Bush and his advisors hoped to do exactly that—to delay action on health reform until after the 1992 election. "What is really essential to make a debate happen in 1992 is that [the] Democrats have a plan," a senior administration official told the *Washington Post* in September 1991. "Until that happens, there is no reason for the President to come forward and take the heat."[14]

But by the end of 1991, growing pressure for reform made delay impossible—and politically unwise. In June 1992, a poll commissioned by the Kaiser Family Foundation reported that Americans considered health care second only to the economy as an issue in the upcoming presidential election. This public sentiment was set in stark relief in November 1991, when Democrat Harris Wofford came from 40 points behind to defeat former Attorney General Dick Thornburgh in the Pennsylvania Senate race. Polls indicated one of three people voting for Wofford did so solely on the basis of his strong support for a national health program.

On February 6, 1992, President Bush presented his own health-care package, which included a health-insurance tax credit and deduction to help low- and moderate-income families afford insurance; use of managed care to control health costs; market reforms to make health insurance more affordable for low-income families and available to people with chronic health problems; and programs to limit medical malpractice litigation.

In introducing the plan, Bush noted, "We need common sense, comprehensive health care reform and we need it now.... My plan puts the emphasis on expanding access while preserving the choice people now have over the type of health care coverage and health care they receive."

He concluded, "Providing affordable care, efficient care, wringing out excess waste and controlling federal growth will create the kind of market-based reform plan that will give Americans the kind of health care they want and deserve and put an end to the worry that keeps them awake at night."[15]

The president's proposal earned praise from insurers and some business leaders, and criticism from many in the health-care community. The Health Insurance Association of America, the industry trade group, was enthusiastic: "We wholeheartedly agree with the President that only a strengthened private/public health insurance partnership can deliver the health care Americans need, at a price they can afford to pay, while retaining the cutting edge quality they have grown to expect."[16]

Some health-care advocates argued the program would not, as the president promised, improve access or control health costs. The president of the National Leadership Coalition for Health Care Reform pointed out that under the proposal, "uninsured families of very modest means would have to spend at least $3,375 a year on health insurance—money that most of them can't even conceive of piecing together—in order to get only a $375 tax credit. This would keep them firmly in the ranks of the uninsured."[17]

Some representatives of small business welcomed the proposal, but other business leaders doubted the plan would rein in health costs. Families U.S.A. found fault with the proposal's reliance on managed care to control costs: "Managed care premiums have been increasing at virtually the same rates as other health insurance premiums."[18] Congressman Dan Rostenkowski (Democrat, Illinois) pointed out that the administration had included few details about how the plan—expected to cost about $35 million a year—would be funded.

"When I talk to health policy experts—and I'm not just talking about liberals—the president's proposal is just dismissed," said Rashi Fein, a professor of the economics of medicine at Harvard Medical School. "It's very sad because his proposal is the culmination of almost four years of study. A good bunch of people working very hard could have come up with that plan in two weeks."[19]

Dr. Arnold Relman, professor of medicine and social medicine at Harvard Medical School and editor-in-chief emeritus of The New England Journal of Medicine, also criticized the Bush plan. "Bush believes that the free market is the answer to all our domestic problems," Relman said. "But the free-market model is inappropriate for health care because it doesn't lead to cost-effective or equitable care. You simply cannot treat health care as a business."[20]

Relman believes the powerful health-care industry, which he calls the "medical-industrial complex," is a major—perhaps the major—obstacle to comprehensive health reform. And as Common Cause magazine pointed out in a 1992 investigation, "The same insurance companies, doctors, hospitals and drug manufacturers that

live off the $700 billion-a-year health-care industry are battling comprehensive reform on Capitol Hill and at the White House." According to Common Cause, the health industry contributed over $60 million to congressional candidates between 1980 and early 1991. And the health industry's influence was not limited to political contributions: Deborah Steelman's job as a lobbyist is only one example of the often fuzzy line between advising government on health issues and lobbying it on behalf of corporate interests opposed to reform.[21]

Given these significant obstacles to reform, changing the U.S. health system is not going to be easy—or popular. It is going to require challenging interests that have won tremendous profits under the current system, educating the public about complex issues, and mobilizing support for difficult policy choices. And, as Relman points out, that is what leadership is all about. "President Bush is very proud that he led us to victory in a war against Saddam Hussein, a war that many people opposed," Relman said. "He is proud that he stood up to that opposition. Why doesn't he have the same courage on domestic issues?"

In a wisecrack aimed at the Senate Democratic leadership, Bush himself may have best captured his administration's strategy on health reform: "Ask them about the side effects of their proposal, and they'll say, 'Take two aspirin and call me after the election.'"[22] ■

At any given moment the president faces pots simmering, or overboiling, everywhere. Policy emphasis is a judgment call. But if those calls result in a pattern, we can discern presidential priorities. George Bush did not see health care as a major problem in this country or, if he did, he apparently saw it as unamenable to government solution. His faith was in free enterprise and his solution was to let the market work it out. Meanwhile, he would do more "presidential" things, such as fighting wars and capturing Manuel Noriega.

"HEY! WHO MOVED THAT TO THE *FRONT BURNER?!!*"

Though some Americans might wish it otherwise, presidents represent all of us but reward those who put them in office. Citizens who forget this will find the policies of the Bush administration more puzzling than they need be. Until recently, we defined our health-care problem as one involving the poor and minorities. Those people are more often Democrats than Republicans. On the other hand, doctors, the insurance industry, and the medically insured are more often Republicans. Those groups did not push for health-care reform, and Bush did not deliver it.

RX: BUY SOME INSURANCE.

Health care in America is essentially a part of our private enterprise economy. When some kind of national health-care program drew widespread public support in the 1940s and 1950s, the medical establishment blunted the drive by inventing health insurance. The more powerful and affluent elements of the population, who were capable of paying insurance premiums, were removed from the problem. Later, the medical establishment supported Medicare, theoretically removing Grandma from the health-care equation. Left to fend for themselves were the impotent and the impoverished.

To be profitable, the health-insurance industry must contain its costs to levels below its premium income. If you can find some hint of humane concern for the ill in that axiom, you have a vivid imagination. Ours is a system measured by money. Insurance companies offer an array of plans to match the premium you are willing to pay. They can eliminate coverage for one malady or another and alter the percentage of cost borne by the insured. Employers have resorted to both to escape the burden of escalating health-care costs. To be assured you're well insured, you better read your policy.

In this society, people have traditionally received only as much health care as they could afford. But during the last 50 years, a philosophical shift in public perception has taken place. Most Americans now see health care as a human right. At issue is the means to provide that care. The bottom line is that health care for the poor must be paid for, one way or the other, by the rest of the population. The issue is exacerbated by the constantly escalating costs established by the private vendors' services.

DANZIGER
The Christian Science Monitor
Los Angeles Times Syndicate

The financial reality is that in order to hold down premiums and turn a profit, insurance companies must hold down claims. One obvious way to do so is to refuse to insure those with high-risk potential. Another is to refuse coverage for "preexisting" conditions. Both leave those citizens most in need of health care without effective coverage. Refusing coverage is an absolutely rational policy decision on the part of the insurers. Now all we have to do is explain that to the chronically ill.

The AIDS epidemic has tested not just science, but human compassion as well. Its transmission was associated with activities most Americans frowned upon. That the Bush administration was slow and hesitant to respond to the epidemic was probably inevitable. Had the disease remained safely isolated in the gay and drug communities, the national response to AIDS would probably continue to be damned little effort—reluctantly made. Well, it didn't, and precious time was squandered debating morality with a microbe.

When syphilis first reached Europe, the pious clucked about the wages of sin while the disease swept the continent. Now 500 years later, our leaders have done the same while the AIDS epidemic swept the world. We debated the morality of condom ads and issued rubber gloves to police. We were horrified at those who suggested distributing clean needles to drug users. Too few of us were able to see the victims as just "sick." We continued to be put off by how they got that way. Our children will pick up the tab for our moral squeamishness.

BEWARE OF THE MEDICAL-INDUSTRIAL COMPLEX.

Eisenhower warned us about the military-industrial complex and the power it might wield over our elected government. In fact, the health-care industry dwarfs the defense industry both in money spent and numbers of people involved. And it is a major presence in every congressional district. Since Eisenhower's time we have invented political action committees (PACs) and perfected the organization and application of special interest group power. Medical policy in this nation is essentially made by the health-care interest groups. There just ain't no sick people PACs.

Most presidential programs begin as rather vague and general ideas, eventually clarified and made specific by a president's advisors and the bureaucracy. George Bush believed in small, unobtrusive government. His advisors and speech writers were faced with the paradox of trying to establish a governmental response to our health-care crisis that would support the president's belief that government should stay out of the way. The reports and recommendations that emerged from the Bush administration, or from the study groups Bush created, reflected his self-limiting attitude. We had "sitting on your hands" as policy.

If we assume the purpose of most legislation is to silence citizen criticism or satisfy constituent demand (and we probably should), then it is unrealistic to expect comprehensive health-care reform. Congress and the president will provide limited solutions with programs having the most visible and vocal supporters. Such a piecemeal approach might actually have its virtues. Comprehensive reform could bring about a coalition of the health interest groups. Imagine uniting the power of doctors, nurses, druggists, hospital workers, nursing home operators, and the drug and the insurance industries! Congress does.

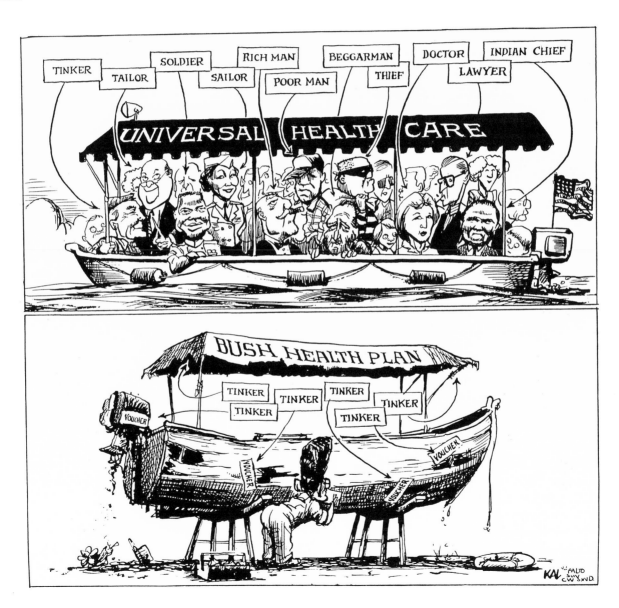

ABORTION

The struggle for consensus

Eileen McNamara

Eleven days before the inauguration of George Bush, the U.S. Supreme Court agreed to hear arguments in a Missouri case that would revive the divisive national debate about abortion just as the 41st president took up residence in the White House. The Court's decision to uphold new restrictions on abortion six months later was the first of many during the Bush years to narrow the constitutional right to abortion established in 1973 in *Roe v. Wade.* That landmark ruling made clear that the right to abortion was not absolute. Dividing pregnancy into three trimesters, *Roe* said state interest in regulation increased as the fetus developed. During the first trimester, a woman had an unrestricted right to abortion. During the second, states could intervene to protect a woman's health. Once the fetus was viable (meaning it could survive outside the womb), during the third trimester, states could protect the fetus by banning abortion except to preserve a woman's life or health.

Although the post-*Roe* decisions granting states greater latitude to limit the circumstances under which women could terminate unwanted pregnancies came during the Bush administration, the groundwork had been laid by his predecessor. President Ronald Reagan had packed the federal judiciary with abortion opponents; he had named three similarly minded jurists to the Supreme Court; and he had imposed regulatory prohibitions on federal funding for health clinics that offered abortion counseling or for medical research that involved the use of fetal tissue.

In abortion-related matters, George Bush merely maintained the Reagan status quo. In 1980 Reagan took the lead on the abortion issue when he chose the more moderate Bush as his running mate. Reagan's and Bush's position on abortion had differed marginally when both were vying for the GOP nomination. Like Reagan, Bush opposed federally funded abortions, but unlike the eventual nominee, he did not support a constitutional amendment to ban abortion. Bush, in accepting the vice-presidential slot, abandoned his former position because doing so was critical to his being accepted by the dominant right wing of the Republican Party.

Just how critical was evident in a front-page editorial written by William Loeb, conservative publisher of the *Manchester Union Leader,* before the 1980 New Hampshire primary. "All prolifers in New Hampshire should be alerted to the fact that George Bush is proabortion," Loeb wrote. "Ronald Reagan, on the other hand, has indicated time after time on the public record, that he supports the human life amendment to the Constitution as necessary to protect the unborn child."[1]

Despite Bush's recanting of his stand on abortion, for abortion opponents, he remained suspect throughout Reagan's two terms. Reagan continued to call for a constitutional prohibition on abortion, but the vice president said during a campaign stop in 1984 that he could support the right to abortion in rape cases. He spent the better part of the next week back-pedaling to get in line with Reagan's position.

Part of Bush's problem with the volatile abortion issue was that he lacked the passion and moral certitude with which Reagan spoke on the subject. At times, in defense of his antiabortion position, Bush almost sounded prochoice. In a 1991 letter to House and Senate leaders during a move by Congress to broaden access to federally funded abortions to include rape and incest victims in addition to women whose lives would be endangered by continuing their pregnancies, Bush wrote:

"Given the importance of this issue, I am writing to make sure there is no misunderstanding of my views or convictions. I have not reached these decisions easily or lightly. Abortion is a difficult, deeply emotional and very personal decision for all Americans. It is made even more difficult when the underlying issue is whether the government—and ultimately the American taxpayer—is asked to pay for abortions and under what circumstances." This language seemed to echo the choice and privacy themes of abortion rights advocates. But, however ambiguous his wording to this point, the final sentence delivered the strong stance his antiabortion constituency sought: "I will veto any legislation that weakens current law or existing regulations."[2]

Although some in the antiabortion movement

174

would remain wary of Bush, none could argue that he had failed to fulfill his promise to the antiabortion wing of the GOP that had helped him win the White House. Although careful not to call it a litmus test, the Bush administration carefully noted the abortion views of each potential appointee. Douglas Johnson, the legislative director for the National Right to Life Committee, noted that if Bush "did not consider a candidate's position on prolife issues when it was pertinent to the job, it would make the president's campaign promises ring hollow."[3]

Candidates for jobs in the Bush administration either shared his antiabortion views, modified their positions, or withdrew from consideration. Burton Lee, a White House physician considered for Surgeon General, withdrew. Opposition from antiabortion groups also derailed the nominations of a candidate for assistant secretary for family support in the Department of Health and Human Services and another for director of the Legal Services Corporation.

Health and Human Services Secretary Louis H. Sullivan nearly sabotaged his own appointment when he told an Atlanta newspaper he did not support overturning Roe v. Wade. He was confirmed after recanting. In 1991 Bernadine Healy won confirmation as director of the National Institutes of Health only after distancing herself from two advisory panels on which she had served at NIH that had recommended an end to the ban on fetal tissue transplants. The rationale behind the ban, first imposed by Reagan in 1988, was that the transplants would encourage women to have abortions.

Bush may have lacked Reagan's emotional fervor about abortion, but the end result was the same: the constitutional right to end unintended pregnancies established in Roe was eroded throughout his presidency by the U.S. Supreme Court. It is to the conservative shift in the Court that historians will trace the Reagan-Bush abortion legacy.

By 1989 Ronald Reagan had named three justices to the Court. Sandra Day O'Connor, Antonin Scalia, and Anthony M. Kennedy helped form a tenuous 5 to 4 conservative majority that Bush solidified with the appointments of David H. Souter in 1990 and Clarence Thomas in 1991. Having watched the 1987 nomination of Robert Bork to the Court derail over abortion, Bush selected nominees with vague track records on the issue. In addition, both Souter and Thomas declined to discuss their abortion views during confirmation hearings, arguing that to do so could compromise their impartiality in future cases.

As vacancies permitted Bush to remake the face of the Court, abortion cases initiated years earlier in the lower courts began to land on the Supreme Court docket. The Missouri case was first. In Webster v. Reproductive Health Services, the Supreme Court upheld more limits on abortion than had been ruled constitutionally permissible under guidelines established in Roe. States were within their rights, the Court ruled, to ban abortions in hospitals that receive public funds, to bar public employees from performing abortions, and to require doctors to test fetuses for viability—the ability to live outside the womb—after 20 weeks' gestation.

More cases followed, each one broadening the authority of the states to limit access to abortion. In 1990 the focus was on parental involvement in a minor's abortion decision. In Hodgson v. Minnesota, the Court upheld a state law re-quiring a minor to tell both parents of her abortion plans or seek the permission of a judge. In Ohio v. Akron Center for Reproductive Health, the Court held that a teenager could be required to inform one parent before obtaining an abortion.

With each new ruling, abortion rights advocates bemoaned and abortion opponents trumpeted the imminent death of Roe. But, although the Court was chipping away at access to abortion, the majority opinions continued to reaffirm the core of Roe: that a woman has a constitutional right to abortion. In Planned Parenthood v. Casey, the Pennsylvania case that in 1992 gave Bush's two Supreme Court appointees their first opportunity to review Roe, Thomas fulfilled the president's expectations, calling for the overturn of the landmark ruling. Souter, however, sided with the slim 5 to 4 majority, arguing that to abandon Roe "under fire" would be a political act that would damage the reputation of the Court and "the nation's commitment to the rule of law." Whether directly or indirectly, the Court's actions had dramatic political repercussions during the Bush years. In the wake of the Webster decision, states seized the opportunity to regulate or protect the procedure. Louisiana and Utah enacted laws recriminalizing abortion, measures that were immediately enjoined pending appeal to the U.S. Supreme Court. Nevada, on the other hand, enacted a law guaranteeing the right to abortion established by Roe in the event Roe was overturned.

The legislative and legal maneuvering surrounding abortion rights was played out against a backdrop of polarized debate and public ambivalence. The National Organization of Women marched its members to the Supreme Court steps. Operation Rescue dispatched its members to entrances of the nation's abortion clinics. Meanwhile, the far less noisy public, poll after poll, was found to harbor inherently contradictory opinions on the issue.

A clear majority of Americans opposed government interference in a woman's abortion decision; a majority, equally as clear, opposed abortion on demand. Two polls in December 1991 and January 1992 yielded typical results. In the first poll, 64 percent said they would not want to see *Roe* overturned; in the second poll, larger majorities of 70 to 80 percent favored particular restrictions on abortion, including a 24-hour waiting period, a provision in the Pennsylvania law the Court upheld in July 1992.

The restrictions being imposed by lawmakers and affirmed by the Supreme Court found support in a populace clearly unsettled by the sheer numbers of abortions performed in the United States each year: 1.4 million. Bush capitalized on public queasiness that abortion was being used as birth control but did not shift federal funds to family planning initiatives to reduce the numbers. In fact, the federal family planning program (Title X of the Public Health Service Act) was held hostage to the abortion debate throughout the Reagan-Bush years. The family planning program has not been reauthorized since 1985, having been vetoed by both presidents after Congress attached amendments to permit public funding of abortions in cases of rape and incest. The program has continued with interim funding measures.

Bush's liberal use of his veto power thwarted all efforts in support of abortion rights initiated by Congress. And Congress, attentive to the electorate's ambivalence on the issue, consistently failed to muster the necessary two-thirds major-

ity to override the president. Abortion rights activists introduced the Freedom of Choice Act in Congress to thwart the Court's abortion decisions. Sponsors said it would simply codify *Roe* into federal law. Opponents argued it would deprive states of the right to regulate late-term abortions. The bill did not get out of committee until 1992 when it faced a certain Bush veto.

Bush's veto was an insurmountable hurdle for the abortion rights movement, which looked to electoral politics after the *Webster* decision to further its cause. Kate Michelman, executive director of the National Abortion Rights Action League, warned that the "prochoice majority" would prove to be a "sleeping giant" that would turn antiabortion politicians out of office. The task did not prove so simple. Abortion was a major issue in the 1990 elections, but the results were mixed, with wins recorded for both sides at the state and congressional levels.

The protracted public debate about abortion showed few signs of abating as George Bush's first term came to a close. At least one abortion rights advocate thought that the discussion, no matter how acrimonious, was a healthy process for the country. When the Supreme Court legalized abortion in 1973, the nation had just begun its modern political debate about the issue, noted Jane Hodgson, an obstetrician-gynecologist who lost her Supreme Court challenge to Minnesota's parental consent law in the first year of Bush's presidency.

In the years just before Justice Harry A. Blackmun wrote the *Roe* decision, 4 states had repealed antiabortion statutes and an additional 13 had modified abortion laws to permit the procedure in cases of rape, incest, severe fetal defect, or when a woman's health would be

harmed by continuing the pregnancy. This gradual liberalization of abortion laws echoed the nation's earliest experience. Until 1821 abortion was legal in all states. Soon thereafter, states began limiting abortion to the weeks before "quickening," when a woman felt the fetus move (in about the fourth month of pregnancy).

The more restrictive laws that followed—those being repealed in the late 1960s and early 1970s—were not prompted by religious debates about fetal life. The impetus, according to Professor James C. Mohr of the University of Maryland, was both the death rate among women having pregnancies aborted by quacks and the declining birth rate among white, Protestant women. "There can be little doubt that Protestants' fears about not keeping up with the reproductive rates of Catholic immigrants played a greater role in the drive for antiabortion laws in nineteenth-century America than Catholic opposition to abortion did."[4]

Jane Hodgson argued in 1989 that the modern political paroxysms wracking the nation over abortion were the price of democracy. "I think *Roe* is a beautiful decision. I am full of admiration for Justice Blackmun for the intelligence of that ruling," she said. "But the truth is he was ahead of his time. The doctors weren't ready for it. The public wasn't ready. We need to reach a national consensus on this issue. It may take another 30 years."[5] ∎

Ironically, two of the most vocal and powerful institutions in the national debate over abortion are dominated by men. The hierarchy of the Catholic Church is adamantly male (most antiabortion Protestant sects show a preponderance of male leadership as well). And, although Congress is somewhat less exclusively male, women are few enough to be of marginal importance in a test of strength between "prolife" and "prochoice" forces. More than any other issue, the abortion question has driven home to women their relative powerlessness in the decision-making process. Move over, gentlemen, the ladies are coming.

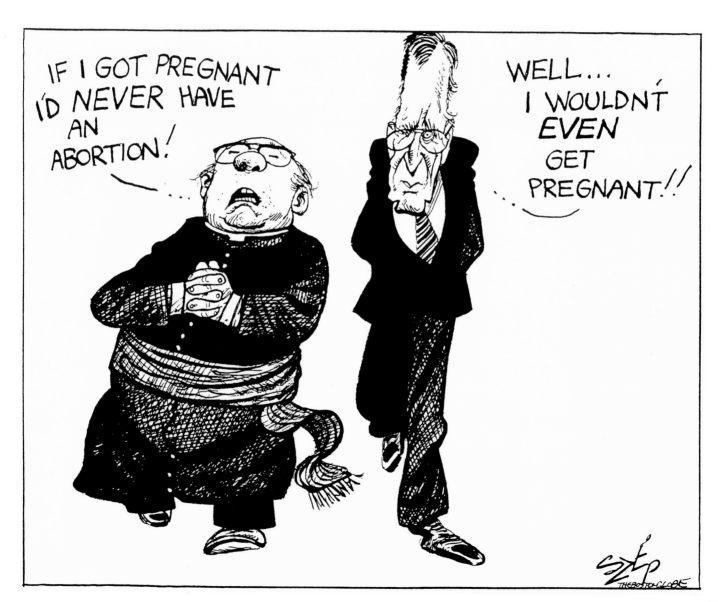

No responsible prochoice spokesperson advocates abortion as a substitute for contraception. In an ideal world, every child would be conceived by parents with the desire, the emotional stability, and the means to provide a safe and rich environment in which that child could grow. But public policy must deal with the real world. Religions may debate whether the woman should have become pregnant. Government is being asked to deal with the fact that she is.

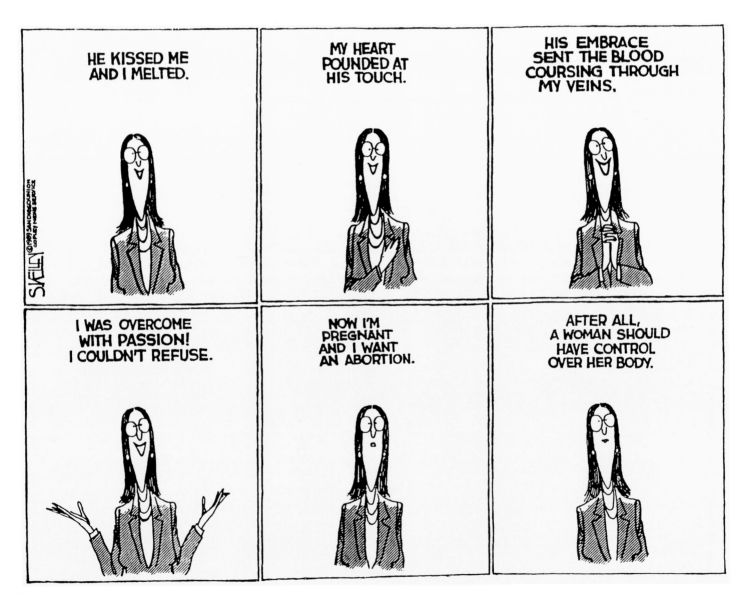

At the core of the abortion issue are two major philosophical questions. When does life begin, and at what point do we deal with that life as separate from the mother's. The picture of Congress debating such issues is, regrettably, ludicrous. In hindsight, it might have been best if the problem had remained outside of the political arena. But it's there now, and governments cannot avoid the issue. They will try to delay the decision, but ultimately they will have to impose the values of one group upon the other. Well, nobody promised that democracy would be easy.

"A FOOLISH CONSISTENCY IS THE HOBGOBLIN OF LITTLE MINDS." RALPH WALDO EMERSON

Both sides in the abortion controversy delight in exposing the inconsistencies in their opponent's position. That process may win points in college debates, but it is irrelevant to a political system struggling to make policy. It doesn't make much difference how voters reach the positions they have assumed; the politician must consider not only the positions taken by his constituents but the intensity of their convictions as well. Though polls indicate a majority of Americans support a woman's right to abortion under certain circumstances, that support is broadly defined and subject to qualifications. Conventional wisdom holds that the abortion issue is more central to the political thinking of antiabortion activists than it is to most proabortion advocates. In a political world of rewards and punishments, politicians are more certain of punishment for a proabortion stance than they are of reward for supporting a woman's right to choose.

Government's role, in part, is to establish laws governing the conduct of one citizen toward another. But government is notoriously ineffective when it attempts to police actions its citizens do not see as impositions on the rights of others (issues such as drinking, drugs, consensual sex). Abortion is a "victimless crime" unless one accords the rights of an individual to a developing fetus. The key contradiction many critics of the Bush administration perceive is its strident concern for the rights of the fetus and its lack of concern (expressed in various forms of government assistance) for children already born.

Perhaps the most obvious characteristic of the abortion controversy is the dominance of extremism. The two sides talk past each other rather than to each other. They work not to persuade but to beat down and morally condemn the opposition. Prochoice advocates see any restriction on abortion as inevitably leading to the demise of any right to abortion under any circumstances. Prolife supporters see any form of legal abortion as demeaning the value of human life and opening the door to euthanasia. Our politicians must invent a middle ground.

Prochoice advocates were incensed when the Bush administration ordered personnel at clinics receiving federal monies to halt any discussion of abortion as an option for women using those clinics. The argument ran something like this: "Women have no freedom of choice if they are not presented with all of the options." And, from the other side: "Tax revenues collected from those opposing abortion should not be used to encourage that very act." The holes in both arguments are rather obvious. Women can learn about abortion from other sources. And government consistently spends tax dollars on programs opposed by significant numbers of voters (the Vietnam War, for instance).

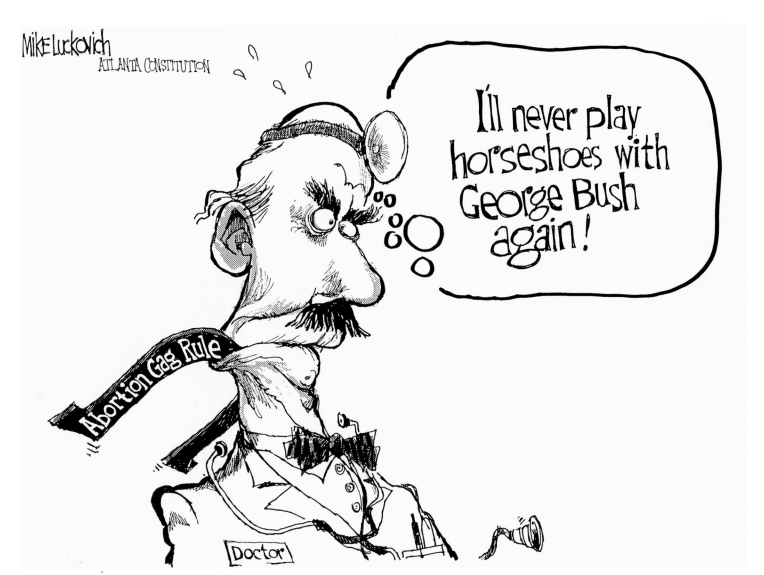

One great irony of the Bush administration's antiabortion campaign was the fact that the only abortions the administration was in a position to restrict were abortions for the poor. Middle-class women could avail themselves of the services of private doctors. Only the poor depend on government-funded clinics for abortions. To the extent that the Bush campaign succeeded, it would maximize the number of births to those groups least able to support and care for children. And, it would increase the number of people receiving the welfare aid that Bush conservatives so resented.

Any decision by government to interfere with a woman's decision regarding abortion carries with it a responsibility to ensure that the resultant child gets a chance at a decent life. To do less means that we have protected our moral sensibilities at the expense of the mother and child. A look at Bush administration policies and budget allocations for programs involving children revealed no such commitment. George Bush was like the stereotypical unwed father— very involved in the first part of the process and absent thereafter.

For the last 12 years the American public has been witness to a unique era in the history of the Supreme Court. During the Reagan-Bush years, prospective appointees have been screened in the Reagan-Bush White House for their "correctness" on a single issue—abortion. Given the multitude of problems facing this nation and the Court's vital role in resolving many of them, there is something bizarre about the president's fixation on the reversal of ROE V. WADE.

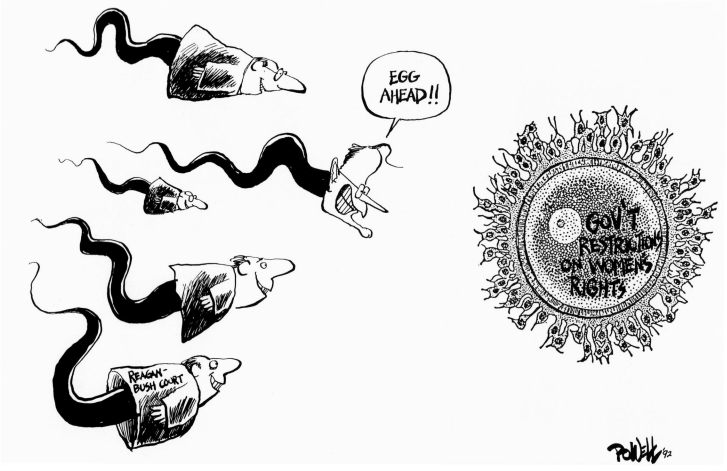

For most of our national history, abortion was not considered within the realm of governmental action. Congress saw the issue as a no-win situation and left the question in the hands of the states. After 1900, state governments bowed to reform pressure and passed widely diverse restrictive legislation. Illegal abortion mills followed and women died or were mutilated in frightening numbers. Because elected politicians would not take the heat involved in modifying state abortion laws, the Supreme Court felt compelled to act. If ROE V. WADE is reversed, state governments will again come under pressure to enact anti-abortion laws. We'll be back where we started, and it's hard to see that as a good place. There must be a better way!

The Supreme Court, if and when it reverses ROE V. WADE, will not make abortions illegal. Congress or state governments alone are empowered to do that. The Court will have merely stepped out of the way. One might debate whether it should step aside, but the fact remains that it is our elected officials who will, or will not, eliminate a woman's right to an abortion. That the clear national majority favoring a woman's right to choose is reluctant to allow the issue to be decided by our elected representatives is a sad comment on our democratic institutions. But the public may be right, and that is a sadder comment still.

If you don't like a Supreme Court decision, wait a little while. The Constitution is silent on abortion. The decision in ROE V. WADE was an interpretation of that document, an extension that functioned much like an amendment. The Bush administration has attempted to rescind that interpretation. In a very real way, you can change what the CONSTITUTION means by changing the jurists who interpret it. A president can direct its interpretation if he knows in advance how his appointees will vote on a particular issue. What this nation may or may not do will be decided by one appointed individual—the fifth vote.

For many women, perhaps the most irritating aspect of the whole abortion debate is the reality that, while they are not telling other people how to conduct their lives, other people are trying to dictate to them. Thus, many women who would not personally consider an abortion rise to vehemently defend the right of other women to make that choice. ROE V. WADE was ideologically offensive to some people, but it forced no change in how they conducted their personal lives. The same cannot be said of restrictive abortion legislation.

George Bush came rather late to his commitment to the antiabortion position. He was, indeed, once a member of Planned Parenthood. As this nation shifted to the right in the late 70s, and because the conservative wing of the Republican Party was crucial to winning the presidential nomination, Bush became a true believer. At the Republican Convention in 1992, conservative forces were still strong enough to push through an antiabortion plank. But national polls hint that such a stance may have cost more votes than it attracted. Within days after the convention, George and Barbara Bush began making moderate noises.

WAR ON DRUGS

The enemy is us

Jefferson Morley

In September 1989 President George Bush went on national television pledging a three-part strategy to wage war on drugs. He promised to get tougher on drug offenders—"much tougher than we are now." He promised to "intensify our efforts against drug smugglers on the high seas, in international airspace and at our borders." And he promised more treatment for drug users: "It's time we expand our treatment systems to do a better job of providing services to those who need them."[1]

Three years later, President Bush could plausibly say he had delivered on his promises. The government had indeed gotten tougher. The number of people serving time in prison for drug offenses had increased as had the average length of drug-related sentences.[2] The drug war outside the United States had escalated. In December 1989 the United States invaded Panama to capture President Manuel Noriega, the first time the nation had gone to war for the sake of drug policy. The Bush administration had also increased spending for drug treatment and prevention by $1 billion to $2.5 billion a year, an all-time high.[3]

What Bush and the country could not say was that his policies had reduced Americans' propensity to use and abuse drugs. Alcohol and nicotine use accounted for the vast majority of U.S. drug-related deaths and countless injuries and hospital visits. The illicit drug economy remained as large as ever with gross receipts ranging from $20 billion to $40 billion. Cocaine remained cheap and readily available in most cities. Heroin grew more popular.[4] Although the use of crack cocaine waned after its initial vogue in the 1980s, a sizable group of habitual users—most of them poor and unemployed—remained.

Bob Martinez, director of the Office of National Drug Control Policy, claimed the Bush administration had made "substantial, undeniable progress" in reducing drug use among the middle class. Between 1988 and 1991, Martinez noted, the number of people using cocaine dropped 22 percent.[5] However, this decline was concentrated among infrequent users, whose drug use posed the least threat to themselves or others. By comparison, the number of heavy users (people using cocaine at least once a week) remained unchanged between 1988 and 1991. By any standard of success more exacting than reducing the number of casual drug users in America, the results of the war on drugs were, at best, modest.

Internationally, the drug control effort produced few results. In Panama, according to the Drug Enforcement Administration, drug trafficking and money laundering returned to preinvasion levels.[6] The Peruvian government withdrew from a U.S.-sponsored coca eradication program because it would hurt Peruvian farmers and fail to reduce the cocaine supply. Colombia pursued its own accommodation with cocaine traffickers. Leading Colombian drug producers surrendered to authorities in return for short prison terms; the volume of cocaine exported from Colombia, however, did not decrease. Honduras and Guatemala, longtime U.S. allies, emerged as new transplant points for smugglers, who presumably were acting with the complicity of local military officers.

The failure of the war on drugs is rooted in the economics and the structure of the drug business and the policies applied in fighting drugs.

The economic realities of the drug business undermined Bush's war on drugs in two ways. The first reality is the paradox of prohibition: prohibition creates a substantial part of the drug trafficker's profit margins.

Criminal sanctions against the sale of drugs discourage sellers of drugs in three ways: by limiting the supply of drugs, by imposing the risk of going to prison, and by removing drug entrepreneurs from the protection of the law, thus exposing drug traffickers to violence and theft. In turn, the drug entrepreneur capitalizes these three factors into the price he or she charges for the drugs. The paradox is this: while prohibition, by limiting the supplies and increasing prices, may force drug users to modify or abandon their usage, it typically creates conditions of scarcity and rising prices, which, in turn, encourage new entrepreneurs into the drug market. Thus prohibition makes drug trafficking an attractive livelihood, providing economic opportunity in America's poverty-ridden inner cities.

The second reality undermining the war on drugs is the organization of the illicit drug business, particularly its boom sector, the cocaine trade. Rhetoric on the drug issues often includes such terms as cartels, kingpins, and drug lords, suggesting the drug business is controlled by an oligarchy atop a hierarchy. Remove the drug lords, Bush suggested, and the cocaine industry would falter. Noriega's conviction, the president declared, would "send a message to drug lords everywhere."[7]

In fact, the cocaine business is not structured hierarchically. Rather, it is an informal network of independent contractors—producers, transporters, facilitators, distributors, middling traffickers, and street dealers. They come together for specific drug deals and then go their separate ways. In this underground economy, General Noriega was not a "drug lord." He was a facilitator for drug traders. His conviction and long prison term no doubt came as a relief to Colombian drug traffickers. Noriega was no longer in a position to inform on them or extort bribes.

President Bush's first important move in drug policy was to appoint William Bennett as director of the Office of National Drug Control Policy, a position he dubbed the "drug czar." Bennett, secretary of education in the second Reagan administration, welcomed the title. He viewed the nation's drug problem as primarily a moral issue, "an offense against God." Therefore, the challenge facing the drug policymaker, he felt, was to focus on reducing not just drug abuse, but all forms of drug use. The successful treatment of addicts, Bennett said, was not enough because it did nothing to curb the use of drugs by nonaddicted users.[8]

Bennett's mindset puzzled many and scandalized others. His influence on federal drug policy, however, was not lasting. After 13 months on the job he resigned, to become head of the Republican Party. After Bennett quit, the moralistic themes of Bush's war on drugs got less play. Bob Martinez, the former governor of Florida, succeeded Bennett. Martinez, who was neither flamboyant nor ambitious, had no expertise in drug treatment or drug enforcement. Soon drug-related issues stopped attracting front-page and network news coverage. Rather than expound on the urgency of controlling casual drug users, Martinez advocated a federal antidrug policy of "pressure on all fronts."[9]

Along with these administrative appointments, Bush increased federal spending for drug treatment and prevention by $1 billion, funding that went largely to so-called zero-use programs. Zero-use programs are based on the premise that habitual drug users must cease all drug consumption forever. Although most drug treatment professionals favor zero-use regimes, critics have noted the poor record of such programs, especially among users without jobs or education. For example, among poor crack users who undergo zero-use treatment, four of five will use again.[10] Responsible use programs, while not advocating drug use, encourage addicts to reduce consumption and dangerous practices, such as sharing needles. The General Accounting Office concluded the Bush administration had "unnecessarily limited the search for successful drug abuse prevention programs by considering only those espousing zero-use."[11]

In any case, increased funding was more than offset by budget cuts at the state and local levels. These governments, hard hit by the recession, reduced funding for drug treatment programs.

Nationwide, the number of publicly funded treatment slots available for drug abusers declined from 2.2 million in 1991 to 2 million in 1992.[12]

The Bush administration also favored interdiction of drug shipments, a policy dating from the early 1980s. In March 1982 President Reagan had named Vice President Bush to head the South Florida Task Force, the Reagan administration's first high-profile campaign against drug trafficking. A year later, Reagan created the National Narcotic Border Interdiction Service, putting Bush in charge.

By all measures, government drug interdiction failed in the 1980s. While federal efforts had succeeded in reducing the flow of marijuana into the country, domestic producers quickly stepped in to meet the demand. In turn, international traffickers flooded the market with the less easily detectable cocaine. Between 1982 and 1985, while Bush oversaw U.S. drug interdiction efforts, the amount of cocaine arriving in the United States at least doubled.[13] The best indication of the cocaine glut was falling prices. In 1982, Drug Enforcement Agency undercover agents in Miami were paying $47,000 for a kilo of cocaine; by 1985, a kilo could be purchased for $30,000. The price of a gram of cocaine on the street was also falling—from an average of $115 in 1982, to about $80 in 1985. The purity of cocaine sold on the street rose from 30 percent to 55 percent in the same period.[14] And cocaine-related deaths more than doubled from about 300 nationwide in 1983 to close to 700 in 1985.[15]

The glut of cocaine on the streets of America meant more competition among drug dealers. Cocaine was plentiful, prices were falling by the month. To attract new customers, dealers began cooking powdered cocaine into crystalline rocks that could be smoked in a pipe. Crack, as smokable cocaine became known, enabled drug dealers to sell cocaine in $10 and $20 packages instead of at the $50 to $70 per gram cost of powdered cocaine. Crack use spread quickly across the country. According to drug treatment professionals, the popularity of crack had subsided by 1990, not because of law enforcement or treatment, but because awareness of the drug's devastating effects had become widespread.[16]

When Bush became president in 1989, he launched a second interdiction campaign. Funding for federal efforts to reduce the supply of drugs rose from $7 billion in 1989 to nearly $8 billion in 1991.[17] No discernible effect on the availability or price of cocaine or heroin in the streets of America resulted. Between 1989 and 1991 less cocaine was imported into the United States. But the volume of heroin coming into the country probably doubled. Interdiction efforts were, once again, overwhelmed.

In pursuit of drug policy goals, Bush deployed the military more widely, and to less effect, than his predecessor Ronald Reagan. The participation of U.S. military personnel in antidrug operations was first made possible by amendments to the Posse Comitatus Act in the early 1980s. However, throughout the 1980s, Secretary of Defense Caspar Weinberger heeded the advice of the Joint Chiefs of Staff and limited the role of the armed forces in the drug war.

This policy was reversed late in the Reagan administration by Weinberger's successor, Dick Cheney. When Bush was elected, Cheney remained defense secretary and the militarization of the drug war accelerated. In August 1989 the Bush administration provided U.S. military support to the Colombian government's nationwide crackdown on drug traffickers. Three months later, the president called for the invasion of Panama, and approved deployment of Green Berets to Colombia, Peru, and Bolivia. The Bush administration even countenanced the first deployment of active-duty U.S. military personnel by sending U.S. National Guardsmen in to board up crack houses in southeast Washington, D.C.

Perhaps the most far-reaching effect of the war on drugs has been its effect on Americans' civil liberties. By the end of 1991, 4.3 million Americans were in jail, on probation, or on parole, an increase of 7 percent over the year before and a 44 percent increase since 1985. More than half of all federal prisoners had been convicted of drug offenses.[18] Since 1987, drug offenders made up three quarters of all new inmates. The introduction of mandatory minimum sentences in 1987 has also deprived judges of the right to exercise leniency when appropriate, leading many judges to call for changes in the law.[19] The federal prison population is expected to double by 1996. The burden of Bush's pledge "to get tougher" was borne principally by African American men, ages 18 to 40. Studies showed that between 25 and 40 percent of these men were in jail, awaiting trial, on parole, or on probation. Half were in the legal system because of drug offenses.[20]

The war on drugs has also compromised the rights of citizens never convicted of any drug offense. The federal government seized $644 million in assets from suspected drug offenders in 1991; state law enforcement agents seized another $150 million in assets. The *St. Louis Post Dispatch* tracked 330 seizures in Missouri and Illinois and found 59 percent of the people whose property was seized were never convicted of any crime and the property was not returned.[21]

Only after the Los Angeles riot in 1992 did President Bush respond to the entrenchment of the illicit drug economy in American cities. In July 1992 the Bush administration gained congressional approval to create 50 urban enterprise zones around the country in which businesses would receive tax breaks in return for inner city investment. The legislation included $2.5 billion for "weed and seed" programs. The idea is that, after law enforcement officers weed out drug dealers, target neighborhoods will be seeded with enhanced law enforcement, job training, and social service programs. Some members of Congress saw the passage of the program as a "breakthrough," but Raymond Flynn, mayor of Boston and former chair of the U.S. Conference of Mayors, described it as "meaningless."[22] Critics charge the programs put little emphasis on social service needs, instead focusing on increasing law enforcement.

In any case, "weed and seed" programs were certain not to have any effect on the nation's drug problem in the near future. In his inaugural address in January 1989, President Bush had said of the nation's drug problem, "This scourge will end." Four years later, the end was still not in sight.■

Our drug problem is a self-inflicted wound. Although it's a cliche to point out that there would be no market if there were no buyers, the fact remains that drug use, not the drug trade, is the kernel of the problem. Psychologists, urbanologists, sociologists, and other qualified social commentators offer a broad array of explanations for our illicit drug consumption. The consensus is that drug use is symptomatic of other circumstances: unemployment, family disintegration, racial and ethnic prejudice, alienation, urban decay, and a host of other problems endemic in modern society.

MARLETTE ©1989
NEW YORK NEWSDAY

Ours is a bellicose century. We have declared war on poverty, pornography, and pollution. As commander-in-chief, the president automatically leads us into battle. George Bush enthusiastically and voluntarily took command of our war on drugs. It was a war against urban guerrillas sustained by millions of American collaborators. There were a thousand fronts and a foxhole in every neighborhood. He couldn't win, he wouldn't quit, and he certainly could not surrender. He could have claimed martyrdom and hoped for a sympathy vote.

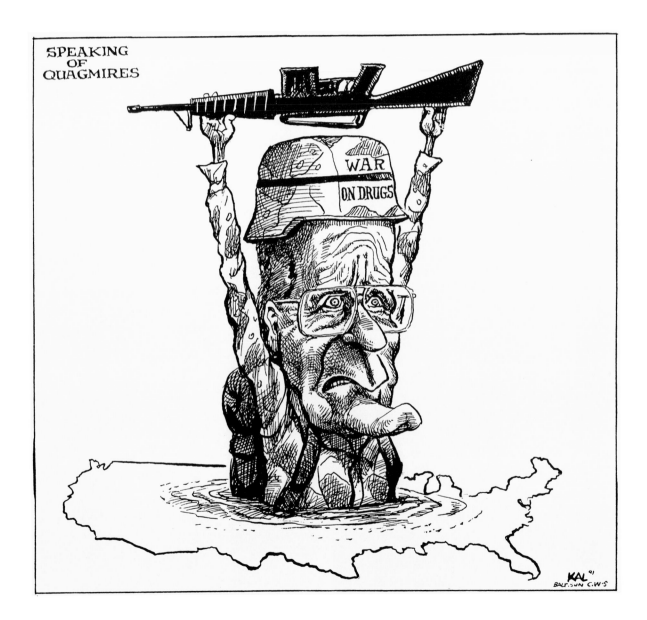

President George Bush quickly recognized that dealing with the domestic roots of the drug problem would be a slow, undramatic, and costly process. But the public wanted a "quick fix" (the problem as part of the language) and "action." Perhaps Bush got carried away with "supply-side" rhetoric. Emphasis was placed upon inhibiting foreign production and halting importation. We had no jurisdiction and minimal clout in dealing with the producing nations. Our message seemed to be: "We pay big money for it, but please don't produce it." And we found once again that the American border is not a wall but a gateway.

Had his performance matched his self-confidence, we'd all be drinking buttermilk. William Bennett was Bush's "Mission Impossible" appointee, first in the department of education and then as drug czar. Fundamentally bombastic and prone to oversimplification, Bennett acted more like the commander of the Salvation Army than J. Edgar Hoover. All too soon, it became obvious that it would take more than bell ringing to lead America out of the drug problem. Besides, Bennett decided there wasn't enough money in the pot and left for a better-paying job.

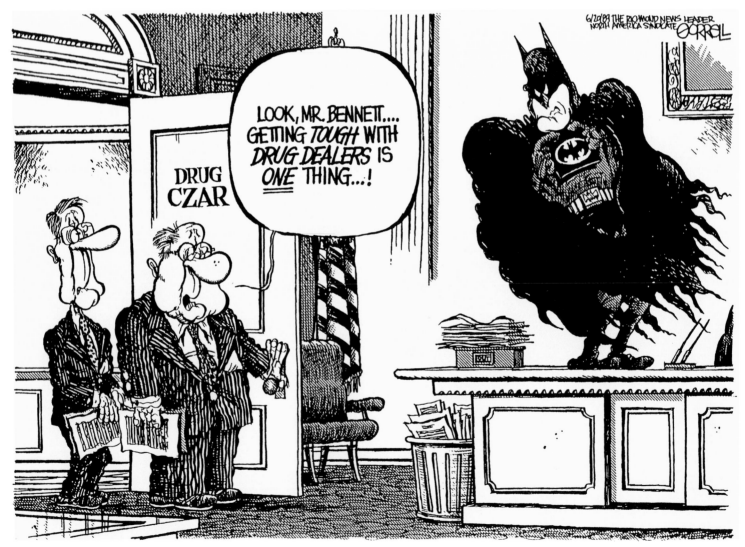

Modern technology is constantly reducing those areas of life that were once essentially private and safe from outside scrutiny. The line between the "right to privacy" and the public "right to know" has always been hard to define. Our commitment to presumption of innocence has usually prohibited testing for alcohol or drugs until after an infraction of the law has occurred. Still, some groups (athletes, for instance) have been required to accept periodic drug testing. William Bennett advocated expanding that program to private industry and many corporate leaders applauded. It also became a civil rights issue. "I refuse to pee on the grounds it may tend to incriminate me."

The slogan "Just Say No" was probably terribly effective with young people who would have said "No" anyway. And it may have helped inhibit middle-class youngsters contemplating casual use of drugs. But it penetrated the ghetto like spit on a windshield. The response on the street was, "And then what?" We have to offer them something to move toward if we expect them to move away from the drug culture. The sight of a teenage drug pusher with a Rolex on his wrist and a chauffeured BMW under his bottom looks irresistible to ghetto kids with an employment future of menial jobs in an eddy of mainstream America.

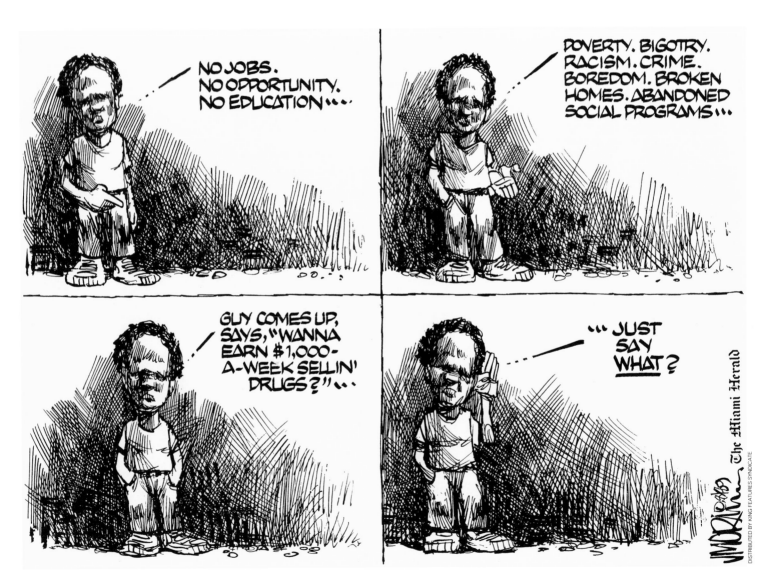

There's a tendency for drugs to come out of the urban jungle but for the attendant social disintegration to remain behind. Those who can flee, do so, and those who can't, live a life of fear and progressive degradation. There is nothing particularly new in the situation. Every city in history seems to have selected out a section to which the poor and the broken are relegated and neglected. It is the task of the police to assure that most of the threat generated in those areas stays there. Another casualty is created when those areas expand or new areas are taken over, and the old, the poor, and the helpless are unable to get out. Mrs. Stumpberger must be one of those, God help her.

MISS ELVIRA STUMPBERGER TAKES UP THE BUSH ADMINISTRATION SUGGESTION THAT SHE CHASE AWAY LOCAL DRUG DEALERS.   MEMORIAL SERVICES NEXT TUESDAY.

CZARS MAY COME AND CZARS MAY GO, BUT PUSHERS ARE FOREVER.

Nice society and moral Americans are susceptible to spasms of concern and reform. And sometimes there is a residue of improvement. But the general pattern is one of political pontification, short-term remedies directed at symptoms rather than root causes, and the rise of apathy when quick solutions are not forthcoming. And, as long as the basic causes of the problem go unaddressed, the social parasites that feed and flourish on such misery need only lay low, or change their modus operandi, and wait out the reformers.

Once we had settled on the phrase "War on drugs," it was probably inevitable that there would be suggestions to use the army. Half the nations in the world maintain armies to be used primarily against domestic foes. The United States has generally resisted that temptation and insisted that the army be employed against foreign foes. Indeed, that may be one of the reasons we're still a democracy. But the real drug problem is here, not somewhere else. That means that the U.S. army, trained for foreign wars, will be, at best, ineffectual. At worst, it means the military will involve itself in areas better left to civil authority.

Every president is a symbolic stand-in for the nation as a whole, but the president must not confuse what is truly a threat or affront to the nation with what is actually a personal confrontation between heads of state. George Bush crossed that line. Though most Americans saw Manuel Noriega for what he was, a two-bit dictator, Bush reacted more personally. He was being defied and challenged. That, and Bush's continued inability to make significant progress in the drug war, produced the frustration that led to our ill-conceived adventure in Panama.

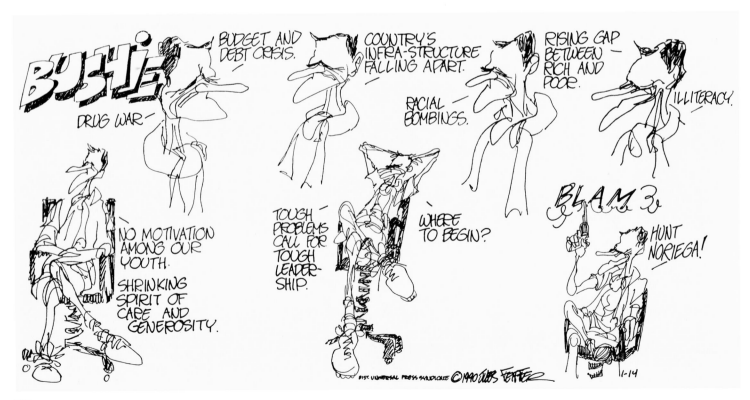

It is entirely possible that an occasional outburst of limited irrationality is a useful tool in international affairs. A course that is entirely predictable and responsible leaves one open to continued and annoying harassment by those less responsible and less rational. Ronald Reagan's airstrike on Libya might be a case in point. The attack certainly sobered Momar Khaddaffi up. Bush may well have been attempting the same sort of thing in Panama. If so, the results were far less salutary. The attack was too large scale, the execution too clumsy, and the objective too insignificant. In the end, Bush didn't look scary, just petulant.

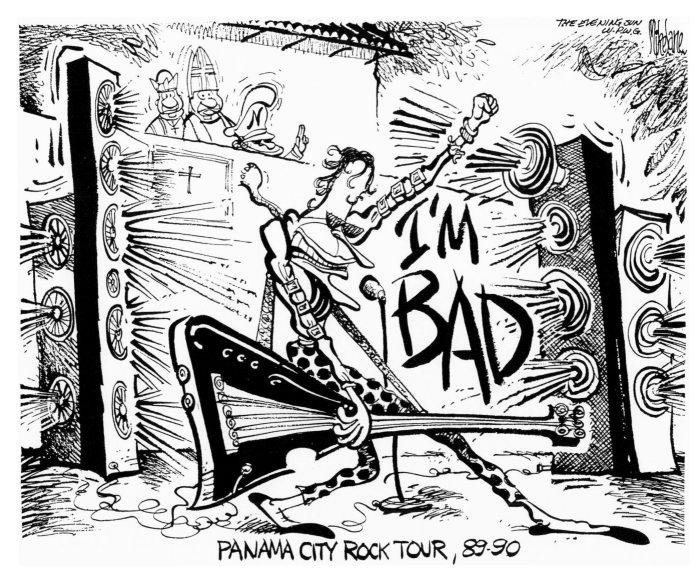

As they have proven to the governments of Colombia and Peru, the leaders of the Latin American drug trade are dangerous and effective foes. But at no time did Manuel Noriega rank among them. Eliminating Noriega left the drug production and distribution system unimpaired. No American user went unsatisfied, and no crime motivated by the need for drug money went uncommitted. The whole affair seems strangely irrelevant to the very real problem America has with drugs. It's nice when our foreign policy works, it's acceptable when it occasionally fails, but it's unsettling when it's entirely irrelevant.

The trial of Manuel Noriega had overtones of a quarrel among thieves. The CIA, in its Latin American operations, found its informers and agents anywhere it could get them. The DEA, in order to gather information, had to make deals with the societal dregs of several nations. The Reagan and Bush administrations, ever paranoid about leftist regimes in Latin America, did the same thing. All of them had, at one time or another, been involved with the "grimy" Noriega, and all of them had muddy skirts. What this administration needed was a laundry, not an invasion of Panama.

THE UNINDICTED CO-CONSPIRATORS

There is a very old punch line that says, "You can't get there from here." In the case of the drug war, the "here" is the decision to fight the problem by cutting off the supply. The paradox that makes the goal almost unattainable is the fact that our successes leave the market undiminished and serve only to raise the sale price. Suppliers are encouraged rather than discouraged, and the potential profits now make the risks more worthwhile. They redouble their efforts and so must we. Perhaps we need a new compass.

5

MAJOR EVENTS:
THE GULF WAR
S&L SCANDAL
IRAN-CONTRA
AFFAIR

THE GULF WAR

A censored victory

Joost R. Hiltermann

On August 2, 1990, Iraqi forces overran the small but oil-rich emirate of Kuwait. Six days later, on August 8, President George Bush sent American troops to the Persian Gulf, declaring that "a line has been drawn in the sand" against Iraqi aggression.[1] In using these words, the president evoked, perhaps inadvertently, the region's colonial legacy, an understanding of which is essential to any discussion of the crisis that evolved in the Gulf in 1990–91.

Like all Middle Eastern states, Iraq is an artificial creation. Its boundaries were drawn by France and Britain in the Sykes-Picot Agreement of 1916, which anticipated the collapse of the Ottoman Empire at the end of World War I. Iraq became a British mandate territory under the League of Nations in 1920, despite a popular revolt against British rule, and finally gained its independence in 1932. In 1922 the British high commissioner in Iraq, Sir Percy Cox, unilaterally redrew the frontiers between Iraq, Saudi Arabia, and Kuwait.[2] These "lines in the sand" reflected British interests in the Gulf, where large deposits of oil were suspected to exist, and left Iraq virtually landlocked.

In 1980 Iraq President Saddam Hussein ordered an invasion of neighboring Iran over a border dispute involving access to the Gulf. The war, in which an estimated 1 million people were killed, was financed in large part by the Gulf states, who feared the revolutionary expansionism of Ayatollah Imam Khomeini's Islamic Re-

public. By 1988, its war with Iran over, Iraq was saddled with a $90 billion war debt, $17 billion of it owed to Kuwait.[3] Kuwait loaned $17 billion to Iraq during the latter's war with Iran. At this juncture, Iraq pressed for higher oil prices and asked Kuwait and the United Arab Emirates to forgive Iraq its war debts since in Iraq's view, it had fought to protect all the Gulf states.

In early 1990, in violation of agreed-upon OPEC quotas, Kuwait and the United Arab Emirates drove down oil prices from $18 to as little as $12 per barrel via excess production. Concurrently, Kuwait refused to discuss the Iraqi debt or other Iraqi grievances. At an Arab summit in Baghdad in May, Saddam Hussein accused the Gulf states of fighting a "war by economic means" against Iraq, and suggested oil prices be raised to $25 per barrel.[4] Precisely what Hussein hoped to get when he invaded Kuwait in August 2—concessions or full control of the emirate—is not clear. Whatever his goals were, he failed to anticipate the strong U.S. response and that of the international community.

International reaction to Iraq's invasion of Kuwait was swift. The invasion threatened the prevailing political order in the Gulf and had given Hussein the opportunity to manipulate oil prices. In response, President Bush put together a coalition of 28 nations. Allied forces entered the Gulf as part of "Operation Desert Shield." On August 8, Bush declared that the United States sought the "immediate, unconditional and com-

plete" withdrawal of Iraqi forces and the restoration of the Kuwaiti government, a position in line with prior U.S. administrations' commitment "to the security and stability of the Persian Gulf."[5]

Bush also said he was "determined to protect the lives of American citizens abroad." Later in the same speech, Bush suggested that because the United States "imports nearly half the oil it consumes," it "could face a major threat to its economic independence" as a result of the invasion. He also implied that because Iraq had a "history of aggression … to assume Iraq will not attack again [i.e., attack Saudi Arabia] would be unwise and unrealistic."

Bush enjoyed broad domestic and international support for the defensive deployment of troops in Saudi Arabia and the lobbying of the U.N. Security Council to impose an arms and trade embargo (excepting food and medicines) on Iraq. He also galvanized public and congressional support when reports of Iraqi atrocities in Kuwait surfaced. Further actions were more controversial, however. On November 8, Bush announced he had sent more troops to the Gulf "to ensure that the coalition has an adequate military option should that be necessary to achieve our common goals."[6] This action, suggesting a willingness to go to war, stirred an intense debate, both domestically and internationally. Congress, for example, strongly supportive of the initial troop deployment and sanctions, appeared reluctant to go to war, and endorsed the use of force only after much deliberation, on January 12.[7] Other than Israel, few countries openly called for the use of force. The final U.N. resolution made before the advent of the war was broad and deliberately vague, authorizing U.N. member states "to use all necessary means" to uphold previous U.N. resolutions. The use of force was not cited.[8]

Congressional and international support for the war waned because evidence suggested that Bush was not fully pursuing alternatives to war. He had allowed only five months for sanctions to take effect, and had brushed off diplomatic efforts by Arab leaders to negotiate a settlement. Playing up a possible Iraqi military threat to Saudi Arabia in August, he had won the support of key Arab regimes like Egypt. However, U.S. intelligence operatives in occupied Kuwait reported at the time that the elite Republican Guard divisions that had led the invasion had withdrawn within days and had been replaced by regular army units of conscripts and reservists.[9]

There are remarkable parallels in the behavior of Bush and Saddam Hussein during the crisis: each played political hardball, shunned substantive negotiations, rejected third-party mediation, and used military force to protect perceived national interests. But Hussein's initial, illegal aggression had isolated him in the world community, and he had further miscalculated Bush's ability and willingness to retaliate. Bush confidently turned Operation Desert Shield into Operation Desert Storm because the Gulf crisis occurred at a historic juncture: the end of the Cold War. Now that the Soviet Union had more or less removed itself from the international military equation, Bush was able to recruit the United Nations to his agenda and unleash conventional American military power against Iraq.

The U.S. military mobilization was the largest since the Korean War.[10] Facing what was touted as the "fourth largest army in the world" (1 million Iraqi soldiers, 5,500 tanks, 700 combat planes, an arsenal of missiles and chemical weapons), the U.S.–led coalition of 28 Western and Third World nations fielded over 700,000 soldiers (500,000 from the United States), 3,600 tanks, 1,800 aircraft, and 150 warships.[11] Estimates of Iraqi power turned out to be largely exaggerated. According to one U.S. analyst, "The war proved that Iraqi [military] capability was ludicrously poor."[12]

Iraqi troop strength in Kuwait had also been miscalculated: not 500,000 but 183,000 Iraqi soldiers faced allied forces when the ground war began, a 4-to-1 advantage for the coalition.[13]

In a punishing six-week bombardment, allied forces dropped 88,500 tons of ordnance on targets in Iraq and Kuwait. Air attacks pulverized Iraqi forces in Kuwait. When allied troops entered the emirate on February 23, thousands of demoralized Iraqi soldiers eagerly surrendered. The "war" was a rout. Greenpeace has estimated that 100,000–120,000 Iraqi soldiers died during the bombing, ground war, and subsequent strafing of fleeing troops on the "highway of death."[14] American soldiers killed in combat totaled 144.[15] Before and during the war, 343 allied soldiers died; of the 266 U.S. casualties, 122 were accidental.

In launching Operation Desert Storm on January 16, 1991, Bush's declared goals were to force the Iraqi army from Kuwait and to destroy Iraq's weapons of mass destruction. Presumably, such actions would preempt any further Iraqi claims to hegemony in the Gulf. Bush stated that allied forces were attacking only military targets in Iraq and Kuwait. "We have no argument with the people of Iraq," he said.[16] Despite this claim, allied bombs wiped out Iraq's civilian infrastructure: power plants, oil refineries, telecommunications, bridges, and, indirectly, water and sewage treatment plants and pumping stations were destroyed.[17]

Thousands of civilians also died during this war, victims of its so-called collateral damage. Because of the domestic chaos in Iraq during and after the war, no precise figures are available. But a widely cited Greenpeace study concluded that 5,000–15,000 Iraqi civilians were killed during the bombing, and an additional 35,000–50,000 civilians died during subsequent uprisings in Iraq and refugee flight.[18] Moreover, a team of Harvard researchers observed "a tripling of infant and child mortality" caused by malnutrition and waterborne diseases related to the destruction of the Iraqi civilian infrastructure and U.N. sanctions.[19]

The cost of the war must be calculated in other terms as well. The Iraqi invasion displaced 2.6 million persons from Kuwait, Saudi Arabia, and Iraq.[20] Uprisings that followed the war displaced an additional 2.5 million people.[21] Of these, an estimated 650,000 Iraqis were still living in temporary shelters in northern Iraq, Iran, and Turkey one year after war's end.[22] War-related environmental damage will be difficult to quantify. It may be nothing short of catastrophic. In one of the more callous acts of the conflict, Iraqi soldiers set afire 732 oil wells in Kuwait, causing immeasurable air, soil, and water pollution. Greenpeace estimated in May 1991 that 2.5 to 3 million barrels of oil were spilled into the

Persian Gulf, covering "hundreds of square miles of Gulf water as well as hundreds of miles of beaches."[23] In the words of a U.N. official, the oil spill and fires together created an "ecological disaster."[24]

In financial terms, the war has been a regional disaster. Some analysts estimate the war may have cost $500 billion in physical damages, military expenditures, and economic dislocations.[25] In contrast, the United States received $54.6 billion in pledges from the Gulf states, Japan, and Germany to cover the coalition's expenses, which the U.S. government estimated to be $60 billion, a figure contested as "unsupported" and "high" by the U.S. General Accounting Office.[26]

Clearly, an unstated goal of the U.S. military campaign in the Gulf was to prevent Iraq's emergence as a regional superpower. What remains obscure is the extent to which George Bush felt U.S. interests would be best served if Hussein remained in power after the war's conclusion. A leaderless Iraq or an Iraq ruled by forces hostile to the United States could further destabilize the region and threaten continued Western access to oil. Perhaps the Iraqi regime was seen to be best equipped to keep the country together, as was so capably demonstrated by its swift suppression of the domestic uprisings that followed the military campaign.[27]

In any final assessment of the war, the record of U.S.–Iraqi relations in the 1980s must also be examined. Details of this relationship were coming to light more fully only in 1992. A Soviet ally in the 1970s, Iraq became of more interest to the United States after the fall of the Shah of Iran in 1979. In 1980 Zbigniew Brzezinski, President Jimmy Carter's national security advisor, declared that "[w]e see no fundamental incompati-bility of interests between the United States and Iraq."[28] In the following decade, the United States provided Iraq with military intelligence in its war with Iran, with helicopters, and with military equipment sold through third parties.[29] An Italian-owned bank in Atlanta, Banca Nationale de Lavoro, made $5 billion in unauthorized loans to Iraq, loans in part guaranteed by the U.S. Department of Agriculture. Some of this agricultural aid was allegedly diverted to military, and possibly nuclear, purchases.[30] As one U.S. Middle East analyst put it, referring to Saddam Hussein, "We knew that he was an SOB, but he was our SOB."[31]

After the war, U.S. federal agencies and congressional committees began investigating the nature of the U.S.–Iraqi relationship. These investigations have focused on a secret presidential order Bush signed in October 1989, National Security Decision Directive 26, which declared that "[t]he U.S. Government should propose economic and political incentives for Iraq to moderate its behavior and to increase our influence with Iraq." It also stated that "[n]ormal relations between the U.S. and Iraq would serve our longer-term interests and promote stability in both the Gulf and the Middle East," and that "access to Persian Gulf oil and the security of key friendly states in the area are vital to U.S. national security."[32] What began to emerge is what is referred to in establishment circles as evidence of a "tilt to Iraq." U.S. actions were an attempt to "ply Iraq with aid."[33] The "tilt" continued well after the perceived Iranian threat to U.S. "vital interests" had receded, and was in evidence right up to Iraq's invasion of Kuwait.[34]

U.S. policy in part explains why Saddam Hussein greatly miscalculated U.S. response to the invasion. Even as late as July 25, 1990, the U.S. Ambassador to Iraq, April Glaspie, told Hussein that the United States had "no opinion on the Arab-Arab conflicts, like your border disagreement with Kuwait," and that "President Bush wanted better and deeper relations with Iraq."[35]

A year after the war, some 18,000 U.S. troops remained in the Gulf. U.N. sanctions were still in place, inflicting hardship on the Iraqi people while Hussein consolidated control of the country. The United States remained the top weapons provider to the Middle East, sending $4.4 billion in arms to the region in 1991.[36] For the people of the Middle East, basic inequalities and injustices, those problems that gave rise to what one commentator has termed the "rage that Saddam Hussein exploits," remain unaddressed.[37] ∎

The Western industrialized nations had managed to accept, and adjust to, the existence of OPEC and its domination of world oil prices. Experience had shown that the member nations were generally unwilling to sacrifice their national agendas in the interest of OPEC unity. It was important, then, that the cartel continue to speak with many voices. However, Iraq was moving toward domination of the system, the international economy was sluggish, and the major economic powers were in no mood to risk energy blackmail. Because there was a glut of petroleum on the world market, Iraqi and Kuwaiti oil production was not immediately essential, and military action that might interrupt that flow was not inhibited. Saddam Hussein badly misread the era.

There's more than one way to bring in a "gusher." Iraq chose the quickest—as well as the most dangerous. In spite of the fact that the governing regime in Kuwait was, by all definitions, a feudal aristocracy, the United States had a long-standing "special relationship" with the nation. The collapse of the Soviet Union had changed the power equation in the Middle East. George Bush could maneuver free of the fear that military action against Iraq might escalate into a broader confrontation with the USSR. Iraq was guilty of unprovoked aggression and George Bush would get to wear the white hat.

Following the oil embargo of the early 1970s, the United States went through a temporary spasm of energy conservation and awareness. By 1991 much of that had dissipated and the nation was more dependent on Middle Eastern oil than before. Little of that oil came from Iraq or Kuwait. The Saudis were the major supplier for the United States. The rise of Iraq as an aggressive, military superpower in that region would leave Saudi Arabia vulnerable to military threat when OPEC polices were being formulated. The Saudis were "reasonable" autocrats; Saddam Hussein was an irresponsible fanatic.

Both Saddam Hussein and George Bush proved willing to follow that old adage "any port in a storm." To protect his rear, Hussein returned to Iran the pitiful territorial gains made in his costly war with that nation. Bush cuddled up to Syria's Assad in an effort to thwart Hussein's attempts to portray the conflict as anti-Muslim. Ignored, if not forgotten, were the earlier charges that Syria sponsored international terrorism. We would fight to protect an autocratic feudal aristocracy with dictators as our allies. It's hard to take the moral high ground when you drag such scruffy friends along.

President George Bush had to navigate a political minefield. Israel was our traditional friend in the Middle East and had the area's most respected army. The Israelis were eager to participate. With the earlier removal of the Shah in Iran, Israel had lost a counterbalance to the hostile Iraqis. Still, Bush feared that Jewish participation in the conflict would discredit Operation Desert Storm in the eyes of the Muslim states and topple his precarious coalition. The Israelis agreed to stay out and refused to be provoked into retaliation by Iraqi missile attacks later in the war. For the moment, at least, she did not demand "an eye for an eye."

A WAR BY ANY OTHER NAME MIGHT JUST BE LEGAL.

The United States has not declared war for 50 years. Still, what happened in Korea and Vietnam looked very much like war to the people involved. Congress, granted the constitutional right to declare war, has generally acquiesced to presidents wishing to fight "undeclared" wars. Congress sees such an arrangement as both safe and clever. If the action is successful, it can point with pride to its support for the president. If the war is lengthy and costly, it can be called "Mr. Bush's War." Bush seized the initiative and pressured Congress for a quick approval of military action. A few Democrats offered token opposition, but Congress meekly followed the president, and the polls, into war. Fortunately, the young men and women we sent to fight were more courageous than those who sent them there.

Everyone in the U.S. government agrees that the basis of successful democratic government is an informed general public. Having said that, those in power enthusiastically join in an effort to "manage" the news. The Reagan-Bush administrations raised that process to an art form. The military, hardly democratic at any time (ask any army private), was more than happy to join the news-manipulation parade. A limited number of reporters were taken on chaperoned "tours" of the Gulf War front. Their insights were something like popcorn, lots of fluff but damned little nourishment.

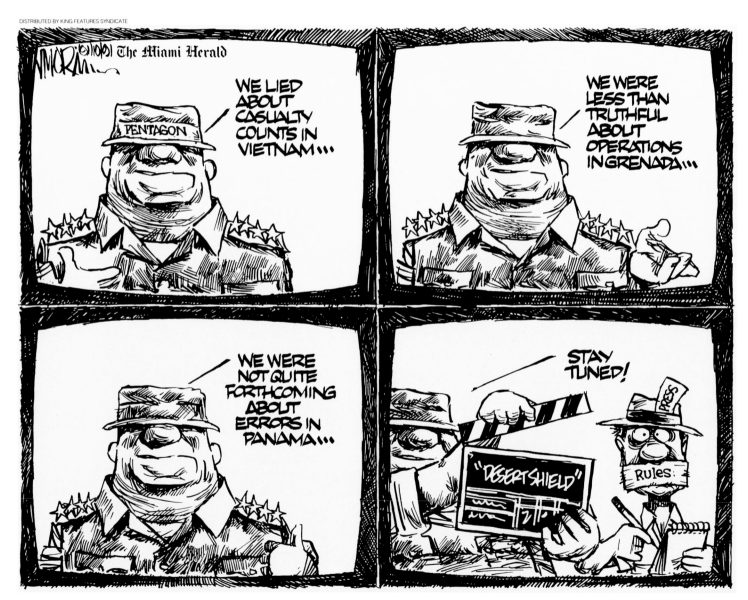

Sometimes you just get lucky. Bush had in place three competent and media savvy commanders. Secretary of Defense Dick Cheney came across as careful and in charge. General Colin Powell was smooth and diplomatic. That he was black disarmed critics who might have objected to the high percentage of African Americans who would be put at risk. But the real charmer was General Norman Schwarzkopf. He was frank, tough, and deeply concerned for his troops. In a terribly impersonal and automated war, he had the personal touch. It was a bravura performance, on the field and on the tube.

THE BOSTON GLOBE

Someone once said that generals, unfortunately, always prepare for the last war while getting ready for the next. That may well be the only area in which Saddam Hussein qualified as a general. He dug his troops into the desert as if he expected American troops to mount the kind of suicidal frontal attacks he had faced with the Iranians. His air force was unaccountably dispatched to Iran to sit out the war unscathed but useless. Saddam Hussein seemed genuinely nonplussed by our decision to delay a ground offensive while allied air power destroyed the capacity of his stationary army to mount a creditable defense. The Iraqi dictator was reduced to name calling and deluded predictions of victory. Bombast is no substitute for bombs, but it's easier to deliver.

Modern efforts to make warfare more humane are laudable but enormously difficult to put into practice. Indeed, the very nature of technological warfare blurs the distinction between military and civilian targets. Saddam Hussein's practice of putting military installations near civilian populations was an attempt to take advantage of our moral inhibitions or to make propaganda victories out of our refusal to be inhibited. When striking a legitimate target might bring about civilian casualties, military commanders tend to accept the recommendation of a 12th-century Christian leader fighting heresy, "Kill them all and let God choose."

Saddam Hussein developed a new twist on an old American dictum. As amended, it would read, "If you can't lick 'em, pound on somebody else." Unable to stop the onrush of U.S. allied troops, the Iraqis launched SCUD missiles against civilian targets in Israel. There was widespread fear that the missiles would release poison gas or other chemical agents. There is no doubt that Saddam Hussein would have done just that had his military been sufficiently advanced. At that stage of the game, it is highly unlikely that Israeli retaliation would have been more than a minor complication for Bush. Muslim disaffection from the coalition was unlikely and would have been too late in any case, for total victory would come in a matter of days.

George Bush discovered that Third World dictators are much like the venerable cockroach. They may be ugly, repulsive, and irritating, but they have an amazing capacity to survive. A major reason some Third World dictators stay in power is that the major powers see some advantage in maintaining their rule. Repression offers stability, and Western industrialized nations perceive stability as economically advantageous. Saddam Hussein's ambitiousness destroyed the fragile stability of the Gulf region. That was a mistake. Still, Saddam Hussein may well be in power long after President Bush has been retired. Political longevity is much enhanced if you can just shoot your opponents.

Cynics have claimed that the concept "military intelligence" is a contradiction in terms. Despite an amazing array of high-tech gadgets, our intelligence services vastly overestimated the fighting capacity of the Iraqi army and had trouble getting information to the forces in the field. The overestimates may have been intentional. It was certainly one way to ready the American public for bad news and/or to make a quick victory more impressive. Ultimately, Saddam Hussein's "mother of all battles" became a traffic jam of surrendering Iraqi soldiers.

Any credence one might have given to Saddam Hussein's claim to be the champion of Muslims against the rapacious "West" went up in flames. He ordered the senseless demolition of the Kuwaiti oil industry and anything else not portable enough to be looted. His decision to order the release of millions of barrels of Kuwaiti petroleum into the waters of the Persian Gulf may well be the first episode of state-sponsored environmental terrorism. He left his supporters among the Palestinians and in Jordan vulnerable and discredited. Finally, he managed to make Bush's earlier vitriolic personal attacks seem like prophesy. Every president should be so lucky.

The war ended abruptly—and perhaps too soon. Much of Hussein's personal army, the Republican Guard, was left intact. Hussein himself survived in some well-equipped bunker. Seeing the regime totter, religious and ethnic factions rose in rebellion. Bush urged Hussein's overthrow, but his goal was a unified Iraq with someone other than Saddam at the helm. When disunion rather than reform seemed to be the rebels' goal, Bush cooled on the revolts. As usual in the Middle East, everyone had a different agenda. The victims would be those who misread the other guy's intentions.

The degree to which the Bush administration is guilty of having encouraged a revolt by Iraqi Kurds is open to question, but revolt they did. As with so many issues in the Middle East, this one tended to slop over national boundaries. Kurdish enclaves existed in both Turkey and Iran. At issue, then, was the political stability of a good-sized section of the Middle East. Bush tried to juggle the humanitarian instincts of the American people and our geopolitical interests. In the end, the interests of the Kurds slipped through his fingers.

"WELL, AT LEAST WE'RE RID OF THE VIETNAM SYNDROME....."

During the Cold War, we persuaded ourselves that the only foreign policy issue of consequence was Communism. Nowadays, things are murkier in a world awash in competing nationalism and ethnic animosities. More and more the United States is faced with the choice of accepting some "tragic situation" or committing some "reprehensible" act. For the last 40 years, American presidents had the comforting knowledge that, when solutions to domestic problems eluded them, they could always move to some foreign policy initiative. George Bush found that haven less attractive. But then, if you can't stand the heat…

As the euphoria over the swift success of Operation Desert Storm dissipated, critics of the Bush administration began to suggest that Bush's political bumbling during the year before the war with Iraq may have been responsible for the whole costly adventure. The record shows that the administration went to embarrassing lengths to woo and appease Saddam Hussein. President Bush found it hard to remain a hero when his own follies may have made heroism necessary. Presidents face two juries—voters and historians. Voters speak first—and emphatically.

SAVINGS AND LOAN SCANDAL

Deregulation and the billion dollar "Jackpot"

Stephen P. Pizzo

The domestic financial problems that would plague the Bush presidency had their roots in his vice presidency. They are also rooted in the core philosophy of the Bush-Reagan administrations: that big government is bad, and in their campaign promise to "get government off the back of business."

One of Vice President George Bush's duties was to chair Ronald Reagan's "The Task Force On Regulatory Relief." The group's task was to slice through the regulatory clutter the administration claimed was stifling American business—one target, the activities of financial institutions.

In October 1982 President Reagan made good on a campaign promise to begin deregulating U.S. financial institutions by signing into law the Garn–St. Germain Act. The legislation cut the nation's savings and loans loose from the restrictive federal regulations by which they had been governed for half a century. "I think we've hit the jackpot," President Reagan said as he signed the bill.

Savings and loans had, for 50 years, been relegated to a quiet corner of the American banking system. Congress had given these thrifts a charter after the Great Depression which limited them to providing home loans. In return, thrifts would be allowed to pay just a bit more interest than banks on savings accounts.

The idea worked. Thanks largely to the nation's S&Ls, millions of blue-collar workers, unable to get bank loans, found an institution willing to make them the loans they needed to become homeowners. Home ownership exploded after World War II, driving a home building industry that became a prime force in a growing and dynamic American economy.

But during the 1970s this successful formula faltered. The advent of the unregulated money market funds began to drain the savings and loans of deposits as customers switched to these funds which paid higher interest rates. To compete, thrifts asked Congress in 1979 to deregulate their interest rates so they could offer depositors the market rate. Congress agreed and also increased federal deposit insurance at thrifts from $40,000 per account, to $100,000.

By 1981 it was clear that thrifts could not pay higher market interest rates and still make the low-interest, fixed-rate, 30-year home loans required by their charters. They went back to Congress and asked that they be allowed to invest deposits in more than home mortgages. Their request coincided with the advent of the first Reagan-Bush administration. Most experts now agree that all thrifts really needed at the time was the power to make "adjustable rate mortgages." ARMs had interest rates that fluctuated monthly or quarterly to reflect changes in the current market rate. ARMs would also have protected thrifts from the inflationary surges plaguing the economy at the time.

But encouraged by the new administration's talk of deregulation and free markets, the thrift industry asked for more. They requested wide-ranging investment powers that would allow them to directly invest depositors' federally insured savings into virtually anything the thrifts thought they could make money on. The resulting legislation was the Garn–St. Germain Act.

Over the next six years savings and loans across the country, some 1200 savings institutions in all, would become insolvent as this new regulatory largess permeated the market. Within two years of the Rose Garden signing, the alarm was already being sounded by some regulatory experts, but neither President Reagan nor Vice President Bush reacted.

But as early as 1984 grim reports were rolling into the Washington offices of the nation's top thrift regulator, Ed Gray. His field examiners were daily telling him horror stories. Empire Savings in Texas had dumped $300 million of its deposits into the miles of unneeded and unfinished condominiums along dusty stretches of I-30. The condos languished unsold in the Texas sun; Lincoln Savings and Loan was investing hundreds of millions of dollars in poor investment quality or junk bonds; Vernon Savings in Texas, with $1 billion in deposits, had a loan default rate of 96 percent.

When Ed Gray, a Reagan appointee, warned in 1984 that the Reagan administration had to immediately hire at least 1000 more regulators to control the situation, the administration turned on him. "They told me I didn't understand the administration's philosophy," Gray said. "They told me that deregulation meant fewer regulators, not more."

The looming financial crisis was ignored. In 1986 Gray had more bad news for both the administration and Congress—the Federal Savings and Loan Deposit Insurance Corporation (FSLIC), the agency that guaranteed depositors' money, was broke. Congress would have to allocate at least $15 billion to bail it out. Without the money, Gray said, regulators could not close insolvent thrifts and repay the depositors.

The General Accounting Office estimated at that time that insolvent thrifts were racking up additional loses of $30 million a day, yet the fight to recapitalize the FSLIC stalled in Congress for nearly a year and a half. Neither the administration nor Congress wanted to allocate the money. For the administration, backing the measure would be admission that its policy of deregulation had been a failure. For members of Congress, it would also mean alienating thrift owners who had become valued Congressional campaign contributors.

Congressional action on the "recap" bill was stopped cold in its tracks by House of Representatives Speaker Jim Wright (Democrat, Texas). Wright appeared to use the bill to pressure Ed Gray to extend regulatory concessions to several Texas thrift constituents. If Gray refused, the recap bill would not move to the House floor for a vote. The bill did not pass until August 1987.

By late 1987 the Reagan presidency was winding down and his replacement, George Bush, began planning for his run for the presidency. The planning had actually begun as early as 1987 when the severity of the S&L crisis had not yet reached the American public. With an election looming, the Reagan administration had every reason not to want the public to learn the depth of the growing crisis.

For George Bush this scandal was also deeply personal. His youngest son, Neil, was a director of Silverado Savings in Denver. The thrift, with $1.2 billion in deposits, teetered on the verge of insolvency. Regulators had been complaining about Silverado's questionable practices since 1985. If Silverado were closed, it would become an election year embarrassment to George Bush. And closing it was exactly what the head S&L regulator for the State of Colorado, David Paul, wanted to do. He reported that the thrift was insolvent and was losing millions of dollars each day it remained open. But Mr. Paul testified later before Congress that he was told by Washington regulators to hold off on closing Silverado.

Controlling information about the growing S&L crisis became a major concern for the Reagan administration. As the end of Ed Gray's term in office neared, the administration began a search for his replacement. White House Chief of Staff Donald Regan had criticized Gray for talking too much in public about the problems facing the S&L industry. Regan told others in the administration that Gray was "off the reservation."

In June 1987 the administration replaced Gray with M. Danny Wall, who had been the chief aide to Senator Jake Garn (Republican, Utah), co-author of the Garn–St. Germain Act. Wall proved to be a team player. He spent the next 18 months assuring Congress and the public that, although S&Ls were having some problems, it was not a crisis and no taxpayer money would be needed to bail them out. He said that losses would not exceed $30 billion.

But private economists, among them Dan Brumbaugh, formerly of the Federal Home Loan Bank, were even then placing losses at over $100 billion. Why were Wall's numbers so much lower? When Federal Home Loan Bank Board member Roger Martin asked FDIC chairman Bill Seidman why Wall's numbers were so low the answer shocked him. "Because (the administration) told him to lie," he said. "They asked me to lie too, but I'm not going to do it."

In August 1988 the Republican National Convention chose George Bush as its candidate for president. The same month Neil Bush resigned his directorship at Silverado Savings.

On Tuesday, November 8, 1988, George Bush was elected president. The next day, federal regulators closed Silverado Savings, where loses were now placed at close to $1 billion. In January 1989 George Herbert Bush was sworn in. Less than one month after the inauguration, M. Danny Wall testified before Congress again, this time admitting for the first time that losses at the nation's thrifts would amount to at least $100 billion.

President Bush abolished the Federal Home Loan Bank Board and replaced it with a new agency, the Office of Thrift Supervision. Its new head was M. Danny Wall. In February 1989 George Bush announced his plan for a $200 billion bailout of the S&L industry.

But such a huge expenditure would undoubtedly force a rise in personal income taxes. To avoid this political bombshell to the public, the President decided to place the S&L bailout "off budget." That is, instead of taking the money from the U.S. Department of the Treasury, it would be borrowed through a series of bond sales. This plan would allow the administration to say it had stayed within its budgetary goals and would blunt the immediate cost to taxpayers by stretching it out over several decades.

But taking the bailout off budget also increased its cost astronomically. The price of buying political cover had never been so high. Even the most conservative estimates placed the final cost of financing the $200 billion S&L bailout to around $500 billion. A 1990 Stanford University study placed the total cost over 40 years at a staggering $1.3 trillion.

Whatever its final cost, clearly S&L deregulation had been a painful experience. Some in Congress, particularly House Banking Committee Chairman Henry Gonzalez (Democrat, Texas), who had opposed thrift deregulation in 1982, hoped that President Bush would no longer see deregulation as a cure-all. These hopes were quickly dashed.

No sooner had President Bush approved the S&L industry bailout than the nation's banks began experiencing financial difficulties. Between 1998 and 1989, over 200 banks failed, the highest failure rate since the Great Depression. Another 1000 were on the government's so-called problem list. FDIC Chairman Bill Seidman, sounding like the ghost of Ed Gray, warned that by 1991 the banks' deposit insurance fund would be broke and asked Congress for $70 billion to recapitalize it.

President Bush's response to the developing bank crisis was to propose a radical deregulation of the nation's banks. The "Bush Bank Reform" package, presented to Congress in early 1991, called for the repeal of the 60-year-old Glass-Steagall Act, which had barred banks from the securities markets. The reform package would also allow banks to underwrite insurance, open branches nationwide, and allow private corporations to own banks.

Some members of Congress, Representatives Gonzalez and John Dingell, Jr. (Democrat, Michigan), were horrified. Representative Dingell's father had been the prime force behind the Glass-Steagall Act and its repeal would have to get by his powerful committee first. Banking expert and author Martin Mayer testified against the plan. "I began writing about these subjects 40 years ago, and I make a living by having a good memory…[and]…it [the Bush plan] is Garn–St. Germain all over again."

In the fall of 1991 a nervous Congress, still feeling the heat from voters over the S&L mess, rejected the Bush Bank Reform Package and went one step further by tightening existing banking regulations.

But despite the enormous mess caused by thrift deregulation, President Bush remained convinced of the evils of government regulation. The rejection of his bank reforms in late 1991 came just as the nation fell deep into a recession. Bush saw in that recession yet further reason for deregulation of banks. He said that old-fashioned bank regulations were choking off loans to "worthy borrowers," which had created a "credit crunch," which in turn had thrown the country into recession.

With Congress blocking his vision of a deregulated banking industry, President Bush resorted to the use of executive powers to gain deregulation of banks. Using the administrative authority of the Department of the Treasury and the Federal Reserve, bank regulations were loosened and bank examiners were ordered to "lighten up" on bankers.

The Federal Reserve Board, chaired by staunch deregulation advocate Alan Greenspan, began using its administrative authority to allow banks to re-enter the securities business on a case-by-case basis, ignoring the Glass-Steagall Act entirely. The changes were a bold end run around the legislative branch and should have sparked a fierce congressional challenge. But Congress, engrossed in its own check-kiting scandal involving the House Bank, mounted no significant challenge.

As Bush completed his first term in 1992, and a new election loomed, a sense of déjà vu permeated the air. George Bush, as his mentor Ronald Reagan, talked only of the evils of government regulation and ordered a sweeping six-month ban on all new federal regulations.

A decade earlier, the savings and loan industry needed to be saved from "choking federal regulations," now it was the banks. And, as if to bring the whole matter full circle, President Bush formed the Council on Competitiveness, the successor to The Task Force On Regulatory Relief he chaired as Vice President. His own vice president, Dan Quayle, would lead it. Quayle's job, like Bush's before him, would be to continue the battle to "get the government off the back of business."■

Congress is responsible for something called an oversight function. They are supposed to keep track of the effects and operation of the laws they pass. As our system works, that function is primarily carried out by the executive branch under the president. Deregulation of banks and savings and loans was the reversal of policies that, for a half a century, had produced stability in our financial institutions and security for their depositors. Deregulation was an experiment that should have been closely monitored. Vigilance was particularly required of the Reagan-Bush administration as they had pushed hard for the policy in the first place. Ronald Reagan says he didn't know the mess was brewing. George Bush says nobody told him. They seem to have a problem with the distinction between oversight and overlook.

THE GREAT SAVINGS AND LOAN ROBBERY

The irresponsible practices of banks and the stockmarket led to the Great Depression. Both turned to government to save them from themselves and, indeed, wrote most of the regulations that were later put in place. In the case of the banking industry, the public agreed to insure the banks' deposits when the banks agreed to regulation. The Reagan-Bush administrations removed the regulations but kept the insurance in force. It turns out we were issuing fire insurance to a client with a record of pyromania. History may not repeat itself, but human nature probably does.

The 1980s witnessed a frenzy of paper manipulation and financial machinations not seen since the 1920s. Mergers, leveraged buyouts, junk bonds, and insider trading became the hallmarks of the American financial establishment. A rather callous disregard for stockholders, employees, and the general public took hold. Reflective of the times, greed became admirable. In the end, factories were closed, solid firms dragged into bankruptcy, and too few crooked financiers were held accountable. The 1990s have, so far, been one long hangover. The party's over.

A great many working class Americans share the perception that our judicial system charges forth to crush crime in the streets but smiles benignly at crime in the suites. Somehow directors who loot a savings and loan or CEOs who defraud the defense department seem immune to prosecution. Meanwhile, the Bush administration talked about law and order while it reduced the number of accountants and attorneys assigned to root out white collar crime. But then, burglars don't make campaign contributions or go skiing in Aspen.

George Bush's son Neil was director of an institution that lost hundreds of millions of dollars. George sympathized with that. Most of our presidents seem to suffer some kind of family embarrassment. But few presidents are so directly responsible for the origin of the problem. It was the deregulatory policies established by Ronald Reagan and continued by Bush that set the scene for the collapse of Silverado Savings and Loan, the institution Neil directed. The situation was a bit sticky during the 1988 election, but it's not as if Neil had smoked pot or something.

The regulator directing the investigation of Lincoln Savings and Loan was summoned to Washington, D.C. to face an inquisition by five U.S. senators. California's Alan Cranston led the attack. When the whole shoddy affair was exposed later, the public learned that William Keating (Lincoln's wheeling and dealing director) had contributed several million dollars to these senators' re-election campaigns. The regulator was told to back off from closing Lincoln and the investigation was put on hold. Lincoln's eventual crash cost the taxpayer roughly a billion dollars, a cost that could have been largely avoided.

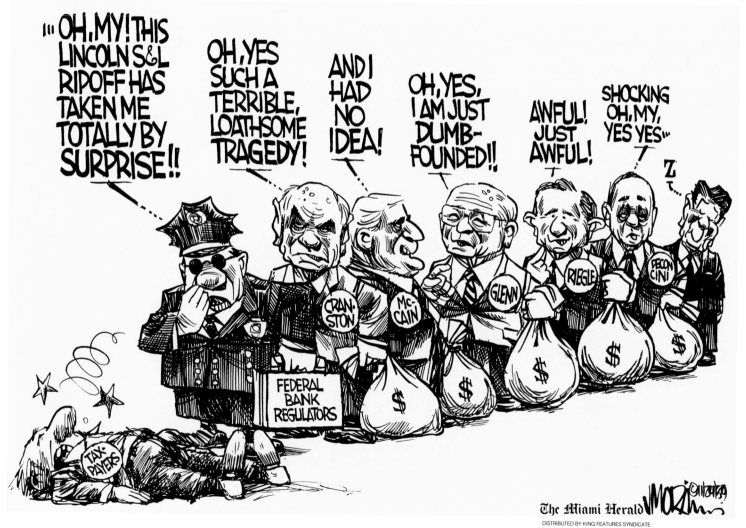

The U.S. senators who intervened to protect William Keating became known as the "Keating Five." When the mess around Keating grew bad enough, the Senate was forced to make housecleaning noises. The senators, brought before the Ethics Committee, accused their accusers of similar practices and explained their action as "constituent services." They were only ensuring that an American citizen was not being harassed by his government. They would do as much for any citizen; the money had nothing to do with it. The members of the Ethics Committee scolded them, but their hearts weren't in it.

Because Bush and Congress agreed to deregulate the S&Ls but to continue insuring their deposits, the collapse of the S&Ls meant the American public had to reimburse depositors. A call for tax increases to cover the losses would have been political suicide. Bush and Congress chose the safer but less honorable way out. They borrowed the money. That would shove the problem onto the next president, the next congress, and the next generation. Interest paid on the borrowed funds would double and redouble the cost to the public, but somebody else would have to deal with it.

Response to the S&L crisis ran the gamut from "let 'em sink or swim" to "make them pick up the tab for their own industry." It was feared that more failures among our financial houses would have a domino effect; pension funds, insurance companies, and healthy businesses could go down with them. Efforts to shift the losses onto the surviving healthy institutions would have created yet more casualties. Even the imposition of stricter controls posed political hazards. And the economy didn't need a credit crunch. In the final analysis, only the public was punished.

'YOU'RE FREE TO GO, MR. S&L, SIR — WE CAUGHT THE REAL FELON.'

A bankrupt institution is required to liquidate its assets and distribute those revenues to its creditors. It was only when the government began that process with the failed S&Ls that the full scope of the irresponsibility and criminality of those who'd managed them came to light. There were damned few assets. Some S&Ls had been raped and pillaged by their directors. In others, stupidity combined with cupidity to produce disaster. Little collateral for loans had been demanded and much of that proved worthless. With pitifully little to salvage, the bailout bill got bigger and bigger.

Although the causes of such remain stubbornly obscure, there do seem to be eras of rampant public and business corruption. In the cases of the Grant and Harding administrations, for example, the nation was led by a popular but befuddled president, by elected and appointed officials who raced to join a get-rich-quick ethic in the private sector, and by financiers snuggled up close to the seats of power. In the 1980s…my word, have we discovered a pattern here? It's hard to identify the prime culprit in the S&L mess, but surely there's enough guilt to go around.

When the government seized the assets of the defunct S&Ls, the Resolution Trust Corporation was given the task of selling off the tattered remains and off-setting, as much as possible, taxpayer losses. But the tangled mess the Corporation put up for sale appealed only to those with broad connections in the financial community and experience with convoluted business practices. These sales brought pennies on the dollar and were negligible to the taxpayer investment. In a few instances, buyers were found among those involved in the original fiasco. We hadn't cleaned house—we'd just rearranged the trash.

We may face another financial disaster. America's commercial banks emerged from the 1980s in bad shape. An astonishing number of bad loans had been made. Third World development loans were being written down and real estate values had plummeted. Commercial banks use healthy loans as assets upon which to base further loans. A base loan default may bring down the pyramid. Banks are trying to rebuild their reserves (in part by holding credit card interest rates at usurious levels), and a general economic recovery could eventually save them from their own mistakes.

Until the New Deal era, commercial banks went bust with regularity. When something frightened depositors, they rushed en masse to withdraw funds. No bank maintains sufficient reserves to cover such "runs." The Roosevelt administration established the Federal Deposit Insurance Corporation (FDIC) to allow banks to insure their customers' deposits. The premiums were agreeably low and "runs" stopped. Deregulation allowed banks to take more risks, but their insurance premiums weren't raised. FDIC reserves would prove ridiculously inadequate should major banks fail.

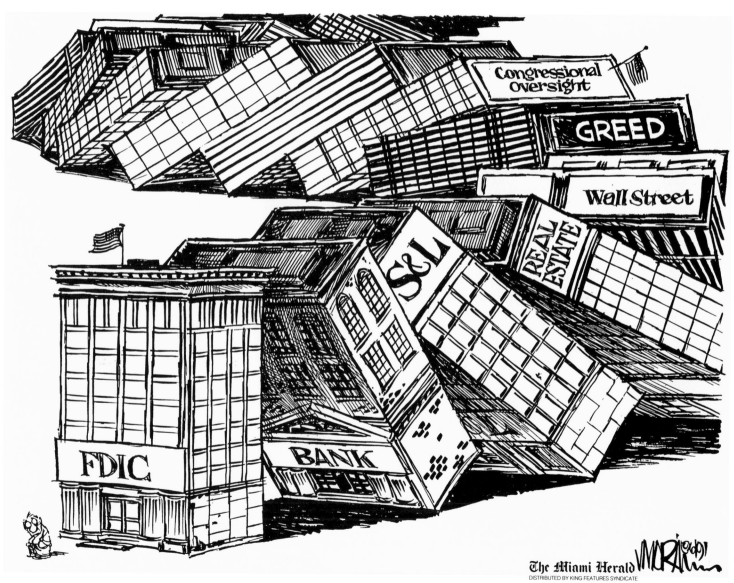

The Miami Herald
DISTRIBUTED BY KING FEATURES SYNDICATE

IRAN-CONTRA AFFAIR

Quid pro quos and the shadow of impeachment   Thomas S. Blanton

The most enduring puzzle from the Iran-Contra scandal remains, "Where was George Bush?" Then–Vice President Bush had served as ambassador to the United Nations and to China, as director of the Central Intelligence Agency, and as head of the Reagan administration's task force on terrorism—amassing as much foreign policy experience as any member in the Reagan cabinet and, indeed, more than most.

Yet none of the official investigations launched after the scandal broke in November 1986 have concluded much about his precise role in the affair—the worst American foreign policy scandal since Vietnam. The public has been left to Bush's claim that he was "out of the loop"—which he defined to Dan Rather in 1988 as having "no operational role" in any deals involving arms for hostages in Iran and cash to Contras in Nicaragua.[1]

The Iran-Contra deals began in the early 1980s with the Reagan administration's secret initiatives to mount multiple, covert operations against real and perceived communists around the world. These deals, with countries such as Taiwan, Costa Rica, and Saudi Arabia, came to light only after the Iran-Contra scandal was exposed. By the time George Bush became president, he had ceased all comment on Iran-Contra matters. But these quid pro quos were still a sensitive subject for him—reason enough to cast aside his blanket of silence when, in 1989, press exposures of an earlier deal with Honduras provoked Bush into vehement, personal denial: "The word of the president of the United States is, there was no quid pro quo."[2]

Bush reacted so strongly because he knew how high the stakes were. At the key 1984 White House meeting about the need to raise money for the Nicaraguan Contras once Congress cut off its funding to them, then–Secretary of State George Shultz warned that third-country fundraising could be "an impeachable offense" because "the U.S. government may raise and spend funds only through an appropriation of the Congress."[3]

George Bush spoke only once in 14 single-spaced pages of minutes of that meeting. "How can anyone object to the U.S. encouraging third parties to provide help to the anti-Sandinistas under the finding [signed by Reagan in 1981]?" Bush asked. "The only problem that might come up is if the United States were to promise to give these third parties something in return so that some people could interpret this as some kind of an exchange."[4]

Only four people at this meeting realized the discussion was more than academic. They knew that the United States had already approached Saudi Arabia for Contra aid, and that Prince Bandar bin Sultan, Saudi ambassador to the United States, had pledged $1 million a month starting that very month. None of the four mentioned the Saudi solicitation, not the man who made the approach, national security adviser Robert McFarlane, nor his military aide Admiral John Poindexter, nor the two men McFarlane briefed for their approval—President Ronald Reagan and Vice President Bush.[5]

Congress was never informed of the Saudi solicitation. Nor was it informed of other initiatives that were under way. For example, the Reagan administration expedited aid—$23 million in military assistance, $35 million in economic aid—to the Honduran generals in return for their help in moving supplies to the Contras. George Bush personally delivered this quid to Honduran president Roberto Suazo in March 1985. A Robert McFarlane memo on the subject specifically noted that "our security commitment" was regarded by the Hondurans "as the main quid pro quo for cooperating with the FDN [Contras]."[6]

The full story of arms deals with Iran during the 1980s will never be told until the Iranians reveal their side of the bargains. But the fundamentals are clear from thousands of pages of declassified U.S. documents released during the Iran-Contra investigations. Israel was the key to the deals. It pursued a strategic relationship with Iran no matter who was in power—the Shah, the Ayatollah Rohollah Khomeini, or Hojatolislam Hasheimi Rafsanjani—because Iran was a useful counterweight to the Arabs menacing the Jewish state. Israeli-supplied arms flowed to Iran before, during, and after the period when American hostages were held in Tehran.[7]

The first documented evidence of high-level U.S. involvement in Israeli arms deals with Iran occurs in the summer of 1985. After a contentious high-level meeting on August 6, President Reagan authorized an Israeli-brokered swap of TOW antitank missiles to Iran for the release of four American hostages in Lebanon. Later in August, 96 Israeli TOWs were delivered, but no hostages came out. Then 408 more TOWs were delivered in September, and one hostage, the Reverend Benjamin Weir, was released.[8]

The participants in the August 6 meeting later suffered memory lapses about Bush's position on this deal. Bush's staff claimed that he was not even present, citing their records in conflict with White House logs. Bush himself told the press once the scandal broke that "I sensed that we were sending arms. And I sensed that we were trying to get hostages out. But not arms for hostages." He claimed in his autobiography that he did not learn of the arms-for-hostages arrangements until 16 months after the first deal, "until it was fully debriefed" by the chair of the Senate Intelligence committee in December 1986.[9]

After Benjamin Weir's release, however, Bush told a very different story to the families of the hostages. Led by Peggy Say, sister of Associated Press Bureau Chief Terry Anderson, the hostage families had demanded a meeting with the president. Bush was sent to calm them down. During the meeting on September 20, 1985, Weir kept returning to a single theme: "If you don't do something, the hostages are going to die!" Bush finally retorted, "I don't care what you think. I'm telling you that we are responsible for you sitting in that chair today."[10] George Bush, under pressure, was admitting he was "in the loop."

During the time of the Israeli TOWs-for-Weir deal, Bush had been briefed twice on the arrangements at the president's daily 9:30 a.m. national security briefing. According to declassified documents and news reports, those daily briefings during 1985 and 1986 became the venue for all the major Iran-Contra decisions—and Bush was there every time.[11]

The most detailed evidence of Bush's knowledge of the arms-for-hostages deals comes from notes made by Bush's own chief of staff, Craig Fuller, during a meeting with Israeli operative Amiram Nir, who negotiated the deals.[12] During the meeting held on July 29 in Bush's suite at the King David Hotel in Jerusalem, Nir reviewed the history of the Iran initiative. Nir told Bush the arms deals were direct U.S. transfers, with Israel providing logistical cover, to "the most radical elements" in Iran in order to get the hostages released. Nir concluded, ."We have no real choice but to proceed."

Bush asked only two questions during the briefing: whether Nir had attended a failed Tehran meeting in May led by McFarlane and whether Nir had briefed his boss, Prime Minister Peres, on the most recent hostage release (he had done both). The notes read, "The VP made no commitments nor did he give any direction to Nir."[13]

In the meantime, more weapons had gone to Tehran, but the two ransomed Americans (Weir and Jenco) were replaced with new hostages, Joseph Cicippio and Frank Reed.

On October 1986, the Iran-Contra affair started unraveling—but not because of a watchdog Congress or an alert press. Two events in foreign countries share responsibility for Iran-Contra coming to light. First, a teenage Sandinista infantryman with a rocket on his shoulder blew the

wing off Eugene Hasenfus's Contra resupply airplane the first week in October. Then, excerpts from leaflets on the arms-for-hostage deals, published by a radical Iranian faction in an attempt to embarrass the Rafsanjani government for talking to the "Great Satan," were printed in a Lebanese newspaper the first weekend in November. Both events triggered widespread coverage in the media throughout the United States and abroad.

The double exposure panicked the Reagan administration. Top CIA and State Department officials lied to Congress about government involvement in the Hasenfus operation, and President Reagan stated on national television to the effect that no deals with the Ayatollah Khomeini had occurred. Two cover-ups resulted, with George Bush instrumental in both. One (on the Contras) succeeded, and the other (on the Iranian arms deals) is only now, in 1992, falling apart.

The first U.S. government entity to hear of the Hasenfus shootdown was George Bush's office. A top Bush aide had helped place Felix Rodriguez, aka Max Gomez, a Cuban-American former CIA agent and Bay of Pigs veteran, in El Salvador, where he helped coordinate the secret Contra supply operations. When Rodriguez heard of the shootdown, he did not call the CIA, where he had put in 15 years as a self-described "secret warrior." He did not call Oliver North's office, though he knew North was the chairman of the board of the resupply operation. Instead, he called the office of George Bush's national security advisor.

Within four days, the *Miami Herald* blared the headline "Vice President, NSC Tied to Secret Contra Flights." Hasenfus had talked about the Ilopango operation—the name for the Contra resupply operation. The story set off a flurry of reporters' calls to Bush's office. In response, Bush spokesman Marlin Fitzwater issued a narrow denial: "Neither the vice president nor anyone on his staff is directing or coordinating an operation in Central America. Allegations to that effect are simply not true." Fitzwater, Bush aide Don Gregg, and the National Security Council spokesman all refused to comment further.[14]

Fitzwater's statement created the alibi George Bush would use from then on—out of the loop, no operational role. Bush's staff had carefully crafted the denial to protect themselves.

They knew they were not "directing or coordinating" because Oliver North was. The denial obscured the real questions of how much did they know about the Contra operation, and what exactly did they do about it. The answers ultimately turned out to be an awful lot and precious little, respectively.

On the Iranian side, the cover-up was tougher. President Reagan went on national television three times in November 1986 to explain away the arms deals, but each time the story changed, his statements had to be corrected afterward, and his credibility shrank. Reagan's standing in the polls was plummeting, and Republicans took a huge hit in the congressional elections that month, losing the Senate.

The notes of the top-level meetings of Reagan aides—always including George Bush—between November 10 and 24, 1986, make for fascinating reading.[15] When not yelling at each other, the aides scrambled for an alternative version of events that would take the heat off the president. They were worried not just about public lies—it's no crime to lie to the American people—but about specific Iran-Contra operations President Reagan had personally authorized. In 1985, for example, Reagan had thanked King Fahd of Saudi Arabia for his Contra contribution, which promptly doubled. In another secret meeting later that year, Secretary of Defense Caspar Weinberger had listed for Reagan the laws broken by shipping arms to Iran, and Reagan had responded: "Well, Cap, the American people would never forgive me if I failed to get the hostages out over this legal question."[16] The president had authorized arms deals he knew to be illegal, and had participated in fund-raising that his secretary of state told him would be "an impeachable offense."

As the scandal grew, Attorney General Edwin Meese III undertook an investigation into the Iran-Contra affair. The trail from the Contras in Nicaragua and the Iranian arms deals led to a man who would become the most associated with this whole affair, Colonel Oliver North. In Oliver North's files, Edwin Meese found memos documenting covert operations, including one that mentioned the transfer of Iran arms deal profits for the use of the Nicaraguan Contras. And hundreds of other memos describing "diversions" in all directions such as Saudi money to the Contras being used by North for hostage ransom attempts.[17]

But Meese apparently was not interested in how the whole off-the-books White House slush fund worked. Instead, Meese asked North and his superior, Admiral John Poindexter, whether they had told the president about the Iran-to-Contras diversion. When they said no, Meese had the story he needed, complete with fall guy (White House aide Oliver North), negligent supervisors (national security advisors Robert McFarlane and John Poindexter), complicated and perhaps not even criminal crime (the diversion), and an out-of-the-loop vice president.

The press and Congress bought Meese's story, which remains the heart of the conventional wisdom on Iran-Contra to this day.

And the official line from the Bush administration has been: "The president's role in the Iran-Contra affair was completely examined in the congressional inquiry, and we have nothing to add."[18]

But the facade is cracking, and the diversion is beginning to look like a diversion. Independent counsel Lawrence Walsh indicted former Secretary of Defense Weinberger in June 1992 for concealing his personal notes of top-level meetings and lying to Congress about the Saudi fund-raising and the 1985 arms deals. Also, polls during the 1992 presidential campaign showed that, by a margin of 2-to-1, the American people did not believe Bush's story of being "out of the loop" on Iran-Contra.

Even President Bush's dramatic Christmas Eve pardons of Weinberger and five other defendants did not bring final closure to the Iran-Contra story. In a statement in response to the pardons, Walsh revealed that Bush himself had withheld his notes related to Iran-Contra, and accused the President of "misconduct." Walsh stated that the pardons "demonstrate[s] that powerful people with powerful allies can commit serious crimes in high office, deliberately abusing the public trust, without consequence."

No smoking gun ended Bush's political career, but his role in the Iran-Contra affair as well as the pardons will forever scar George Bush's place in history.■

There is no real evidence that George Bush selected Dan Quayle as his running mate as a hedge against any future impeachment proceedings. But regardless of intent, that effect is undeniable. Even the most rabidly anti-Bush Democrat would have sober second thoughts about initiating the impeachment process with Quayle next in line. Our current practices in nominating a vice-presidential candidate are obviously inadequate. Quayle became vice president with the "vote" of one man—George Bush. The rest of us got Quayle as part of a package deal—the "prize" at the bottom of the Crackerjacks. There has got to be a better way.

" SO, IMPEACH ME! "

Congress reduced U.S. support for the Nicaraguan Contras to "humanitarian aid." The Reagan administration refused to accept that reduction and embarked upon a program that would allow it to sidestep the law. They would try to accomplish through deceit, subterfuge, and in some instances, illegal activities what they could not do openly. A clear majority of the American public opposed military support of the Contras. Congress passed the laws necessary to end it. The Constitution charges the president to "faithfully execute" the laws of Congress. Obviously, the Reagan administration didn't care very much what the public wanted or what the Constitution said.

Vice President George Bush was aware that he would be in violation of the law if he offered a reward to the government of Honduras in return for Honduran aid to the Contras. Such an arrangement would be a quid pro quo and thus an illegal effort to circumvent a law. An embarrassing charade followed: all parties knew exactly what was happening, but no one verbalized the arrangement. Bush later explained that the sudden increase of financial aid to Honduras was unrelated to a subsequent increase of Honduran aid to the Contras. Just a coincidence, I guess.

Whether he admits it or not, George Bush must see his 8-year hitch as President Reagan's vice president as a mixed blessing. Not really able to control that administration's policies, he was nonetheless involved and supportive. Any chance he might have had to distance himself from those policies was forfeited when he portrayed himself as the Reagan heir in the 1988 election. The Iran-Contra affair has been particularly painful for Bush. If we take him at his word, he was one of the most ill-informed, ignorant, and ignored men in the history of the vice presidency. Gee, is that any way to groom a successor?

IRAN·CONTRA ALIEN

Unfortunately, there are no Jimminy Crickets in politics. Every officeholder is the keeper of his or her conscience, and some of those consciences get exceptionally tough and casual. Years of being pragmatic and realistic can do that. Bush's insistence that there was no relationship between arms sales to Iran and the hostage issue, no connection between U.S. gifts to Honduras and the subsequent Honduran aid to the Contras, left the public with the choice of believing Bush was abysmally naive or was lying. It is really very hard to see a former director of the CIA as naive.

Politicians tend to get callouses on their consciences—no, lesions. Callouses come from working something too hard. One could fill this page with the euphemisms they have created for a failure to tell the truth. They can conjugate the term "lie" and never use that word twice. They automatically say whatever will bring them immediate gain and deal with the consequences later. Most depressing is that the public has generally accepted this behavior. They expect politicians to deliver self-serving pap and are not upset when it arrives. George Bush said he knew nothing about the Iran-Contra arrangement.

There is something essentially undignified and degrading about the unraveling of conspiracies. It's really enough to give any self-respecting plotter pause. At the first crack in the wall of secrecy, the conspirators run squealing to the investigators to protect themselves at the expense of their coconspirators. Those heading the investigation, empowered to grant immunity or reduce punishment to cooperating witnesses, need only catch one well-informed underling with his hand in the cookie jar and the recriminations begin. Parties to conspiracy on the whole don't seem to be very loyal or honorable people. Ah, well, what can one expect of conspirators? Presidents really ought to keep better company.

THE WORM TURNS

And, if somebody did know, it was William Casey, head of the Central Intelligence Agency, and he's dead. The people who ran the Iran-Contra operation apparently learned something from the Watergate scandal. The time to engineer a cover-up is while the operation is developing rather than scrambling about after it's discovered. The trick is to cut the linkage of responsibility at some point far enough down the line to leave only expendable personnel vulnerable. That was achieved by allowing underlings to interpret the wishes of those in charge without ever actually ordering actions.

PANDORA'S BOX

The most bizarre character in the whole seamy episode was Colonel Oliver North. He enthusiastically confessed to shredding evidence, lying to Congress, and a host of other illegal activities. Showing no remorse, he insisted he was right and that Congress and the laws were wrong. There was something almost honorable in such frankness until one remembered the harsh reality beneath his patriotic posturing. He had worked against the very system he had sworn to uphold and had undermined the institutions he was supposed to defend. All those years of covert activities had produced a kind of myopic morality; he could do no wrong.

Oliver North was morally obtuse. His vocal champions were also that—and dangerous as well. One might forgive violations of law and morality committed by those on the field of battle. But North's environment had been the marble halls of Washington and plush-carpeted board rooms. He understood, or should have, the constitutional basis of this government. He was not bludgeoned into undermining that system, but was a wholehearted, exuberant volunteer. Colonel North no doubt loves the flag; he's probably even fond of the Constitution, as long as he doesn't have to read it.

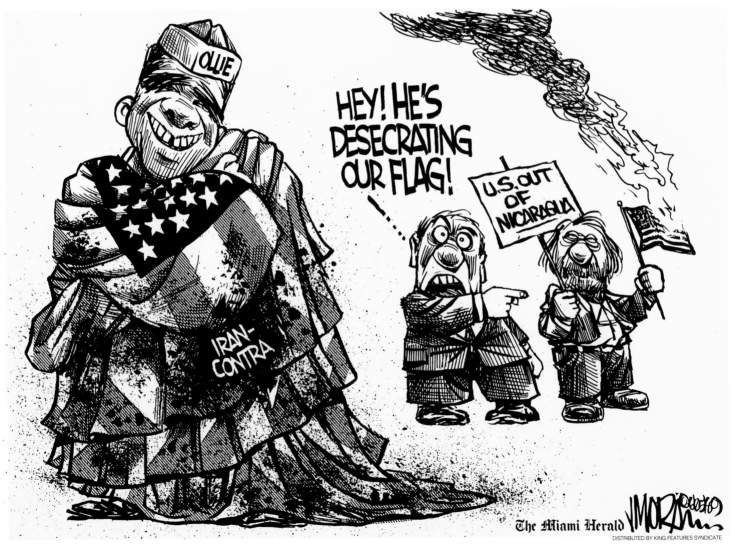

Throughout the probes, investigations, hearings, and trials arising out of the Iran-Contra episode, then-President Ronald Reagan left a trail of extremely strange statements. Each was quickly followed by corrections, clarifications, and amendments issued by his staff. The picture that emerged was of a man only remotely president, only vaguely in charge, and only marginally responsible. We didn't have a captain, we had a crew run amok.

HONOR AMONG STOOL PIGEONS AND OTHERS.

After Ronald Reagan left office, the investigators screwed up sufficient courage to request that he testify about his role in the Iran-Contra affair. He graciously consented to send them a videotaped discussion. The tape might be seen as artful (he certainly didn't incriminate himself) or as embarrassing (he was thoroughly muddled), but it clearly was not informative. The refrain was "I don't recall"; the chorus was "I seem to recollect." It was vague, imprecise, and intellectually mushy. A tape is not susceptible to cross-examination and you can't refute "I don't remember." Nobody wanted to push for a genuine confrontation. Score a victory for Reagan and confusion.

It was a thoroughly pathetic parade. A thoughtless, gung-ho colonel, a third-level bureaucrat with more responsibility than he could handle, and a desk-bound milquetoast admiral with a taste for cloak-and-dagger machinations. Behind them a trail of ruined careers and shattered reputations. Above them a chain of command anxious only to protect itself, and the president in whose interest the culprits had acted. And still Ronald Reagan's supporters insist he brought "respect" back to the presidency. Maybe in Grenada.

As we learned more details about the Iran-Contra operation, the absurdity of the whole episode became inescapable. It had the appearance of a rejected script for a film to be called THE KEYSTONE KOPS VS. GODZILLA. In the theater, tragedy is defined as a tale of great people toppled by inner flaws. Whether Iran-Contra is a tragedy depends on what you think of those in charge. But its last act was certainly in character with the whole bumbling performance. The Ortega regime was removed from power by the one device the plotters refused to consider: free elections.

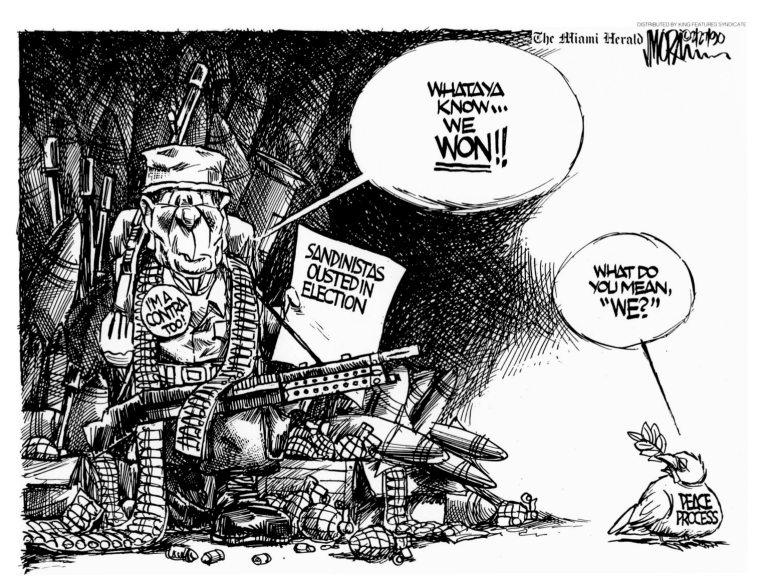

Most Americans feel hostile toward Iran. President George Bush may well have felt apprehensive as well. Circumstantial evidence, and sometimes a bit more, links Bush to the hostages-for-arms deals that took place during his tenure as vice president. Less substantial but still worrisome evidence suggests that the Republican ticket in the 1980 election negotiated with the Iranians to delay release of the hostages held in the U.S. embassy there until after the November election to deny the Democratic candidate Jimmy Carter the popularity boost that would come with their release. The conclusive proof, one way or another, lies in Iran. Will the other shoe drop?

THE CARTOONISTS
NOTES TO ESSAYS
SUGGESTED
READING

THE CARTOONISTS

Reflections from the drawing board   Jack Ohman

As I write, George Bush has become the fourth incumbent president in this century to lose his re-election bid. Bill Clinton will be the 42nd president of the United States. Some may cheer this news, but political cartoonists are banging their heads against their drawing boards and drinking india ink to drown their sorrow. They have just ended a Golden Age thing.

We never knew how good we had it with George Bush.

The popular perception of George Bush when he took office in 1989 was that of a generally nice guy who was given to occasional ruthless moments to keep his résumé burnished. In time, public awareness that that facade of old school manners was a patina covering some truly reprehensible public policy ultimately prevented Bush's re-election. There were two George Bushes. The first George Bush was the Trilateralist Yalie with a Skull and Bones Rolodex and the easy preppy manner. The other George Bush was the man who claimed to listen to country music every morning, the man who asserted—seriously—that his favorite magazine was *Bassmaster,* and the man who owned a Kennebunkport beach house but claimed Texas as his ancestral home. At age 68, George Bush didn't seem to know who he was; finally, neither did the American people.

Cartoonists seized upon this dichotomy as well. Many cartoons appeared depicting George Bush as hopelessly removed from real-life concerns, as an accidental tourist in the American experience, more involved in the problems of Beijing than Peoria.

As a subject for caricature, George Bush had all the ingredients to make even fourth-rate cartoonists seem like satirical Spinozas. Eyebrows perpetually arched in a quizzical squint/frown, a truly lopsided grin starting one inch below the right ear and terminating directly below the nose, a nice little piece of hair dangled permanently over the forehead, and body language known only to George Bush and Dana Carvey—it was cartoonist heaven.

During the Bush presidency, political cartoonists really got to indulge their professional passion for rendering large mechanical objects of destruction, such as tanks and planes, and missiles and Saddam Hussein. That's another reason cartoonists ought to be grateful to George Bush. He gave us a Bad Guy. In the '70s and '80s, cartoonists had the Ayatollah; in the '50s and '60s, there was Khrushchev; in the '30s and '40s, there was Hitler. In the '90s New-World-Order-Where-We're-All-Trading-Partners-Era, who do we have to really sink our teeth into? That fiendish Canadian Prime Minister?

Let us also now praise infamous men, such as John Sununu, the only chief of staff ever to attain five million frequent flier miles. Recall Clarence Thomas, the man responsible for the election of four new women in the U.S. Senate. Let us praise famous dogs, too, such as Millie.

And finally, let us not forget Vice President Dan Quayle. Although we should probably wear his scorn as a badge of honor, we should also note that he was invaluable to political cartoonists: the one man in the Bush Administration we could depend on to provide us with high-quality humor respected throughout the free world. Why was he such a durable subject? Well, it may be because he was the only vice president of the United States on a golf scholarship, or that he had addressed the United Negro College Fund thus, "What a waste it is to lose one's mind, or not to have a mind at all. How true that is." We will miss him and his spat with Murphy Brown, who was right to keep the child and wrong not to name him Dan.

How do we put the presidency of George Bush in a historical context? Cartoonists don't think in historical contexts; it interferes with the creative process when they think about future historians breathing down their necks and critiquing their line quality and lettering. But when we assembled the material in this book, we noted that the cartoonists had rendered history about as accurately as the columnists and pundits, and with 36 percent less pretense.

My favorite quote of former President Bush's is this one: "The doctor told me to relax. The doctor told me to relax. The doctor told me to relax. The doctor told me. He was the one. He said, 'Relax.'"

Relax, Mr. President. It's over. Read our lips.

No more cartoonists.■

Cartoonists Presented:

Chronos Publishing expresses its great appreciation to
the cartoonists and syndicates named on these pages
for their participation in this unique book project.

Jim Borgman
Cincinnati Enquirer
King Features Syndicate

John Branch
San Antonio Express-News

Paul Conrad
Los Angeles Times
Los Angeles Times Syndicate

Jeff Danziger
Christian Science Monitor
Los Angeles Times Syndicate

Kevin Kallaugher
Baltimore Sun
Cartoonists & Writers Syndicate

Mike Keefe
Denver Post

Steve Kelley
San Diego Union
Copley News

Mike Lane
Baltimore Sun

Jim Morin
Miami Herald
King Features Syndicate

Jack Ohman
The Oregonian
Tribune Media Services

Pat Oliphant
Universal Press Syndicate

Mike Peters
Dayton Daily News
Tribune Media Services

Paul Szep
Boston Globe

John Trever
Albuquerque Journal
North America Syndicate

Dan Wasserman
Boston Globe
Los Angeles Times Syndicate

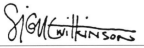

Signe Wilkinson
Philadelphia Daily News
Cartoonists & Writers Syndicate

Kirk Anderson
The Capital Times
Madison, Wisconsin

Tony Auth
Philadelphia Inquirer
Universal Press Syndicate

Brian Basset
Seattle Times

Steve Benson
Arizona Republic
Tribune Media Services

Jules Feiffer
Village Voice
Universal Press Syndicate

Bob Gorrell
Richmond Times-Dispatch
Copley News Service

Jack Higgins
Chicago Sun Times

David Horsey
Seattle Post-Intelligencer
North America Syndicate

Chan Lowe
Fort Lauderdale Sun-Sentinel
Tribune Media Services

Mike Luckovich
Atlanta Constitution
Creators Syndicate

Doug Marlette
Newsday
Creators Syndicate

Tom Meyer
San Francisco Chronicle

Joel Pett
Lexington Herald Leader

Dwane Powell
Raleigh News and Observer
Los Angeles Times Syndicate

Mike Priggee
Spokane Observer

Dana Summers
Orlando Sentinel

Scott Willis
San Jose Mercury News

Don Wright
Palm Beach Post
Tribune Media Services

Notes to Essays

Introduction

1. Arthur B. Laffer, "Reaganite's View of Bush," *San Francisco Chronicle,* October 17, 1992.

2. Postelection survey, conducted for Times Mirror Corporation by The Gallup Organization, November 1988. Number of respondents = 2,022 voters.

3. James Perry, "For President Bush, the First 100 Days Offer Little to Provide Strength for Tough Times Ahead, Political Experts Contend," *Wall Street Journal,* April 28, 1989.

4. Charles O. Jones, "Meeting Low Expectations: Strategies and Prospects of the Bush Presidency," in Colin Campbell and Bert A. Rockman, eds., *The Bush Presidency: First Appraisal* (Chatham: Chatham House, 1991).

5. Quoted in *Newsweek,* January 30, 1989.

6. Jonathan Alter, *Newsweek,* December 3, 1990.

7. These quotes and helpful interpretations come from Kerry Mullins and Aaron Wildavsky, "The Procedural Presidency of George Bush," *Political Science Quarterly,* Spring 1992, 31–62.

8. Bert A. Rockman, "The Leadership Style of George Bush," in Colin Campbell and Bert A. Rockman, eds., *The Bush Presidency: First Appraisal* (Chatham: Chatham House, 1991), 12.

9. John Sununu, quoted in *Time,* August 24, 1992. His statement was made in a November 1990 speech.

10. Transcript of radio address, November 7, 1992, after his defeat, reprinted in *New York Times,* November 8, 1992.

11. Ronald Reagan, remarks at the August 1992 Republican convention, quoted in "George Bush [an editorial]," *Wall Street Journal,* August 20, 1992.

12. Paul Brace and Barbara Hinkley, *Follow the Leader: Opinion Polls and the Modern Presidency* (Basic Books, 1992), 144.

13. *New York Times,* November 8, 1992.

The President and Congress

1. U.S. Constitution, Article 1, Section 7, Clause 2. See also, Wm. Holmes Brown, Parliamentarian, "Constitution, Jefferson's Manual, and the Rules of the House of Representatives," (Washington, D.C.: U.S. Government Printing Office) 45–50.

2. Woodrow Wilson, *Congressional Government* (New York: Houghton Mifflin, 1885), 52.

3. U.S. Senate Library.

4. Charles E. Cook, "The Anti-Incumbent Mood Is On Again, This Time for Good," *Roll Call,* October 11, 1990, 6. See also, Glenn R. Simpson, "Pundits Ponder Case of Reappearing Marginals," *Roll Call,* November 12, 1990, 10.

5. Kim Mattingly, "Gingrich Defection on Budget Forces Michel to Set Up Own Ad-Hoc Whip Organization," *Roll Call,* October 4, 1990, 16.

6. "Our group was outnegotiated by the other side," Congressman Bill Frenzel, as quoted in the *Congressional Quarterly Almanac,* vol. XLVI (Washington, D.C.: Congressional Quarterly, Inc.), 113.

7. Kim Mattingly, "GOP Strategists Advise Hill Republicans in Tight Races to Run Against President," *Roll Call,* October 15, 1991, 1.

8. Susan B. Glasser, "House Members to File Lawsuit Over Bush Action in Persian Gulf," *Roll Call,* November 19, 1990, 11.

9. U.S. Constitution, Article 1, Section 6.5.

10. *Congressional Record,* January 3, 1991, S7.

11. Ibid., S8.

12. Letter from George Bush to Thomas Foley, dated January 8, 1991. Full text of letter published in *Congressional Record,* January 3, 1991.

13. *Congressional Record,* January 12, 1991, H390.

14. Ibid., H391.

15. Craig Winneker, "Congress Supports Gulf War in Encore," *Roll Call,* January 21, 1991, 1.

16. Glenn R. Simpson, "House Bank Prosecutors: Experienced and Zealous," *Roll Call,* June 1, 1992, 1. Among other opinions and commentaries, Wilkey dissented in *Nixon v. Sirica* (1973), the so-called Watergate Tapes case involving President Richard Nixon's claim of executive privilege with regard to congressional subpoenas.

17. Quoted from a letter from Thomas S. Foley to colleagues, *Congressional Record,* April 24, 1992.

18. U.S. Constitution.

19. Norman J. Ornstein, "Wilkey's Subpoena Sets a Dangerous, Sweeping Precedent," *Roll Call,* April 30, 1992, 5.

20. Congressional Record, April 29, H2764. Statement of Representative Fred Grandy. The April 30 and May 4 issues of *Roll Call* carried extensive discussion of these issues.

21. Letter from Representative Henry B. Gonzalez to Judge John Garrett Penn, May 1, 1992. Published in *Congressional Record.*

22. Susan B. Glasser, "Court to Rule Today on Bank Subpoenas," *Roll Call,* May 4, 1992, 1.

The Supreme Court

1. Justice Harry A. Blackmun, dissent in *Planned Parenthood v. Casey,* United States Supreme Court, 1992.

2. *Congressional Quarterly Almanac,* Vol. 16, 1990, published by Congressional Quarterly, Inc.

3. Ibid.

4. The decisions were *Wards Cove Packing Co. v. Antonio, Martin v. Wilks, Lorance v. American Telephone and Telegraph Co., Patterson v. McLean Credit Union,* and *Price Waterhouse v. Hopkins,* United States Supreme Court, 1989.

5. Justice Harry A. Blackmun, dissent in *Wards Cove Packing Co. v. Antonio,* United States Supreme Court, 1989.

6. Justice Thurgood Marshall, dissent in *Payne v. Tennessee,* United States Supreme Court, 1991.

7. Justice David Souter, majority opinion in *Planned Parenthood v. Casey,* United States Supreme Court, 1992.

Foreign Policy

1. Federal Information Systems Corporation, May 29, 1992.

2. Marci McDonald, "A Fall from Grace," *MacLean's,* January 20, 1992:

3. For an account of these traditions, see George Kennan, *American Diplomacy* (Chicago: University of Chicago Press, 1951); and John B. Judis, *Grand Illusion: Critics and Champions of the American Century* (New York: Farrar, Straus and Giroux, 1992).

4. John B. Judis, "Scowcroft and Statecraft," *The New Republic,* February 24, 1992.

5. Walter Isaacson, *Kissinger: A Biography* (New York: Simon and Schuster, 1992), 398.

6. Alan Tonelson, "Prudence or Inertia: The Bush Administration's Foreign Policy," *Current History,* April 1992.

Military Spending

1. President George Bush, "National Security Strategy of the United States," (Washington, D.C.: U.S. Government Printing Office, August 1991).

2. *Defense Almanac 91* (September–October) (Washington, D.C.: U.S. Government Printing Office).

3. Presidential television address, quoted in *Washington Post,* September 28, 1991.

4. Senator Jim Sasser, "President Bush's 1993 Budget: Review and Analysis," prepared by the Staff of the U.S. Senate Committee on the Budget, January 31, 1992, 52.

5. Carnegie Endowment's National Commission: *America and the New World, Changing Our Ways* (Washington, D.C.: Carnegie Endowment for International Peace), 1992.

6. Statement to the Senate Budget Committee, February 5,1992, 3.

7. General Colin Powell, Chairman Joint Chiefs of Staff,

"National Military Strategy," (Washington, D.C.: U.S. Government Printing Office, January 1992).

8. As quoted by Benjamin M. Friedman in "The Morning After," *New York Review of Books,* August 13, 1992.

The Economy

1. David E. Rosenbaum, "On the Economy, Bush Followed Reagan's Lead, Not His Success," *New York Times,* June 29, 1991.

2. These economic statistics, and those throughout this essay not otherwise identified, are calculated from the Council of Economic Advisers, *Economic Report of the President* (Washington, D.C.: Government Printing Office, 1992) and "Economic Indicators," prepared for the Joint Economic Committee of the U.S. Congress by the Council of Economic Advisers, May 1992.

3. CBO Staff Memorandum, "Measuring the Distribution of Income Gains," (Washington, D.C.: Congressional Budget Office, March 1992).

The Cities

1. "Cover Story: The Immigrants: How They're Helping to Revitalize the U.S. Economy," *Business Week,* July 13, 1992, 118.

2. Richard Nathan and John Logo, In Intergovernmental Fiscal Roles and Relations, *Annals of the American Academy of Political and Social Science, No. 509,* May 5, 1990, 42.

3. *New York Times,* January 19, 1988.

4. Victoria Irwin, *Christian Science Monitor,* May 17, 1988.

5. Robert Pear, "White House Spurns Expansion of Nation's Anti-Poverty Efforts," *New York Times,* July 6, 1990.

6. U.S. Department of Housing and Urban Development, Office of Policy Development and Research. *The President's National Urban Policy Report.* (Washington, D.C.: U.S. Government Printing Office, 1991).

7. *New York Times,* May 14, 1992.

The Environment

1. World Commission on Environment and Development. *Our Common Future,* Oxford: Oxford University Press, 1987.

2. Ross Gelbspan and Dianne Dumanoski. "Environmentalists Assail Bush; 1st Term Gets Low Grade; New Proposals called Election Ploy," *Boston Globe,* January 27, 1992, 1.

3. Sally Lehrman. "Biotech Firms Persuaded Bush to Reject Earth Treaty," *San Francisco Examiner,* June 10, 1992, 1.

4. Op. Cit., 1.

5. Rae Tyson. "How Green is Bush?" Gannett Company, Inc., September 18, 1991.

Health Care

1. Employee Benefits Research Institute, "Sources of Health Insurance and Characteristics of the Uninsured," February 1992.

2. Children's Defense Fund, "Children and Health Insurance," January 7, 1991.

3. Alliance for Health Reform, "Chartbook: Healthcare in America," May 1992.

4. Advisory Council on Social Security, "Income Security and Health Care: Economic Implications 1991–2020," December 1991.

5. Daniel Q. Haney, "Cost of Treating One American With AIDS for a Year: $38,000," *Associated Press,* July 22, 1992.

6. National Commission to Prevent Infant Mortality, "Troubling Trends Persist: Shortchanging America's Next Generation," March 1992.

7. Robert Blendon and Jennifer Edwards, eds., "System in Crisis: the Case for Health Care Reform," Faulkner & Gray's Healthcare Information Center, 1991.

8. The Public Agenda Foundation, "Faulty Diagnosis: Public Misconceptions About Health Care Reform," 1992.

9. U.S. Department of Health and Human Services, and Public Health Service, "Healthy People 2000," September 1990.

10. Marlene Cimons, "Government Proposes Sweeping Health Goals," *Los Angeles Times,* September 7, 1990.

11. Advisory Council on Social Security, op. cit.

12. Ibid.

13. Eric Weissenstein, "Reform Panel Remains Divided," *Modern Healthcare,* December 9, 1991.

14. Ann Devroy, "Bush on Health Care: Case Study in Caution," *Washington Post,* September 26, 1991.

15. Remarks by President Bush to the Greater Cleveland Growth Association, Cleveland, Ohio, February 6, 1992.

16. Carl J. Schramm, President of the Health Insurance Association of America, press release, February 6, 1992.

17. Henry E. Simmons, "Cheaper Health Care (for the Rich)," *New York Times,* May 15, 1992.

18. Families U.S.A., "The Bush Health Plan: Gain for Insurance Companies, Medical Industry; Pain for America's Families," February 1992.

19. Rashi Fein, interview with the author, June 1992.

20. Dr. Arnold Relman, interview with the author, June 1992.

21. Vicki Kemper and Vivica Novak, "What's Blocking Health Care Reform?" *Common Cause,* January/February/March 1992.

22. Remarks by President Bush, op. cit.

Abortion

1. William Loeb, quoted in the "Political Circuit," *Boston Globe,* December 29, 1979.

2. George Bush, June 4, 1991 letter to Congressional leaders, *Congressional Quarterly Almanac 1991* (Washington, D.C.: Congressional Quarterly, Inc., 1992) 334.

3. Douglas Johnson, statement issued by National Right to Life organization, printed in *Congressional Quarterly Almanac 1989* (Washington, D.C.: Congressional Quarterly, Inc., 1990), 305.

4. James C. Mohr, *Abortion in America: The Origin and Evolution of National Policy* (New York: Oxford Uni-

versity Press, 1973) 167.

5. Dr. Jane Hodgson, *Boston Globe*, November 29, 1989.

War on Drugs

1. The President's drug war speech is included in "Drug Prohibition and the Conscience of Nations," p. 10. Edited by Arnold S. Trebach and Kevin B. Zeese; (Drug Policy Foundation) Washington, D.C., 1990.

2. Marshall Jonathan. "How Our War on Drugs Shattered the Cities," *Washington Post,* May 17, 1992.

3. "National Drug Control Strategy: Budget Summary," Office of National Drug Control Policy, (Drug Policy Foundation), Washington, D.C., February 1992.

4. The estimated size of the illicit drug economy is from an interview with Peter Reuter, an analyst of illegal markets for the RAND Corporation in Washington, D.C. The assessment that cocaine, heroin, and marijuana are "readily available" was made by the National Narcotics Intelligence Consumers Committee, NNICC Report, July 1992.

5. Martinez is quoted in "20 Years of War on Drugs, and No Victory Yet," *New York Times,* June 14, 1992.

6. See "Heavy Traffic: Drug Smuggling Overwhelms Panama Two Years after the Overthrow of Noriega," *Dallas Morning News,* January 8, 1992.

7. Bush quoted on Noriega, *New York Times,* April 2, 1992.

8. Ibid. 1, 21.

9. "20 Years of War on Drugs, and No Victory Yet," *New York Times,* June 14, 1992.

10. "De-escalating the War," *Family Therapy Networker,* November–December, 1990, 10–21.

11. "Drug Abuse Prevention: Federal Efforts to Identify Exemplary Programs Need Stronger Design," General Accounting Office, Washington, D.C., 1992, 11.

12. "Budget Cuts Undermining 'War' Against Drug Abuse," *Washington Post,* October 27, 1991.

13. "Controlling Drug Abuse: A Status Report," Comptroller General of the United States (General Accounting Office), Washington, D.C., 1988, 7.

14. "The National Narcotics Intelligence Consumers Re-

ports," National Narcotics Intelligence Consumers Committee, 1983 and 1987.

15. "Controlling Drug Abuse: A Status Report," Comptroller General of the United States (General Accounting Office), Washington, D.C., 1988, 9.

16. Jerald G. Bachman, Lloyd D. Johnston, and Patrick M. O'Malley. "Explaining the Recent Decline in Cocaine Use Among Young Adults: Further Evidence that Perceived Risks and Disapproval Lead to Reduced Drug Use," *Journal of Health and Social Behavior,* Vol. 31, (American Sociological Association), Washington, D.C., June 1990, 181.

17. "The Bush Drug War Record," The Drug Policy Foundation, Washington, D.C., September 1992, 3–4.

18. "Probation and Parole 1990," Bureau of Justice Statistics Bulletin, U.S. Department of Justice, Washington, D.C., November 1991.

19. "How Our War on Drugs Shattered the Cities," *Washington Post,* May 17, 1992.

20. Terry Don. "Prison as Usual/A Special Report," *New York Times,* September 13, 1992.

21. "Study says Anti-Drug Property Seizures Often Snare the Innocent," *Dallas Morning News,* May 18, 1992; and "Cover Story: The Government Doesn't Have to Prove Guilt," *USA Today,* May 18, 1992.

22. *New York Times,* May 12, 1992.

The Gulf War

1. Alexander M. Sullivan, "Bush: 'A Line Has Been Drawn in the Sand,'" U.S. Information Agency, August 8, 1990.

2. Hala Fattah, "From Regionalism to Nation-State: A Short History of Kuwait," Phyllis Bennis and Michel Moushabeck, eds., *Beyond the Storm: A Gulf Crisis Reader* (New York: Olive Branch Press, 1991), 45–46.

3. Figure cited by Yahya Sadowski, "Scuds vs. Butter: The Political Economy of Arms Control in the Arab World," *Middle East Report* 177 (July/August 1992), 5. Kuwait loaned $17 billion to Iraq during the latter's war with Iran. See Joe Stork and Ann M. Lesch, "Why War?" in Cynthia Peters, ed., *Collateral Damage: The 'New World Order' at Home and Abroad* (Boston: South End Press, 1992), 167.

4. See Walid Khalidi, *The Gulf Crisis: Origins and Consequences* (Washington, D.C.: Institute for Palestine Studies, 1991), 11.

5. George Bush, "In Defense of Saudi Arabia," Micah L. Sifry and Christopher Cerf, eds., *The Gulf War Reader: History, Documents, Opinions* (New York: Times Books, 1991), 198. Bush also said he was "determined to protect the lives of American citizens abroad." Later in the same speech, Bush suggested that because the United States "imports nearly half the oil it consumes," it "could face a major threat to its economic independence" as a result of the invasion. He also implied that because Iraq had a "history of aggression...to assume Iraq will not attack again [i.e., attack Saudi Arabia] would be unwise and unrealistic.

6. George Bush, "The Need for an Offensive Military Option," in Sifry and Cerf, 229.

7. For excerpts from the hearings, see Sifry and Cerf, 234–54.

8. Resolution 677, quoted in Sifry and Cerf, 156.

9. U.S. News & World Report, *Triumph Without Victory: The Unreported History of the Persian Gulf War* (New York: Times Books, 1992), 97–98. See also Norman Friedman, *Desert Victory: The War for Kuwait* (Annapolis, Md.: Naval Institute Press, 1991), 108 and 117–19.

10. Harry G. Summers, Jr., *On Strategy II: A Critical Analysis of the Gulf War* (New York: Dell Publishing, 1992), 174.

11. Ibid., 238 and 255. See also Michael T. Klare, "The Pentagon's New Paradigm," in Sifry and Cerf, 470; and Lawrence Freedman and Efraim Karsh, "How Kuwait Was Won: Strategy in the Gulf War," *Internal Security*, vol. 16, no. 2 (Fall 1991): 25. The exact number of U.S. forces in the Gulf was 541,425 (*Washington Post*, May 24, 1992).

12. Norman Friedman, 111–12.

13. John Lancaster, "Report: Allies Faced Only 183,000 Iraqis—Panel Suggests Pentagon Vastly Overestimated Enemy Strength," *Washington Post*, April 24, 1992.

14. William M. Arkin, Damian Durrant, and Marianne Cherni, *On Impact: Modern Warfare and the Environment—A Case Study of the Gulf War* (Washington, D.C.: Greenpeace International, 1991), 15.

15. Ibid., 44–45.

16. George Bush, "The Liberation of Kuwait Has Begun," in Sifry and Cerf, 311–13.

17. Barton Gellman, "Allied Air War Struck Broadly in Iraq: Officials Acknowledge Strategy Went Beyond Purely Military Targets," *Washington Post*, June 23, 1991.

18. Arkin et al., 15.

19. International Study Team, *Executive Summary: Health and Welfare in Iraq After the Gulf Crisis—An In-Depth Assessment* (Cambridge, Mass.: International Study Team at Harvard Law School, October 1991), 5.

20. Eric Hooglund, "The Other Face of War," *Middle East Report*, 171 (July/August 1991): 5.

21. Ibid., 7.

22. Lawyers Committee for Human Rights, *Asylum Under Attack: A Report on the Protection of Iraqi Refugees and Displaced Persons One Year After the Humanitarian Emergency in Iraq,* (New York: LCHR, April 1992), 5–6.

23. Arkin et al., 17.

24. Dr. Mostafa Tolba, Executive Director of the U.N. Environment Programme, quoted in Arkin et al., 17.

25. Quoted in Sadowski, 5.

26. Jonathan Rauch, "War Profiteers: America's First Free War," *New Republic*, June 17, 1991, 14. As of May 13, 1992, the allies had paid $53.8 billion of the money pledged. The total cost of the war was revised upward to $61.1 billion to include costs deriving from the continuing U.S. military presence in the region. (*Wall Street Journal*, June 9, 1992).

27. See Faleh Abd al-Jabbar, "Why the Uprisings Failed," *Middle East Report*, 176 (May–June 1992): 2–14. Although Bush called on the Iraqi population to revolt, he did not offer material support once the uprisings broke out. See Morton Kondracke, "Kurdled: What Did the Administration Really Know?" *New Republic*, May 13, 1991, 10–11; Noam Chomsky, "What We Say Goes: The Middle East in the New World Order," in Peters, 70–71; and Lawyers Committee for Human Rights, 57–59.

28. Quoted in Michel Moushabeck, "Iraq: Years of Turbulence," in Bennis and Moushabeck, 33–34.

29. See Middle East Watch, *Human Rights in Iraq* (New York: Middle East Watch, 1990), 101–105.

30. Sharon LaFraniere, "Judge Joins Call for Special Counsel: After Guilty Pleas, Bank Ex-Official Is Evasive on Baghdad Loans," *Washington Post*, June 3, 1992.

31. Geoffrey Kemp, member of the National Security Council under Ronald Reagan, quoted by Chomsky, 63. At the same time, the United States closed its eyes when Iraqi forces gassed the Kurds in 1987–88 and committed other abuses as part of what a 1989 State Department report referred to as "Iraq's abysmal human rights record" (Middle East Watch, 105–112).

32. "The Tilt to Iraq" (editorial), *Washington Post*, May 26, 1992.

33. Quoted in "'89 Bush Order Says Ply Iraq With Aid," *New York Times*, May 29, 1992.

34. George Lardner, Jr., and R. Jeffrey Smith, "CIA Shared Data With Iraq Until Kuwait Invasion: Despite Saddam's Behavior, Ties Continued 2 Years Later Than Senate Panel Had Reported," *Washington Post*, April 28, 1992. For additional examples, see Chomsky, 63.

35. "The Glaspie Transcript: Saddam Meets the U.S. Ambassador," in Sifry and Cerf, 130. For an account of the crucial last days before the invasion, see Pierre Salinger and Eric Laurent, *Secret Dossier: The Hidden Agenda Behind the Gulf War* (New York: Penguin Books, 1991), chapters 4 and 5; and Bob Woodward, *The Commanders* (New York: Simon and Schuster, 1991), chapters 17 and 18.

36. Elaine Sciolino, "Arms Vendors Fail to Impose Limits: Mideast's 5 Biggest Suppliers Report Stalemate in Talks on Nonnuclear Deals," *New York Times*, May 31, 1992.

37. William Pfaff, "More Likely a New World Disorder," in Sifry and Cerf, 489.

Iran-Contra Affair

1. "CBS Evening News with Dan Rather," January 25, 1988.

2. Associated Press, May 4, 1989; see also *Washington Post*, June 10, 1990, C3.

3. National Security Planning Group, June 25, 1984, 2–3 p.m., White House Situation Room, Minutes, 9. Document no.00463 in the National Security Archive's microfiche documents collection, *The Iran-Contra Affair: The Making of a Scandal, 1983–1988* (Alexandria, VA: Chadwyck-Healey, Inc., 1990).

4. Ibid, 14.

5. Robert McFarlane testimony, Iran-Contra congressional hearings, May 11, 1987, 17–19, 24, 53. George Shultz testimony, Iran-Contra congressional hearings, July 23, 1987, 14–17.

6. "Meeting with Honduran President Suazo," Robert McFarlane memorandum to President Reagan, May 21, 1985. Document number 01156 in the National Security Archive's microfiche documents collection, *The Iran-Contra Affair.*

7. See "Toward a Policy on Iran," Graham E. Fuller memorandum to Director of Central Intelligence, May 17, 1985. Document number 01142 in *The Iran-Contra Affair.*

8. Armstrong Scott, Malcolm Byrne and Tom Blanton, *The Chronology: The Documented Day-by-Day Account of the Secret Military Assistance to Iran and the Contras,* (New York: Warner Books, 1987), 140–146, 148–149, 155–161.

9. Report of the president's special review board (Tower Commission), February 26, 1987, B-20-23; George Bush news conference, Iowa, January 8, 1988; Bush on "ABC Nightline," June 9, 1988; Bush in *Looking Forward* (New York: Doubleday, 1987), 240.

10. Peggy Say, *Forgotten: A Sister's Struggle to Save Terry Anderson, America's Longest-Held Hostage,* (New York: Simon & Schuster, 1991), 78.

11. See Bob Woodward and Walter Pincus, "Bush Regularly Attended Meetings on Iran Sales," *Washington Post,* January 7, 1988, A1; and Tom Blanton, "Where George Was: What North's Diaries Tell Us About Bush's Iran-Contra Role," *Washington Post,* June 10, 1990, C1.

12. "The Vice President's Meeting with Mr. Nir," Craig Fuller Memorandum, July 29, 1986. Document number 03215 in *The Iran-Contra Affair.*

13. Ibid.

14. *The Chronology,* 505–518; "Vice President, NSC Tied to Secret Contra Flights," *Miami Herald,* October 11, 1986: Reuters, October 12, 1986.

15. For example, see documents 03731, 03733, and 03737 in *The Iran Contra Affair,* written by Caspar Weinberger, Donald Regan, and Alton Keel, respectively, on the November 10, 1986 meeting.

16. George Shultz testimony, Iran-Contra congressional hearings, July 23, 1987, 31–32.

17. The diversion memorandum is document number 02614 in *The Iran-Contra Affair,* which also includes 145 other documents under Albert Hakim's name alone, related to diversions and secret bank accounts.

18. *Washington Post,* June 10, 1990, C1.6

Suggested Reading

The books listed herein offer further reading on the subjects presented in *Eyes on the President*. The majority of these titles were compiled and submitted by the authors. The titles followed by an asterisk* have been added by the publisher as they are notable books that either appeared after our authors compiled their lists or that the publisher felt our readers might also receive value from reading.

Introduction

George Bush with Victor Gold. *Looking Forward: An Auto-biography*. New York: Doubleday, 1987.

Colin Campbell and Bert A. Rockman, eds. *The Bush Presidency: First Appraisals*. Chatham, NJ: Chatham House,1981.

Thomas E. Cronin, *The State of the Presidency, 2nd edition*. Boston: Little Brown, 1980.

Michael Duffy and Dan Goodgame. *Marching in Place: The Status Quo Presidency of George Bush*. New York: Simon and Schuster, 1992.

Terry Eastland. *Energy in the Executive*. New York: Free Press, 1992.

Richard Rose. *The Postmodern President, revised edition*. Chatham, NJ: Chatham House, 1991.

Norman Schwarzkopf with Peter Petre. *It Doesn't Take a Hero: The Autobiography*. New York: Linda Grey/Bantam, 1992.

Jean Edward Smith. *George Bush's War*. New York: Henry Holt and Co., 1992.

Bob Woodward. *The Commanders*. New York: Simon and Schuster, 1991.

The President and Congress

Jeffrey H. Birnbaum. *The Lobbyist: How Business Gets Its Way in Washington*. New York: Times Books, 1992.

E. J. Dionne, Jr. *Why Americans Hate Politics*. New York: Simon and Schuster, 1991.

Louis Fisher. *The Politics of Shared Power: Congress and the Executive*. Washington: Congressional Quarterly Press, 1981.

Fred I. Greenstein, ed. *Leadership in the Modern Presidency*. Cambridge: Harvard University Press, 1988.

William Grieder. *Who Will Tell the People?* New York: Simon and Schuster, 1992.

Timothy Phelps and Helen Wintermitz. *Capitol Games*. Westport, CT: Hyperion, 1992.

Arthur M. Schlesinger, Jr. *The Imperial Presidency*. Boston: Houghton Mifflin Co., 1973.

Hedrick Smith. *The Power Game*. New York: Ballantine Books, 1988.

John G. Tower. *Consequences*. Boston: Little, Brown and Co., 1991.

Darrell M. West. *Congress and Economic Policymaking*. Pittsburg: University of Pittsburg Press, 1987.

Wilson, Woodrow. *Congressional Government*.

The Supreme Court

Vincent Blasi, ed. *The Burger Court*. New Haven, CT: Yale University Press, 1983.

Ethan Bronner. *Battle for Justice*. New York: W.W. Norton, 1989.

Lee Epstein and Joseph F. Kobylka. *The Supreme Court and Legal Change*. Durham, NC: University of North Carolina Press, 1992.

Charles Fried. *Order and Law*. New York: Simon and Schuster, 1991.

Timothy Phelps and Helen Wintermitz. *Capitol Games*. Westport, CT: Hyperion, 1992.

Rebecca Mae Salokar. *The Solicitor General*. Philadelphia: Temple University Press, 1992.

Foreign Policy

Sidney Blumenthal. *Pledging Allegiance: The Last Campaign of the Cold War*. New York: Harper Collins, 1990.

Pat Choate. *Agency of Influence*. New York: Simon and Schuster, 1991.

Francis Fukuyama. *The End of History*. New York: Basic Books, 1991.

Shintaro Ishihara. *The Japan That Can Say No*. New York: Simon and Schuster, 1991.

John B. Judis. *Grand Illusion: Critics and Champions of the American Century*. New York: Farrar Straus and Giroux, 1992.

Bob Woodward. *The Commanders*. New York: Simon and Schuster, 1991.

Military Spending

James David Barber. "Empire of the Son: How George Bush Rewrote the Book on the Imperial Presidency," *Washington Monthly,* October 1991, 25–29.

George Bush. In response to mailed questionnaire in 1988. Quoted in "George Bush and Arms Control: The Questions in 1992," *Arms Control Today,* April 1992, 35.

"National Security Strategy of the United States." Washington D.C.: U.S. Government Printing Office, August 1991.

William W. Kaufmann and John D. Steinbruner. *Decision for Defense: Prospects for a New Order, 1991*. Washington, D.C.: The Brookings Institution, 1991.

Peter Montgomery. "Re-Arm the World: The Bush Administration May Be Talking a New World Order, But It's Hawking U.S. Weapons Like Never Before," *Common Cause* (May/June 1991): 25–29.

Walter S. Mossberg and Robert S. Greenberger."Policy Void: Upheaval in Europe Tests Bush Capacity for Leadership of the West," *Wall Street Journal,* November 14, 1989.

Kevin V. Mulcahy. "The Bush Administration and National Security Policymaking: a Preliminary Assessment," *International Journal of Intelligence and Counterintelligence* (Summer 1990): 67–80.

Jean Edward Smith. *George Bush's War*. New York: Henry Holt and Company, 1992.

Rochelle L. Stanfield. "A Bush Doctrine? If President Bush is to Sustain National Support for a Protracted Military Action in the Middle East, He Will Need a Succinct Statement of How It Fits in with National Goals," *National Journal*, September 1, 1990, 2062–6.

The Economy

Donald L. Barlett and James B. Steele. *America: What Went Wrong?* Kansas City: Andrews and McMeel, 1992.

Jonathan Greenberg and William Kistler, eds. *Buying Back America.* Tulsa: Council Oak Books, 1992.

Bennett Harrison and Barry Bluestone. *The Great U-Turn: Corporate Restructuring and the Polarizing of America.* New York: Basic Books, 1988.

Paul Krugman. *The Age of Diminished Expectations.* Cambridge: MIT Press, 1990.

Robert Kuttner. *The End of Laissez-Faire: Economics and National Purpose After the Cold War.* New York: Simon and Schuster, 1990.

Isabel V. Sawhill. "Escaping the Fiscal Trap." *The American Prospect,* no.1 (Spring 1990).

The Cities

Fred Harris and Roger Wilkins, eds. *Quiet Riots.* New York: Pantheon Books, 1988.

Marshall Kaplan and Franklin James, eds. *The Future Of National Urban Policy.* Durham, NC: Duke University Press, 1990.

Charles Murray. *Losing Ground.* New York: Basic Books, 1984.

Gary Orfield and Carole Ashkinaze. *The Closing Door: Conservative Policy and Black Opportunity.* Chicago: University of Chicago Press, 1991.

William Julius Wilson. *The Truly Disadvantaged.* Chicago: University of Chicago Press, 1987.

The Environment

Harrison Brown. *The Challenge of Man's Future.* New York: The Viking Press, 1954.

Rachel Carson. *Silent Spring.* New York: Fawcett, 1962.

Carlo M. Cipolla. *The Economic History of World Population.* Baltimore: Penguin Books Inc., 1962.

Barry Commoner. *The Poverty of Power.* New York: Knopf, 1976.

Albert Gore. *Earth in Balance.** Boston: Houghton Mifflin, 1992.

Jonathan Lash et. al. *A Season of Spoils.* New York: Pantheon, 1984.

Jerry Mander. *In the Absense of the Sacred.** San Francisco: Sierra Club Books, 1991.

Bill McKibben. *The End of Nature.* New York: Random House,1989.

Bill McKibben. *The Age of Missing Information.* New York: Random House, 1992.

Ruth Moore. *Man in the Environment.* New York: Knopf, 1975.

John H. Storer. *The Web of Life.* New York: The New American Library, Inc., 1953.

Education

Benjamin R. Barber. *An Aristocracy of Everyone.** New York: Ballantine Books. 1992.

Chester Finn. *We Must Take Charge: Our Schools and Our Future.* New York: Free Press, 1991.

Edward Fiske. *Smart Schools, Smart Kids.* New York: Simon and Schuster, 1991.

Jonathan Kozol. *Savage Inequalities: Children in America's Schools.* New York: Harper Collins, 1992.

Theodore Sizer. *Horace's School: Redesigning the American High School.* Boston: Houghton Mifflin, 1992.

Health Care

Rashi Fein. *Medical Care, Medical Costs: The Search for a Health Insurance Policy.* Cambridge: Harvard University Press, 1986.

Consumer Reports, ed. *How to Resolve the Health Care Crisis: Affordable Protection for All Americans.* Yonkers, NY: Consumer Reports Books, 1992.

Nancy F. McKenzie, ed. *The Crisis in Health Care: Ethical Issues.* New York: Meridian (Penguin), 1990.

J. Warren Salmon, ed. *The Corporate Transformation of Health Care: Issues and Directions.* Amityville, NY: Baywood, 1990.

Neil Rolde. *Your Money or Your Health.* New York: Paragon House, 1992.

Paul Starr. *The Social Transformation of American Medicine.* New York: Basic Books, 1982.

Paul Starr. *The Logic of Health-Care Reform.* The Grand Round Press (Whittle Direct Books), 1992.

Abortion

Mary Ann Glendon. *Abortion & Divorce in Western Law.* Boston: Harvard University Press, 1987.

Kristin Luker. *Abortion & the Politics of Motherhood.* Berkeley: University of California Press, 1984.

James C. Mohr, ed. *Abortion in America.* New York: Meckler, 1992.

Roger Rosenblatt. *Abortion In The American Mind.* New York: Random House, 1992.

Laurence H. Tribe. *Abortion: The Clash of Absolutes.* New York: Norton, 1991.

War on Drugs

Patricia A. Adler *Wheeling and Dealing: An Ethnography of an Upper-Level Drug Dealing and Smuggling Community.* New York: Columbia University Press, 1985.

James B. Bakalar and Lester Grinspoon. *Drug Control in a Free Society.* Cambridge: Cambridge University Press, 1984.

Michael Levine. *Deep Cover: The Inside Story of How DEA Infighting, Incompetence and Subterfuge Lost Us the Biggest Battle of the Drug War.* New York: Delacorte Press, 1990.

Alfred W. McCoy. *The Politics of Heroin: CIA Complicity in the Global Drug Trade.* Brooklyn, NY: Lawrence Hill Books, 1991.

William O. Walker III. *Drug Control in the Americas.* Albuquerque: University of New Mexico Press, 1989.

Terry Williams. *The Cocaine Kids: The Inside Story of a Teenage Drug Ring.* Reading, MA: Addison-Wesley, 1989.

The Gulf War

Phyllis Bennis and Michel Moushabeck, eds. *Beyond the Storm: A Gulf Crisis Reader.* New York: Olive Branch Press, 1991.

Victoria Brittain, ed. *The Gulf Between Us: The Gulf War and Beyond.* London: Virago, 1991.

Norman Friedman. *Desert Victory: The War For Kuwait.* Annapolis, MD: Naval Institute Press, 1991.

Cynthia Peters, ed. *Collateral Damage: The 'New World Order' At Home & Abroad.* Boston: South End Press, 1992.

Nancy J. Peters, ed. *War After War.* (City Lights Review, no. 5). San Francisco: City Lights Books, 1992.

Walid Khalidi. *The Gulf Crisis: Origins and Consequences.* Washington, D.C.: Institute for Palestine Studies, 1991.

John R. MacArthur. *Second Front: Censorship and Propaganda in the Gulf War.* New York: Hill and Wang, 1992.

David McDowall. *The Kurds: A Nation Denied.* London: Minority Rights Publications, 1992.

James Ridgeway, ed. *The March to War.* New York: Four Walls Eight Windows, 1991.

Pierre Salinger and Eric Laurent. *Secret Dossier: The Hidden Agenda Behind the Gulf War.* New York: Penguin Books, 1991.

Micah L. Sifry and Christopher Cerf, eds. *The Gulf War Reader: History, Documents, Opinions.* New York: Times Books, 1991.

Harry G. Summers, Jr. *On Strategy II: A Critical Analysis of the Gulf War.* New York: Dell Publishing, 1992.

Articles:

Several issues of *Middle East Report* (Washington, D.C.), notably nos. 167 ("War in the Gulf," November/December 1990), 168 ("The Gulf Crisis: No Place To Hide," January/February 1991), 169 ("War in the Gulf: Crossing the Line," March/April 1991), 171 ("The Day After," July/August 1991), and 176 ("Iraq: Why the Uprisings Failed," May/June 1992), as well as the resource packet "Crisis in the Gulf" (September 1990).

Human Rights Reports:

Amnesty International. *Iraq: Human Rights Since the Uprisings—A Summary of Amnesty International' Concerns.* New York: Amnesty International USA, July 1991.

Amnesty International. *Iraq/Occupied Kuwait: Human Rights Violations Since August 2, 1990.* New York: Amnesty International USA, December 1990.

William M. Arkin, Damian Durrant, and Marianne Cherni. *On Impact: Modern Warfare and the Environment—A Case Study of the Gulf War.* Washington, D.C.: Greenpeace International, May 1991.

Commission on Human rights. *Report on the Situation of Human Rights in Iraq. Prepared by Mr. Max van der Stoel, Special Rapporteur of the Commission on Human Rights, in Accordance with Commission Resolution 1991/74.* New York: United Nations Economic and Social Council, February 1992.

International Study Team. *Health and Welfare in Iraq After the Gulf Crisis: An In-Depth Assessment.* Cambridge: International Study Team at Harvard Law School, October 1991.

Lawyers Committee for Human Rights. *Asylum Under Attack: A Report of the Protection of Iraqi Refugees and Displaced Persons One Year After the Humanitarian Emergency in Iraq.* New York: Lawyers Committee for Human Rights, April 1992.

Middle East Watch. *A Victory Turned Sour: Human Rights in Kuwait Since Liberation.* New York: Middle East Watch, September 1991.

Middle East Watch. *Human Rights in Iraq.* New Haven: Yale University Press, 1990.

Middle East Watch. *Needless Deaths in the Gulf War: Civilian Casualties During the Air Campaign and Violations of the Laws of War.* New York: Middle Each Watch, November 1991.

The World Health Organization and UNICEF. *WHO/UNICEF Special Mission to Iraq.* New York: United Nations, February 1991.

Savings and Loan Scandal

James Ring Adams. *The Big Fix.* New York: Wiley and Sons, 1989.

Joe Cotchett, *The Ethics Gap: Greed and the Casino Society.* Carlsbad, CA: Parker and Sons, 1991.

Martin Meyer. *The Great American Bank Robbery.* New York: Random House, 1990.

Stephen Pizzo, Mary Fricker and Paul Muolo. *Inside Job: The Looting of America's Savings and Loans.* New York:

Harper Perennial, 1991.

Benjamin J. Stein. *A License to Steal: The Untold Story of Michael Milken and the Conspiracy to Bilk the Nation.* New York: Simon and Schuster, 1992.

Steve Wilmsen. *Silverado.* Bethesda, MD: National Press Books, 1991.

Iran-Contra Affair

Scott Armstrong, Malcolm Byrne, Tom Blanton, and The National Security Archive. *The Chronology: The Documented Day-by-Day Account of the Secret Military Assistance to Iran and the Contras.* New York: Warner Books, 1987.

Malcolm Byrn and Peter Kornbluh, eds. *The Iran-Contra Affair: A National Security Archive Documents Reader.* New York: The New Press, forthcoming in 1993.

Theodore Draper. *A Very Thin Line: The Iran-Contra Affairs.* New York: Hill and Wang, 1991.

Jeffrey Toobin. *Opening Arguments: A Young Lawyer's First Case: United States v. Oliver North.* New York: Viking, 1991.

Report of the President's Special Review Board (Tower Commission). Washington, D.C.: U.S. Government Printing Office, 1987.

Report of the Congressional Committees Investigating the Iran-Contra Affair. Washington, D.C.: U.S. Government Printing Office, 1987.

Acknowledgements

This book would not have come into being without the kindness, generosity, guidance, enthusiastic support, integrity, forbearance, and hard work of those named below. Chronos Publishing wishes to extend to them our gratitude and respect.

Ron Chamberlain
Richard Faralla
Douglas Foster
Shirley Foster
Aubrey+Jennifer Garaghan
Michele+Sean Garaghan
Catherine, Nathan+Gus Heagerty
Dawn+Jonathan Honneyman
Paul Jaffe
Jack Leissring
Carol, Henry+Scott Levy
Joseph Maas
Jerry Mander
Steve McElroy
Bonnie Montgomery
William L. Montgomery
Frank+Sita Nuessle
Richard Reynolds
John+Meredith Schwirtz
David Sweet
Fran Taylor
editcetera
The fact checkers at *Mother Jones*
All of our authors and cartoonists

Offer to Our Readers

Chronos Publishing wishes to know what you think about this book, *Eyes on the President*. We would like to know if this book does what we intended it to do—to enliven your reading and study of the issues and events of the Bush presidency. If you send us a brief note telling us your thoughts about this book, or perhaps how we can improve it, Chronos will send you four of our favorite cartoons from *Eyes on the President*, enlarged, printed on quality paper, and appropriate for framing. They will be our way of thanking you for taking your valuable time to write to us.

To make it possible for us to make this offer we ask that you send $4 to defray the costs of the cartoonists' royalties, postage, a sturdy mailing package, and handling. If you just want to write us a note and don't want the enlarged cartoons, please say so.

Please remember to include your mailing address. Thank you.

Our address is:
Chronos Publishing
PO Box 487A
Occidental, CA 95465-0487

Design: Bruce Montgomery